Twayne's United States Authors Series

Sylvia E. Bowman, *Editor*

IANA UNIVERSITY

ABOUT THE AUTHOR

RICHARD E. AMACHER was educated at Oberlin College and Ohio University, where he received his A.B. degree in 1939. He attended the University of Chicago where he shared first place with John Frederick Nims in the 1940 all-university John Billings Fiske Poetry Prize competition.

For a brief period he worked as a radio and feature writer for the United Press in Pittsburgh. He took his Ph.D. at the University of Pittsburgh in 1947. He has taught at Carnegie Tech, at Rensselaer Polytech, at Yale, and at Rutgers. From 1954 to 1957 he was chairman of the English Department at Henderson State College in Arkansas. Since 1957 he has been associate professor of English at Auburn University.

Professor Amacher's publications include numerous short articles and reviews in *American Literature, New England Quarterly, Explicator, College English,* and other periodicals. With the help of a grant from the Ford Foundation he published a syllabus entitled *Practical Criticism,* as a part of the Arkansas Experiment in Teacher Education. He edited *Franklin's Wit and Folly: the Bagatelles* for the Rutgers University Press in 1953.

For the year 1961-62 he is serving as Fulbright Professor in American Literature at the University of Würzburg in Germany.

min Franklin

BENJAMIN FRANKLIN

by **RICHARD E. AMACHER**

Auburn University

 12

Twayne Publishers, Inc.   ::   New York

Copyright © 1962 by Twayne Publishers, Inc.

Library of Congress Catalog Card Number: 61-18069

MANUFACTURED IN THE UNITED STATES OF AMERICA BY
UNITED PRINTING SERVICES, INC.
NEW HAVEN, CONN.

To those of my students
(past, present, and future)
who combine
Industry and Frugality
with
Love of Liberty

Preface

TO MAKE an analytical study of an American author as complex as Benjamin Franklin is extremely difficult. For this man was the leading scientist of his age, the outstanding printer in the American colonies, the statesman who more than any other single individual founded our nation, the philosopher of utilitarianism, the star of the American Enlightenment, the defender and champion of justice. Withal he was a man of simplicity and naturalness who rarely erred in matters of judgment or common sense. To understand this complex and versatile mind completely would require an expert not only in history (American, British, and Continental) but also in philosophy, religion, chemistry, physics, journalism, literature, and psychology.

Fortunately there is a shorter and an easier way. In this book I have chosen to limit my approach to Franklin as a writer, for in Franklin's writing the manifold variety of his projects, experiments, and causes come to a focal point that the reader can understand and retain—particularly if he wants to comprehend Franklin's career as a whole. All his life long Franklin was putting pen to paper, as his voluminous manuscripts attest. It is Franklin the writer, then, that I present.

Ironically, little attention has been paid to this important aspect of Franklin's career. He has been studied as a scientist, politician, journalist, American, philosopher, and Deist—but seldom to any great extent as a writer. Tyler apparently planned such a study of Franklin, but did not carry it out for lack of time or for other reasons. Lingelbach and Van Doren have done some trail blazing with limited essays on Franklin's ability as a literary artist. (See bibliography.) *Franklin's Wit and Folly: the Bagatelles* attempted to show something of Franklin's artistry in certain special kinds of literary composition. But no previous volume that I know of has ever been devoted to a full-scale study of the whole life and activity of Franklin as a writer.

Needless to say, a book of this size could not possibly attain anything like completeness; but I do present representative samples of significant aspects of Franklin's career as a craftsman in different literary genres. As a writer, Franklin sometimes permitted his forms to overlap. Considering this difficulty, it is probably best to regard general categories, such as those outlined in this book, as merely broad directional indicators, always realizing that every work of literature must ultimately be approached as an individual, or even unique, object. My purpose has been to show that much of Franklin's enduring fame is due to his ability as a writer.

I wish to express gratitude to the following persons and institutions for permission to quote from manuscript and copyrighted material: The American Philosophical Society—Carl Van Doren's *The Letters and Papers of Benjamin Franklin and Richard Jackson* and Dr. William E. Lingelbach's "Franklin's American Instructor" in the *APS Lib. Bull.* (1952); Howard C. Meyers, Esq. —Smyth's *The Writings of Benjamin Franklin;* the Library of the University of Pennsylvania—Franklin's letters to Lafayette (Sept. 17, 1782) and Elizabeth Partridge (Oct. 11, 1779); the Royal Society—Franklin letters (Phila., May 29, 1754 and London, Nov. 7, 1773); Cornell University Library—Franklin's manuscript of *The Ephemera;* Dr. Robert Newcomb—"The Sources of Benjamin Franklin's Sayings of Poor Richard," an unpublished dissertation (University of Maryland); Yale University Press—Drs. Leonard Labaree and Whitfield Bell's *The Papers of Benjamin Franklin* and *Mr. Franklin;* the University of California Press— Dr. Max Farrand's *The Autobiography of Benjamin Franklin;* Houghton Mifflin Co.—Dr. Russel Nye's *Benjamin Franklin's Autobiography;* Macmillan Co.—F. L. Lucas' *The Art of Living;* Rutgers University Press—my edition of Franklin's *Wit and Folly: the Bagatelles.* For kind permission to reproduce the Duplessis portrait of Franklin, I am indebted to M. le Comte Olivier de Lamothe-Mastin.

I am also deeply appreciative of encouragement and assistance from Dr. Walton Patrick and other colleagues of the Auburn University English Department. Miss Sylvia E. Bowman has made numerous helpful suggestions in her office as general editor of Twayne's United States Authors Series. Special thanks are due to the reference librarians in the Auburn University Library for securing research materials on interlibrary loan and to Miss Patricia Lacerva for typing the manuscript.

Finally, I wish to thank the Auburn Research Council for a grant-in-aid making possible the completion of this book.

Auburn University
July, 1961

RICHARD E. AMACHER

Contents

Chronology

1706 "I was born in Boston." (January 17).

1718 Works as apprentice printer to his brother James.

1721 First publication of *The New England Courant*, August 7, by James Franklin.

1722 Publishes *Dogood* papers anonymously, April 2–October 8.

1723 Publishes the *Courant* (February 11–May 7). Breaks apprenticeship and escapes to Philadelphia, where he works for Samuel Keimer.

1724- Works in London as a printer. Returns to Philadelphia
1726 on October 11, 1726. Writes and prints *A Dissertation on Liberty and Necessity* in 1725.

1727 Forms the Junto.

1728 Establishes partnership with Hugh Meredith.

1729 Writes *Busy-Body* papers (February 4–March 27). Buys Keimer's *Universal Instructor* and changes its name to *Pennsylvania Gazette*.

1730 Becomes printer to the Pennsylvania Assembly. Marries Deborah Read Rogers.

1731 Birth of William Franklin. Founds the Philadelphia Library Company. Sends Thomas Whitmarsh to Charleston, S. C., as partner.

1732 Begins *Poor Richard's Almanack* (first issue in 1733). Birth of Francis Folger Franklin.

1733 Forms partnership with Louis Timothée as successor to deceased Whitmarsh.

1735 Writes and prints defense of Reverend Mr. Hemphill.

1736 Establishes Union Fire Company. Becomes clerk of the Pennsylvania Assembly. Death of Francis Folger Franklin.

1737 Postmaster of Philadelphia.

1741 Publishes *The General Magazine and Historical Chronicle*.

1742 Sends James Parker to New York City as a partner. Invents Franklin stove.

1743 Birth of Sarah Franklin.

1744 Becomes first secretary of the American Philosophical Society.

1746 Begins study of electricity.

1747 Turns over management of printing shop to his partner, David Hall.

1749 Writes *Proposals Relating to Education of Youth in Pennsylvania.* Helps found academy which later develops into University of Pennsylvania.

1750 Helps make treaty with Indians at Carlisle, Pa.

1751 *Experiments and Observations on Electricity* published by Collinson in London from letters of Franklin. Helps Dr. Bond establish Pennsylvania Hospital.

1752 Invents lightning rod. Establishes fire insurance company.

1753 Appointed deputy postmaster general of North America. Honorary M.A. degree from Harvard and Yale. Receives Copley medal from Royal Society.

1754 Proposes a plan for union of colonies at Albany Congress.

1755 Provides supplies for Braddock expedition.

1756 Becomes a member of the British Royal Society. Honorary M.A. degree from William and Mary College.

1757- Serves as agent for Pennsylvania in dispute with pro-
1762 prietaries.

1758 Publishes *The Way to Wealth.*

1759 Doctor of Laws degree from University of St. Andrews. Honorary member of Philosophical Society of Edinburgh.

1760 Writes *The Interest of Great Britain Considered with Regard to Her Colonies.* Joins Dr. Bray's Associates.

1762 Honorary Doctor of Civil Laws degree from Oxford.

1764- Serves for second time as agent representing Pennsyl-
1775 vania in proprietary dispute. Also agent for Georgia, New Jersey, and Massachusetts during part of this time.

1766 Examined in House of Commons on repeal of Stamp Act. Becomes member of the Royal Society of Sciences, University of Göttingen.

1771 Begins writing *Autobiography.* Member of Learned Society of Sciences, Rotterdam.

1772 Foreign member of Royal Academy of Sciences of Paris.

1773 Writes *Rules* and *Edict*. Sends Hutchinson-Oliver letters to Massachusetts.

1774 Examined by Wedderburn before the Privy Council about Hutchinson-Oliver letters. Dismissed as deputy postmaster general. Death of wife, December 19.

1775 Delegate from Pennsylvania to the Second Continental Congress. First postmaster general under the Articles of Confederation.

1776 Helps draw up the Declaration of Independence. Leaves Philadelphia for Paris as one of three commissioners from Congress.

1776- Residence in France. Minister plenipotentiary of the
1785   U.S. to France, 1778-1784. Writes *bagatelles*. Resumes work on *Autobiography* in 1784. Member of Royal Medical Society of Paris (1777); fellow of American Academy of Arts and Sciences (1781); foreign member of Academy of Sciences, Letters, and Arts of Padua (1781); Venerable of *Loge des Neufs Soeurs,* a Masonic order (1782); honorary fellow of the Royal Society of Edinburgh (1783); member of Royal Academy of History in Madrid (1784); associate member of Academy of Sciences, Literature, and Arts of Lyon (1785); honorary member of Manchester Literary and Philosophical Society (1785). Investigates Mesmerism. Signs Treaty of Paris. Returns to Philadelphia in 1785.

1786 Corresponding member of the Society of Agriculture of Milan.

1787 Pennsylvania delegate to the Constitutional Convention. Honorary member of Medical Society of London. President of the Pennsylvania Society for the Abolition of Slavery.

1788 Works on *Autobiography.*

1789 Continues *Autobiography.* Member of Imperial Academy of Sciences of St. Petersburg. Writes papers against slavery.

1790 Writes paper against the slave trade in the *Federal Gazette,* March 23. Dies on April 17.

CHAPTER *1*

A Printer Who Could Write

I *Apprentice in Boston*

"THE TOWN is become almost an Hell upon Earth, a City full of Lies, and Murders, and Blasphemies, as far as Wishes and Speeches can render it so; Satan seems to take a strange Possession of it, in the epidemic Rage, against that notable and powerful and successful way of saving the Lives of People from the Dangers of the *Small-Pox*."[1] The perturbed mind that recorded these words in its diary was Cotton Mather's, not Benjamin Franklin's. The town was Boston, the time was August 24, 1721, and the occasion was a horrendous epidemic of smallpox terribly complicated by a rabid dispute about the effects of inoculation against this disease.

In this dispute young Benjamin Franklin and his older brother James had joined the wrong side, however temporarily, to challenge the power of the churchly hierarchy championed by the Mathers. Since Cotton Mather's father, Increase, was president of Harvard University, the debate grew into an academic as well as an ecclesiastical hullabaloo. The "Six Innoculating Ministers," as they were called, included Increase and Cotton Mather, Benjamin Coleman, Thomas Prince, John Webb, and William Cooper.[2] Those who opposed inoculation did so partly because of their lack of knowledge but more because of their resistance to the tyrannical method by which the Mather group had tried to impose and enforce vaccination procedures. The churchly "Innoculaters" branded their opposition the "Hellfire Club." Among this group of young rebels against the long-standing tyranny of the clergy were James Franklin, the editor of the *New England Courant;* his younger brother Benjamin; a certain "Mr. Gardner"; a certain Captain Taylor; Dr. William Douglass; John Checkley; Mathew Adams; and John Eyre.[3]

All these young men struck hard for liberty. And the pages of their newspaper, the *Courant*, turned into a battleground, focusing the oral debate of the entire town and transforming it into something of a literary war. Thus early (he was then only in his teens) Benjamin Franklin learned by rough experience the power not only of the press but of the individual pens that composed it. He must have learned, too, this young boy who later developed into the most famous and best-loved scientist of his century, the meanness and greatness of passionate and self-interested men trapped in this whirlpool of terror, ignorance, enlightenment, passionate puritanical zeal, and death. And he must have recognized the hard road of the love of liberty and its sometimes disastrous effects on those brave enough to oppose tyranny, whatever its forms, by whatever means. For the controversy over inoculation shook the town more than the epidemic itself.[4] Many years later, when his own uninoculated son had died of the smallpox in Philadelphia, Franklin urged vaccination through the power of his own press.

The Boston that Franklin lived and worked in as a young apprentice printer numbered about ten thousand people. To persons living in London it must have seemed a mere outpost in the wilderness of colonialism, and hardly the proper place for the birth and nurture of a writer because of its contrast to the elegant environments in which some of the Queen Anne wits moved and wrote. One British pundit has tried to argue that Franklin's greatness as a writer was due to his not having had a regular education, to his not having lived "in a refined and literary community," and therefore to his being freer than others to develop his originality.[5] If Franklin had been bred in a college, runs the argument, he might have contented himself with garrulous talk about unimportant aspects of Greek poetry while drinking too much port wine—something like a modern dandy at a cocktail party.[6] But this is mere guesswork, and Boston when Franklin was a teen-ager was not at all what it might have seemed to persons living in London.

For Boston contained many well-educated and highly-cultured readers. Certain Puritan dogmas, it is true, had delayed the progress of the fine arts; for they were considered works of the devil. The power of the church, although waning, still remained strong enough to make it highly dangerous to attack it or its agents. Magistrates and official censors were sensitive to criticism or ridicule and they wielded sufficient power to punish their critic-victims severely—as James Franklin learned by an experience in jail. Literary men in Boston therefore had little chance to express their true feelings in print because of the heavy censorship imposed by such officials.

Boston had three newspapers and five printing presses in 1720, more than any English city except London.[7] Of the newspapers, the *New England Courant* was outstanding for general excellence and liveliness. The Boston *News-Letter,* founded in 1704, had a name as the official organ for executive orders and proclamations, and it therefore did not undertake social criticism. The Boston *Gazette,* a younger paper, came into existence in 1719; but it, too, felt the unfortunate weight of politics and was hamstrung to some degree by its publisher Musgrave's connection with the Post Office. Mild literature it did indulge in, but in such a desultory manner that the Hellfire Club found it completely unsatisfactory for its purpose of airing and promoting much-needed reforms.[8]

The *New England Courant* had come into being as a result of these unhappy conditions. It was to provide young writers an opportunity to speak their minds honestly and freely. Why did these young rebels prefer a newspaper rather than a book to vent their thoughts and sentiments? For one thing, despite Musgrave's Boston *Gazette,* Boston did not enjoy a plethora of light literature in that day. "Few men," one writer tells us, "wielded a ready pen of satire, of verse, or of story, and such writing in the printed book seemed out of place in the community" because of the hard-dying influence of Puritanism.[9] Newspapers, therefore, might offer an outlet to the few gifted young men who desired to dash off a squib or a letter to the editor, a veiled allegory, or an open attack upon a local person or institution.

Since it carried little or no advertising, the *Courant* depended almost entirely upon its literary quality. It closely imitated the *Spectator* of Addison and Steele both in format and content. Its predominantly neo-classical orientation appeared in the Greek and Latin-sounding names of characters in articles. Their names usually indicated their function with respect to some needed reform. Philanthropos, for example, urged wealthy persons to help struggling young businessmen. Hypercarpus (literally, one who carps) discussed pride, the greatest of all

sins for the classical Greeks and for the neo-classical writers of
the eighteenth century. Philomusus (love of the muses) and
Hypercriticus (hypercritical) criticized the very bad and highly
sentimental effusions of versifiers of condolence—the so-called
New England school of elegiac poetry. Proteus or Old Janus,
as these names imply, could be "all things to all men."[10] Other
characters, however, carried self-explanatory English names—
Justice Nicholas Clodpate, Tom Pen-Shallow, Ichabod Hen-
roost (a hen-pecked husband), Abigail Afterwit, Betty Frugal,
Fanny Mournful, Tabitha Talkative, Dorothy Love, etc.[11]

Employing satire with entertaining effects, the *Courant*
rebelled against the abuses of the times. In many ways it
represented a "violent and almost coarse reaction against clerical domination of New England."[12] If it lacked the urbanity
of the *Spectator*, it made up for this lack in punch and stench.
"It was in bad odor from the start," writes Ford, "with those
who had it in their power to make it uncomfortable for the
printer."[13] But it made American literary history, for it carried
Franklin's first published series of essays, the *Dogood* papers
(1722), and it marked the beginnings of a rebellious spirit of
social criticism in journalism and literature that we like to
think of as characteristically American. Crude, coarse, humorous, shrewd, and spontaneous, this little paper bore the leaven
of 1776 in its soul, as the following protest against titles of
rank makes clear. Written by Benjamin Franklin, aged seventeen, it appeared in the *Courant* for February 18, 1723.

In old Time it was no disrespect for Men and Women to be
call'd by their own Names: Adam, was never called *Master*
Adam; we never read of Noah *Esquire*, Lot *Knight* and *Baronet*,
nor the *Right Honourable* Abraham, *Viscount Mesopotamia*,
Baron of Canaan; no, no, they were plain Men, honest Country
Grasiers, that took care of their Families and their Flocks.
Moses was a great Prophet, and Aaron a Priest of the Lord;
but we never read of the *Reverend* Moses, nor the *Right Reverend Father in God*, Aaron, by Divine Providence, *Lord Arch-
Bishop of Israel*: Thou never sawest *Madam* Rebecca in the
Bible, my *Lady* Rachel, nor Mary, tho' a Princess of the Blood
after the Death of Joseph, call'd the *Princess Dowager of Naza-
reth*; no, plain Rebecca, Rachel, Mary, or the *Widow* Mary,
or the like: It was no Incivility then to mention their naked
Names as they were expressed.[14]

The *Courant* appeared for about five years, from August 7, 1721, to sometime between June 25, 1726, and March 9, 1727. On this latter date the Boston *News-Letter* referred to the "late *Courant,*" and Ford's opinion is that the journal probably "fell off in circulation and died for want of support."[15] We know that Franklin wrote the Silence Dogood essay on page one of the thirty-fifth issue of the *Courant* for April 2, 1722. Except for two ballads about the capture of a pirate and a lighthouse tragedy, which he claims to have printed and peddled on the streets of Boston, this was his first known appearance in print.[16] We know, too, that when James Franklin went to jail for refusing to cooperate with the censorship of the Secretary of the Province, the name of Benjamin Franklin appeared on the paper as publisher from the issue of February 11, 1723, until June 4, 1726—almost three years after he had run away to Philadelphia. The September 16th issue of 1723 was probably the last in which he took part.[17]

Although he enacted the role of publisher for the public during the three months his brother was detained in jail,[18] his status did not improve much over his former position as apprentice. Publicly, his old indentures were released to him, he explains in the *Autobiography,* so that it would not appear that an apprentice had taken over publication of the *Courant.* Privately, a new set of secret indentures was drawn up, so that he was still actually an apprentice.

Besides affording him experience as a writer and publisher and providing associations with good writers of satire, the apprenticeship on the *Courant* must have stimulated Franklin's interest in reading. Owners of private libraries of any fairly large size in the colonies before the year 1730 "could be counted on the fingers of one hand"[19] and the library of the *Courant* "in the number and variety of its secular books, could have challenged comparison with the few notable colonial libraries of that date."[20] It owned a copy of *Paradise Lost,* a great rarity in the colonies at that time. Other books that lined its capacious shelves were works of Shakespeare, Milton, and Virgil; Aristotle's *Politics;* Samuel Butler's *Hudibras;* eight volumes of *The Spectator* and two of *The Guardian;* Swift's *A Tale of a Tub;* the works of St. Augustine and of John Tillotson; Bishop Gilbert Burnet's *History of the Reformation* and Thomas Burnet's *Theory of the Earth;* and two highly important books by the Port-Royal writers that influenced some of the best writers and logicians of that age, *The Art of Thinking* and *The Art of Speaking*. And this is only the barest kind of a partial list.

The *Courant* took great pride in its library, advertising "we have also . . . a vast Quantity of Pamphlets."[21] In some respects this library outranked that of Harvard College. One authority writes: ". . . we know that Addison, Steele, Bolingbroke, Dryden, Pope, Prior, and Swift would have been looked for in vain at Harvard a year after the *Courant* had a full set of *The Spectator, A Tale of a Tub,* and Milton."[22] One cannot imagine a young man of Franklin's industry, ambition, sensitivity, intelligence, and keenness of observation neglecting these publications.

Not long after he ran away to Philadelphia—Franklin records in his *Autobiography*—his growing love for books led to his project of founding a library company there. Everything that we know of Franklin as thinker, writer, politician, practical scientist, and moralist points to his having made an early and extensive reading acquaintance with great books. As one writer puts it, "Franklin had grown up in the most highly articulate society in America—Boston. He had, therefore, the concepts and the speech to give voice to popular thought of the colonial people, who were [later in Philadelphia] his subscribers."[23]

II *Philadelphia Printer, Writer, Publisher*

Franklin ran away from Boston to Philadelphia when he was seventeen. He explains fully and satisfactorily in his *Autobiography* the reasons for his departure. Partly he had chafed under the restrictions of a censored press; partly he had felt that his brother had exploited him in the role of apprentice-publisher. The story that he had got a girl pregnant and was running away from her to escape marriage was useful only as a pretext to gain passage on a ship bound for Philadelphia. But Franklin himself must have had enough foresight to realize that, with his name on the masthead of the *Courant,* the same difficulties and imprisonment visited on his brother James undoubtedly awaited him. Prospects in general did not seem too bright. He resolved to try life in a new colony.

Because he could not find work in New York, he traveled on to Philadelphia. Luckily for his development as a writer, Philadelphia in the year 1723 ranked second only to Boston as a literary center. By the close of the colonial period, some fifty years later, it had become, largely by Franklin's own efforts, the place of most concentrated literary activity on the entire continent.[24] "Near the end of the first quarter of the eighteenth century," writes Moses Coit Tyler, "about the time Benjamin Franklin commenced his career there,—Philadelphia, though still dominated by the Quakers, had become the seat of a large population who were not Quakers; it had something of the liberal tone of a metropolis,—where men of cultivation, of vivacity, of literary aptitude, had begun to realize the presence of one another, and of a common literary purpose."[25] But only one other printer, Andrew Bradford, had established himself in the colony of Pennsylvania during the years 1712-1723.[26] Philadelphia, then, represented a fortunate choice for the young man who aspired to excellence in printing and writing.

The fact that he could write, and write well, gave him an edge in competition with other printers. "One of the first good effects of my having learned a little to scribble," Franklin modestly explains in the *Autobiography*, was a great increase in subscribers. "Some spirited remarks of my writing on the dispute then going on between Governor Burnet and the Massachusetts Assembly struck the principal people, occasioned the paper and the manager of it to be much talked of, and in a few weeks brought them all to be our subscribers."[27] Still another of his early rewards as a writer accrued as a result of an anonymous pamphlet he wrote and printed. Entitled *A Modest Enquiry Into the Nature and Necessity of a Paper Currency* (1729), this pamphlet, writes Franklin,

> was well received by the common people in general; but the rich men disliked it, for it increased and strengthened the clamour for more money; and they happening to have no writers among them that were able to answer it, their opposition slackened, and the point was carried by a majority in the House. My friends there, who considered I had been of some service, thought fit to reward me by employing me in printing the money—a very profitable job and a great help to me. This was another advantage gained by my being able to write.[28]

In the controversial *Busy-Body* papers Franklin's superiority as a writer also helped him to a profitable victory over his competitor Samuel Keimer.

As a printer he was, of course, no "slouch." One expert on typography characterizes him as "the best of his time in the mechanical sense" and notes that the early issues of Franklin's *Pennsylvania Gazette* (in the New York Public Library) compare favorably in clarity with twentieth-century reprints.[29] Franklin himself wrote in the *Autobiography* that the first issues of the *Pennsylvania Gazette,* which he had started in October of 1729, "made a quite different appearance from any other papers before in the province, a better type and better printed. . . ."[30] Eventually, thirty years of journalistic experience taught him "all that was to be known in that busy craft."[31]

The style that Franklin evolved as a result of his journalistic work was of necessity clear and forceful, plain and brief. His practical-minded readers found it free of nonsense but full of pithy moralizing. They had no time for hifalutin literary embroidery, but they apparently did not object to a little free preaching from time to time. He knew his audience well; for, according to one historian, Franklin "understood Puritanism well enough to realize it offered assurances of material prosperity to all who followed its code of morals."[32] This historian then accuses Franklin not only of perceiving that the Puritan virtues had immense utilitarian value but of exploiting them in the various *Poor Richard's Almanacks* and elsewhere.[33] There is a great deal of truth in this charge; it needs no great discernment to see that this same Puritanism afflicts our present culture with the false idea that there exists some necessary connection between virtue or intelligence and material prosperity.

In our discussion of the *Autobiography* we shall consider in more detail the question of Franklin as the embodiment of capitalistic success. But it is worth noting here that his agrarianism and liberal economics are inconsistent with the modern capitalistic cult of "pecuniary power and individualism."[34] In politics Franklin belonged to the Pennsylvania agrarian class, a class of farmers who sharply opposed the wealthy merchant class and their British mercantile policies. On the question of paper currency he had seen this same division of interest between farmer and merchant groups in his native Massachusetts.[35] His early and important pamphlet on the paper currency sprang from his sympathy for poor farmers.

As an eighteenth-century writer and publisher, Franklin early encountered and joined in the growing wave of liberalism that flowed from the print shops.[36] Such shops, but particularly their publishers, "became the handmaids of the insurgent class because this class, lacking privilege, needed to claim its rights, and the press became the chief channel for making its claims."[37] In the American colonies as abroad, the great patrons of liberalism were the small shopkeepers, Jews, and Masons. "Franklin had established social relationships with all of these . . . he caught and restated through his mouthpiece, Poor Richard, the *Volksgeist* [spirit of the people] so that his precepts became a part of traditional American mores."[38] As a writer, Franklin's individual shrewdness and broad tolerance created a pattern for modern liberals devoted to modifying the status quo by orderly social change and by the use of free associations of individuals.[39]

Strongly as Franklin may have advocated individual enterprise, his individualism more closely resembled a "circumscribed individualism," that is, an individualism circumscribed by "ultimate social control." His numerous projects for improving Philadelphia attest this point. This kind of social control, Professor Verner W. Crane reminds us, constitutes an integral part of the "authentic American tradition" (54, 51-52). Modern reactionaries who have seized upon Franklin as their figurehead for ruthless individualism sometimes forget not only his attitudes but this part of our heritage. But Franklin's sharp division of human nature into the "wise and moderate" on the one hand and the ambitious and avaricious on the other, underscores the need for control of the latter, whom he regarded as dangerously motivated by "the love of power and the love of money."[40]

His relatively quick success as a printer in Philadelphia was not entirely due to his gifts as a writer. He knew the value of advertising and reputation in the conduct of business, and he indicates his astuteness in the *Autobiography*:

> I took care not only to be in *reality* industrious and frugal, but to avoid all *appearance* of the contrary. I dressed plain and was seen at no places of idle diversion. I never went out a fishing or shooting; . . . [and] to show that I was not above my business, I sometimes brought home the paper I purchased at the stores, thro' the streets on a wheelbarrow.[41]

His uncanny ability to organize his business efficiently and his quickness to sense and seize an opportunity helped him immeasurably. He combined these abilities with an extraordinary insight into human nature. Furthermore, as a kind of great-granddaddy to Madison Avenue, he established a long line of public relations experts.[42] Taking extreme care of his reputation and publicizing at every opportunity the freedom of his paper from dirty journalism—"the Personal Abuse, so scandalously common in our Newspapers"[43]—he created a tidy and well-organized business that later expanded into a chain of printing houses along the Atlantic seacoast.

Franklin's career as a printer in Philadelphia encompassed three large journalistic projects during a span of about twelve years, 1729-1741: the *Pennsylvania Gazette,* a newspaper; *Poor Richard's Almanack;* and the *General Magazine and Historical Chronicle.*

First and most important after his trip to London to purchase type was his acquisition of the newspaper. Franklin and his partner Hugh Meredith took over Samuel Keimer's bankrupt *Universal Instructor in All Arts and Sciences and Pennsylvania Gazette* on October 2, 1729.[44] Franklin's first issue carried the date September 25—October 2, 1729, but appeared on the October date. Franklin immediately shortened the paper's title to *Pennsylvania Gazette,* and also served notice to his readers that the policy Keimer had followed in tediously publishing extracts from Chambers' *Cyclopedia* would stop. (Despite this avowal Franklin actually reprinted some of Chambers' articles; an article on hemp appeared in Number 42, one on inoculation for smallpox in Number 80, and one on Free-Masonry in Number 130.)[45]

The *Pennsylvania Gazette,* which usually contained several columns of foreign and out-of-town news, radiated a kind of cosmopolitan air for its provincial readers. It reprinted essays from English periodicals—sometimes those published by the Junto members and Franklin himself. It abounded in local news —fires, accidents, burials, notices of counterfeiting, suicide attempts, Negro slaves for sale (one by Franklin's mother-in-law), laws passed by the latest sessions of the Pennsylvania Assembly, and advertisements for an early anti-slavery tract published by Ralph Sandiford.[46] The *Gazette* for January 4, 1732, carried the notice "We have no Entries this Week, the River being full of Ice."[47] The following appeared at one time or another in issues of the paper during 1732: advertisements for "Flour of Mustard-Seed" (a cure for sea-sickness), geese-feathers, women's corset stays, and children's coats; announcements of the meetings of Franklin's Library Company; and advance publicity on *Poor Richard's Almanack* (to be published in 1733).[48] One particular advertisement for August 19, 1731, refers to the Widow Read (Franklin's mother-in-law), her "well-known Ointment for the Itch," and "her excellent *Family Salve* for Burns or Scalds."[49]

Franklin's humor helped spice the *Gazette*. One excerpt for October 16, 1729, reads: "And sometime last Week, we are informed, that one Piles a Fiddler, with his Wife, were overset in a Canoo near Newtown Creek. The good Man, 'tis said, prudently secured his Fiddle, and let his Wife go to the bottom."[50] For June 19, 1732, he described a boy struck by lightning in Bucks County: "One Flash came so near [the] Lad, as without hurting him, to melt the Pewter Button off the Wasteband of his Breeches. 'Tis well nothing else thereabouts was made of Pewter."[51] The real test of a sense of humor, of course, is whether a person can laugh at a joke on himself. The following example of Franklin's word-play and punning shows him measuring up to this test:

> Thursday last, a certain P——r ['tis not customary to give Names at length on these Occasions] walking carefully in clean Cloaths over some Barrels of Tar on Carpenter's Wharff, the head of one of them unluckily gave way, and let a Leg of him in above his Knee. Whether he was upon the Catch at that time, we cannot say, but 'tis certain he caught a *Tartar*. 'Twas observed he sprung out again right briskly, verifying the common Saying, *As nimble as a Bee in a Tarbarrel*. You must know there are several sorts of *Bees*: 'tis true he was no *Honey Bee*, nor yet a *Humble Bee*, but a *Boo bee* he may be allow'd to be, namely B.F. N.B. *We hope the Gentleman will excuse this Freedom.*[52]

The *Pennsylvania Gazette* also gave healthy expression to Franklin's penchant for satiric fun. Generally the satire took the form of an essay, or a letter to the editor. *The Speech of Polly Baker* and *The Witch Trial at Mount Holly* are but two of numerous examples. Along with these we may cite the brief character sketches featuring Anthony Afterwit, Alice Addertongue, Celia Single, and Patience Teacroft, all of whom had their counterparts in the *Spectator*.[53]

Franklin's contributions to the *Gazette* eventually made it the best-written paper in America.[54] His enterprises had a way of succeeding, and the *Gazette* was no exception; it soon became a source of power and enlightenment throughout the colonies.

His consciousness of the difficulties and responsibilities required of an author of such a paper probably helped to insure its success.

> The Author of a Gazette (in the Opinion of the Learned) ought to be qualified with an extensive Acquaintance with Languages, a great Easiness and Command of Writing and Relating Things cleanly and intelligently, and in few Words; he should be able to speak of War both by Land and Sea; be well acquainted with Geography, with the History of the Time, with the several Interests of Princes and States, the Secrets of Courts, and the Manners and Customs of all Nations. Men thus accomplish'd are very rare in this remote Part of the World; and it would be well if the Writer of these Papers could make up among his Friends what is wanting in himself.[55]

At the start of the year 1733 Franklin began publication of the *Poor Richard* almanacs. This second large publishing venture in Philadelphia developed into an even greater success than his first. Some idea of its size may be gained from the fact that it sold "over ten thousand copies a year annually for many years" and constituted one of the chief sources of his income.[56] We shall discuss this and other almanacs of the period in Chapter Three.

Franklin's third enterprise during the period 1729-1741 was the founding of a magazine which narrowly missed being America's first. Andrew Bradford's *American Magazine* beat it by three days by appearing on February 13, 1741. But both magazines carried January datelines, which indicates a hot race to be first.[57] Plans for each magazine had been printed in the November issues of the papers of their respective editors. Bradford's announcement appeared a week ahead of Franklin's; but Franklin charged in his announcement that John Webbe, a lawyer whom he had hired to collect Bradford's debts due the post office, had carried the idea of a magazine to Bradford after Franklin had revealed it to the former in confidence. (Webbe had published essays on government in the *Pennsylvania Gazette* in 1736.)[58]

The complete title of Franklin's magazine was *The General Magazine, and Historical Chronicle, For all the British Plantations in America.* Tyler not only states that a magazine by definition aimed at "a more explicit literary intention than the newspapers," but also claims that more space was devoted to

literary news, criticism, and talent than in the newspapers.[59]
But according to F. L. Mott (I, 75), comparatively few pieces
of original poetry or prose adorned the *General Magazine,* for
the two chief subjects running through all six numbers concerned the currency question and the opinions and activities of
the Methodist revivalist the Reverend George Whitefield. Smyth
incompletely describes the contents of the magazine as "parliamentary proceedings, extracts from sermons, a bit of verse
of more than Franklinian foulness [?], rhymes eulogizing Gil-
bert·Tennent, and a manual of arms."[60] Labaree and Bell publish the complete contents of all six numbers.[61] Both Franklin's
magazine and Bradford's published mainly state papers, but the
General Magazine had more pages and more variety than its
rival. Neither succeeded. Bradford's magazine, edited by Webbe,
lasted only three months; Franklin's—only six months, despite his
increasing the size and undercutting his competitor's price by
three shillings a year.[62]

III *Writers Who Influenced Franklin's Style*

The satire of bad verse in the seventh *Dogood* paper would
indicate that, as an apprentice in Boston, Franklin "had read
much poetry carefully."[63] His comments on poetry show that he
liked the British poets William Cowper and James Thomson,
particularly the latter's poem, "The Seasons."[64] But his taste was
far from impeccable. He also admired the verse of the popular
hymn writer Isaac Watts, whose "Psalms of David" underwent
twenty-two editions between 1729 and 1781. Franklin published
his works,[65] and one story relates that on his deathbed Franklin
quoted Watts.[66]

Franklin's early reading had included such works as the following: Tryon's book on vegetable diet; Edward Cocker's book
of arithmetic; John Seller's and Samuel Sturmy's books of nav-
igation; John Locke's *Essay Concerning Human Understand-
ing; The Art of Thinking* by Messrs. du Port Royal; James
Greenwood's *An Essay toward a Practical English Grammar;*
Xenophon's *Memorable Things of Socrates;* the works of such
Deists as Anthony Cooper, third Earl of Shaftsbury, Anthony
Collins, and Bernard Mandeville; William Wollaston's *Religion
of Nature* (also Deistic); John Bunyan's *Pilgrim's Progress;*
Robert or Richard (see note) Burton's *Historical Collections;*
Plutarch's *Lives;* Daniel Defoe's *Moll Flanders, Robinson Cru-*

BENJAMIN FRANKLIN

soe and *An Essay on Projects;* Cotton Mather's *Essays to Do Good;* Joseph Addison and Richard Steele's *The Spectator;* Edward Young's *Satires;* and Samuel Richardson's *Pamela.*[67] He very likely also read Defoe's *Religious Courtship* and *Family Instructor;* Milton's *Paradise Lost* (part of which he quotes in his *Articles of Belief,* 1728); and some works of Edmund Waller, Dryden, Goldsmith, and Pope.[68]

Besides the authors already mentioned he either read or advised others to read the works of Dr. George Turnbull, John Tillotson, Algernon Sidney, Sir William Temple, Swift, Homer, Cato, Virgil, Horace, Rabelais, Fénelon, Robert Greene (1678-1730), William Paley, Tom Paine, Francis Bacon, David Hume, Jeremy Taylor, and Dr. Johnson.[69] And this is only a partial list. Spenser and Shakespeare are conspicuously absent. It has been suggested that Franklin omitted them intentionally as "unsuitable models for a writer of clear, concise language,"[70] but this hardly makes sense.

The question of exactly how reading influences writing has never been solved. That writers resemble other writers in the employment of certain techniques, or even general methods, no one will deny. But precisely how these procedures drift from one writer to another is a difficult problem. As a careful and extensive reader, Franklin learned a good deal about writing through reading, as studies of his work show and as he himself admitted.

Lois M. MacLaurin states that Franklin's works show the effect of "widespread imitation of English authors."[71] She regards Bunyan, Defoe, Addison, and Swift as the principal influences upon Franklin's style and vocabulary. "Like them he wrote to convince, and accordingly chose a language that appealed to the reader by its very simplicity and conciseness."[72] Robert Newcomb, who has made a very careful and extensive study of this problem in *Poor Richard,* notes Franklin's great admiration for Pope, his liking for Addison, Thomson, Young, Milton, Dryden, Rowe, and Watts—especially the latter.[73]

Franklin candidly admits his debt to Addison in the *Autobiography.* He relates how he wrote down "short hints of the sentiment in each sentence" of some of the *Spectator* papers, laid them aside a few days, and then, "without looking at the book," tried to develop in his own style "each hinted sentiment at length and as fully as it had been expressed before."[74] He then compared his finished composition with the original of the *Spectator* in order to discover some of his faults and to correct them. Franklin's *Dogood* papers, especially, reflect many tricks from the *Spectator;* among them are the Latin mottoes for headings, the letters from fictitious correspondents, names suggestive of characters, quotations from the *London Journal,* first-person point of view of an on-the-scene reporter, essay subjects introduced as general observations, and even an imitation of actual paragraph beginnings. "About half of the fourteenth Dogood is a quote from Addison's *Spectator* 185" on religious zeal, and the satiric vision of Harvard in the fourth *Dogood* is "like the allegorical dream of the throne-room of Public Credit in Addison's third Spectator."[75]

Yet one recent critic thinks that Swift rather than Addison should be recognized as the stronger influence on Franklin as a writer.[76] Swift's influence began early and lasted late, long into Franklin's best period of satire, 1766-1775. As has already been mentioned, Swift's *Tale of a Tub* occupied a prominent place on the shelves of the *Courant* library. In 1757 Franklin met in London a certain Dr. John Hawksworth, who two years earlier had edited Swift's works.[77] In their liking for irony and hoaxes Franklin and Swift had a great deal in common. Neither Franklin nor Swift was very optimistic about human goodness, but Franklin lacked some degree of the savage indignation that lacerated the soul of Swift.[78] And while Swift sometimes cannonaded the world at large or man in general, Franklin always sniped away at specific situations.

The most apparent borrowing from Swift appears in the Titan Leeds hoax, which Franklin began in the *Pennsylvania Gazette* and continued in *Poor Richard.* Leeds was a rival almanac maker, or philomath. One function of all publishers of almanacs was to predict the weather because farmers made up a large part of almanac readers. When Franklin predicted his rival's death to the day, hour, and minute, Leeds retorted in print that he was still alive after the above date and called Franklin some rather nasty names. Anyone acquainted with Swift's Bickerstaff papers will instantly see the likeness of the situation. Twenty years earlier, in the Bickerstaff papers, Swift had similarly baited an unfortunate cobbler and almanac maker by the name of Partridge, whose protestations that he was alive became the more ridiculous the more he protested. And so it was with Leeds. Francis X. Davy sees the influence of Swift in other works of Franklin: *Reflexions on Courtship and Mar-*

riage (1746), which Franklin actually bound with Swift's *Letter to a very Young Lady on her Marriage; The Exporting of the Felons* (1751), and *Pax Quaeritur Bello* (1776), both of which resemble Swift's *A Modest Proposal;* and *An Account of the Captivity of William Henry,* which reminds this critic of *Gulliver's Travels.*[79]

Besides Addison and Swift, Defoe merits some critical attention as an influence on Franklin's writing. Davy sees Defoe's "hortatory influence" in the *Dogood* papers, especially in the plan for the relief of widows (*Dogood* No. 10) and in the plan for female education (No. 5).[80] Defoe's *An Essay on Projects,* in which he describes his friendly societies, also probably influenced the eleventh *Dogood* paper, which concerns insurance for old spinsters. The interest that Silence Dogood takes in problems of intoxication and alcoholism as well as in those created by amorous sailors and night strollers, writes Davy, resembles the interest in low life about which Defoe moralized so heavily.[81] Franklin's "vigorous graphic manner" of presenting his subject as a scientist; his "plain, matter-of-fact style which carried conviction by its very lack of imaginative qualities"; his gift for satire; his interest in political, economical, and social problems; and his ability to perpetrate a hoax (cf. *The Shortest Way with Dissenters* and *An Edict of the King of Prussia*)—all these may show the influence of Defoe upon Franklin.[82]

Many other influences operated in the formation of Franklin as a writer, but space does not permit treating each in detail. Prominent among these are "Bunyan's simple rhythm and bald English idiom," the King James version of the Bible, and John Smith's *The Mysterie of Rhetorique Unveiled,* a popular book which "taught the searcher to find art in the language and rhythms" of this same Bible.[83] Since Franklin began conscious practice of rhetorical (persuasive) skills when but a boy, he may have read—or even studied—this book of Smith's as well as the Bible. The classical influence that pervaded the entire eighteenth century certainly must have affected Franklin—particularly the numerous instruction books in rhetoric that usually traced their origin in one form or other to Aristotle's *Rhetoric.* These left their mark deeply on Franklin's writing technique, as we shall show later.

Socrates, Plato, Xenophon, Hesiod, and Plutarch were also Franklin's instructors in the art of writing, for he used their methods of questioning and definition time and time again.

Among the French we must name La Bruyère, La Rochefou-cauld, Montaigne, and Rabelais, although none of them lived in the eighteenth century. The Port-Royal *Art of Thinking* and *Art of Speaking*, as Davy has shown, cannot be disregarded. The latter work, by Bernard Lamy, was available to Franklin in the *Courant* library. Davy is not absolutely certain that Franklin used it, but he sees a striking similarity between some of Lamy's instructions about purity of language and Franklin's statements on style.[84]

Franklin actually used *The Art of Thinking*. A collection of essays first published in 1662 and written by the followers of Descartes, it concentrated on such matters as discovering arguments, logical fallacies, analysis and synthesis, methods of ordering material, definition, syllogisms, and enthymemes. The writers of the Port-Royal group tried to make students "sensitive and critical about words."[85] Other subjects they drew attention to were as follows: how disputes arise from mistakes in meaning, how different ideas become attached to similar words, how ideas gain emotional force from figurative dress, how true and false arguments can be distinguished, and how rhetorical principles may be most effectively applied.[86] Davy concludes that in this book Franklin found "a solid, systematic, and thorough treatment of thinking and of many secrets of persuasion; an insistence that each word and figure do its share of work; a careful discipline in terminology, definition, division; an alert sensitivity for sophism; and an established distaste for fluff and mere decoration."[87]

IV *Franklin's Theories on Writing*

> If you wou'd not be forgotten
> As soon as you are dead and rotten,
> Either write things worth reading
> Or do things worth the writing.[88]

This quotation from *Poor Richard* for 1738 aptly introduces Franklin's ideas about the vital importance of good writing. Despite his numerous and suggestive comments on this subject, little attention has been paid to his theories. In a paper entitled *On Literary Style*, which he prepared as a reply to a question proposed in the Junto and which he printed in the *Pennsylvania Gazette* for August 2, 1733, he asserts: ". . . there is Scarce any Accomplishment more necessary to a Man of

Sense, than that of *Writing well* in his Mother Tongue: But as most other polite Acquirements make a greater Appearance in a Man's Character, this however useful, is generally neglected or forgotten."[89]

Franklin has described in detail in the *Autobiography* the manner by which he himself learned to write. In an already quoted passage we noted that one of his self-imposed exercises was to select something in the *Spectator*, turn it into verse, and translate it back into prose. By this arduous work he hoped to remedy certain defects that were apparent when he compared his version with the original in the *Spectator*. He describes his objective in performing this exercise: "I wanted a stock of words or readiness in recollecting and using them, which I thought I should have acquired before that time if I had gone on making verses; since the continual search for words of the same import but of different length to suit the measure, or of different sound for the rhyme would have laid me under a constant necessity of searching for variety, and also have tended to fix that variety in my mind, and make me master of it."[90]

Another device he used to teach himself writing concerns organization, an even more important principle than that of *variety:* "I also sometimes jumbled my collections of hints into confusion, and after some weeks endeavoured to reduce them into *the best order* before I began to form the full sentences and complete the paper. This was to teach me *method* in the arrangement of the thoughts. By comparing my work afterwards with the original, I discovered many faults and corrected them."[91] (The italics are mine.)

Order and method were all-important to Franklin as a writer; and that *order* is the first law of writing Franklin came to understand while yet a boy.[92] Because order and method are of special importance in rhetorical, or persuasive works, Franklin early conceived his idea of the best style as an orderly one adapted to a plainly visible end or purpose. "Good writing," he thought, "should proceed regularly from things known to things unknown, distinctly and clearly without confusion . . . that is best wrote which is best adapted for obtaining the end of the writer."[93] If persuasion is the object, and it often was Franklin's object, the writer "should proceed gradually from Things already allow'd, to those from which Assent is yet with-held, and make their Connections manifest."[94] The habit of using good *method* "could be acquired by study of a little Geometry or Algebra."[95] Franklin's care with *order* may be seen in one of his marginal comments written opposite the Standing Queries of the Junto: "Memo these Queries are not plac'd in the order I design 'em."[96] In a letter of November 2, 1789, to Benjamin Vaughan, he chides his friend for his "neglect of method" or order. "Thus I would have you put a figure before each thought, to mark its future place in your composition."[97]

From Franklin's early experiments in verse he had learned the necessity of plan or design in writing: ". . . we ought always, before we begin, to form a regular plan and design. . . ."[98] In his early so-called "imitations" of Addison he depended upon the *Spectator* for his general plan, and for this alone, as we have already seen. "In details he worked quite independently," as Davy says, adding that such a method was "entirely in keeping with the notions of his day on the subject of imitation."[99] Later, when he grew more skillful, he formed his own plans.

Franklin's ideas on the teaching of composition appear in his *Proposals Relating to the Education of Youth in Pensilvania.* He suggests in this document that students write letters to each other, make abstracts or a précis of what they read, and write the same thing *in their own words.* He also suggests that they tell or write in their own words stories they have recently read. All this is "to be revis'd and corrected by the Tutor, who should give his Reasons, and explain the Force and Import of Words, &c."[100]

Besides his emphasis on order, method, and formal plan, Franklin posed in his essay *On Literary Style* three other requirements for good writing—that it be "smooth, clear and short: For the contrary Qualities are apt to offend, either the Ear, the Understanding, or the Patience."[101] Brevity, the third of these requirements for good writing (and the one he discussed most amusingly), consisted of this simple rule: use no unnecessary words.

Amplification, the lack of brevity, he defined as "the Art of saying Little in Much." According to Franklin, amplification should be allowed only to public speakers—preachers and lawyers in particular. Amplification is especially useful to a lawyer, in Franklin's opinion, because the ignorant people in a jury "can scarcely believe it possible that a Man can talk so much and so long without being in the Right." The following quotation should clarify any remaining doubt on this subject:

Let them [lawyers and preachers] have the Liberty then, of repeating the same Sentences in other Words; let them put an Adjective to every Substantive, and double every Substantive with a Synonima; for this is more agreeable than haulking, spitting, taking Snuff, or any other Means of concealing Hesitation. Let them multiply Definitions, Comparisons, Similitudes and Examples. Permit them to make a Detail of Causes and Effects, enumerate all the Consequences, and express one Half by Metaphor and Circumlocution; Nay, allow the Preacher to [sic] to tell us whatever a Thing is negatively, before he begins to tell us what it is affirmatively; and suffer him to divide and subdivide as far as *Two and fiftiethly.* All this is not intolerable while it is not written. But when a Discourse is to be bound down upon Paper, and subjected to the calm leisurely Examination of nice Judgment, every Thing that is needless gives Offence; and there all should be retrenched, that does not directly conduce to the End design'd. Had this always been done, many large and tiresome Folio's [sic] would have shrunk into Pamphlets, and many a Pamphlet into a single Period.[102]

Labaree and Bell have attributed to Franklin one of the most entertaining of early satirical essays, a regular *tour de force,* entitled *On Amplification,* published in the *Pennsylvania Gazette* for June 17, 1736, and reprinted in the Boston *Evening-Post* of October 11, 1736.[103] Following a brief résumé of land conveyance since the time of William the Conqueror, the essay, which parodies legal jargon, begins with this remark: "The Lawyer, in one of Steele's Comedies, instructs his Pupil that *Tautology* is the first, second, and third Parts of his Profession, that is to say, *the whole of it:* And adds, *That he hopes to see the Time, when it will require as Much Parchment to convey a Piece of Land as will cover it.*" The essay then takes the form of the petition of a certain Dermond O'Folivey, "an attorney of the Kingdom of Ireland." The petition begins as an unostentatious and modest address to the "Right Honourable Sir William Aston, Knight, and Lord Judge of Assize of the Munster Circuit."

Most humbly, and most submissively, and most obediently, and most dutifully, by shewing, and expressing, and declaring to your Lordship, that whereby, and whereas, and wherein, the most major, and most greater, and most bigger, and the most stronger Part of the most best, and the most ablest, and most mightiest Sort of the People of the Barony of Torrough and

County of Kerry, finding, and knowing, and certifying themselves, both hereafter, and the Time past, and now, and then,
and at the present time, to be very much oppressed, and distressed, and overcharged in all Taxes, . . . etc., etc.

The parody proceeds with its "now, and then, and there, and
here, and anywhere, and everywhere, and somewhere, and
nowhere," with its "all such, and all much, Bailiffs," and finally
reaches its humorous climax with this well-weighed formal
close: "Given, and granted, and dated, and signed, and sealed
by my own Hand and with my own Hand, and so my own
Hand, and under my own Hand and Seal this Day of Anno.
Dom. [signed] Mr. Dermond O'Folivey."

As a critic of writing Franklin tended to judge a work in
terms of how well it contributed to improving either virtue
or knowledge. Quite categorically he states in the essay *On
Literary Style* that *"no Piece can properly be called good, and
well written, which is void of any tendency to benefit the
Reader, either by improving his Virtue or his Knowledge."*[104]
And he adds that every writer should keep this principle in
mind whenever he writes.[105] But Franklin also believed that
good writing should be interesting, and the following statement
indicates still another method and test of writing: "I believe
there is no better Means of learning to write well, than this of
attempting to entertain the Publick now and then in one of
your Papers."[106]

V *Franklin's Practice as a Writer*

For sheer volume and rapidity of production few writers
have matched Franklin. One recent estimate of the number of
documents written by him numbers in the vicinity of twenty
thousand.[107] By turning out copy in great quantity at a great
rate of speed, he naturally aroused the suspicion that he was
careless in composition and spent little time in revision. But
this suspicion is entirely unfounded, as Verner W. Crane, Carl
Van Doren, and others have demonstrated.[108] "There are many
revisions in his manuscripts. He wrote prose as careful poets
write poetry."[109]

To Max Farrand, one of the strongest contributions to Franklin's learning to write well was his ability to think clearly; even
as a young boy he was able to think and write clearly. Defi-

nitely a precocious writer, Franklin, according to Van Doren, exhibited as early as the *Dogood* papers most of the qualities he evinced later. At sixteen he was "already the most charming writer in America."[110]

He seems to have taken literally the advice that "the best way to learn to write is to write and to keep on writing, provided one is critical of one's own work."[111] This self-critical attitude toward writing—and indeed toward his own developing moral and intellectual nature—was almost an innate characteristic with him. Sometimes he wrote notes to himself on how to develop and improve his first drafts.[112] "He taught himself— as every good, pungent, characteristic writer does and should."[113]

Despite Franklin's theoretical emphasis on order, Davy's opinion is that Franklin "was no devotee of rigid formal structure nor so unpracticed a writer as to leave his work divided into clearly marked 'parts' with the gaps showing between them. Rather, the parts fused easily together."[114] But in our opinion Franklin did take great care with matters of literary form, plan, and design. Almost all of his works reveal such a well-developed sense of part-whole structure that they make excellent exercises in literary analysis for beginners.

If, finally, we consider the general kind of writer Franklin represents, we may still feel somewhat nonplussed because he remains so versatile as to seem completely unclassifiable. One recent writer, however, has analyzed quite well the basic method of Franklin as writer and thinker. "If there are two kinds of writers," says Paul Baender, "—those who delight in the peculiarities of things and those who delight in the resemblances among things—certainly Franklin was of the second kind."[115] In his scientific writings, for example, he set up "comparisons between unknowns and knowns" and then assumed a rule of analogy that would guide him to distinctive knowledge of the unknowns.[116] If this method sounds abstract, it may become clearer by reference to his technique in *Poor Richard* in whose sayings and proverbs Franklin also used resemblances. Baender says that Franklin used proverbs and fables to illustrate maxims, presumably in the satires and other writings as well as in *Poor Richard*. "The force of these illustrations," he argues, "lay in the discovery that they were not the odd inventions they seemed but contained informative implications for men in general: their similarities to human experience were more significant than their peculiarities."[117]

In his *Autobiography* Franklin applied this same method but with a different emphasis. Unlike other colonial writers with a background of Puritanism, who might have ascribed their rise in life to "Gracious Influences, the rubric of typology, or some other theological argument that allowed him to study himself in relative isolation from his fellows," Franklin "could explain his rise only through fairly systematic comparisons of himself with people like John Collins and Samuel Keimer, who at various points had jobs and opportunities similar to his."[118] In an almost experimental way, he used "these tentative and partial resemblances to isolate the personal factors" of his success.[119]

In Franklin's writings on ethics and politics Baender also observes this same method of resemblances at work: "Certain resemblances among men were authoritative for Franklin. Over and over in his creeds and political writings he reminded himself and others that 'doing Good to Man' was virtuous because all men were equally deserving."[120] Thus his method in writing was related closely to his thoughts and views on human nature. As one writer put it, "Whatever he wrote seems to have been conceived upon a scale which embraced the whole human race."[121]

CHAPTER 2

The *Autobiography*

FRANKLIN'S *Memoirs*, as he called them, comprise probably the most famous autobiography in the world.[1] Along with *Poor Richard's Almanack*, the *Autobiography*—as we call his *Memoirs*—constitutes an enduring foundation for his fame as a writer. These works, including *The Way to Wealth*, are certainly also his most popular productions.[2] As the first great book written in America, the *Autobiography* not only holds a unique place in our literary history,[3] but will probably remain the one work by which Franklin is best known.

I *Popular Success Story*

Franklin's autobiography effectively withstood the competitive "flood of memoirs deluging the eighteenth century"—possibly because of its simpler style and greater clarity[4]—and by 1890 it had passed through "at least one hundred and seventy editions."[5] Earlier in the century, 1806 to be exact, a critic in Boston had recommended it as useful reading "for all young persons of unsteady principles, who have their fortunes to make or to mend in the world." Apparently, the utility of the book as a guide to morality (this would have pleased Franklin) struck this critic, although he was also pleased because it demonstrated the "comparative uselessness of [formal] learning and laborious accomplishments" in Franklin's career.[6]

To account for the great fame of this little book is not easy. Two possibilities have already been suggested: its clarity and its appeal to readers with little formal learning. For such people Franklin represented a kind of champion who by dint of superior natural endowment outstripped the learned in science, politics, philosophy, or practically any area of knowledge. If Franklin could do this, others could—or at least so they thought. And thinking so was the important thing. The rise of Franklin, described in the *Autobiography*, opened the doors to what many Americans, and others, must have regarded as a brave new world of opportunity—the chance to break the chains with which the intelligentsia and the clergy had shackled them. The brilliancy of Franklin's career suggested the immense possibilities of common sense latent in the tradesman class to which he belonged. In more than mere political freedom, therefore, Franklin epitomized the spirit of liberty to his fellow men.

Another closely allied reason for this book's success is related to the great American dream: a poor person can become very wealthy—and even great—in the American community if he plays his cards properly. Numerous critics and writers have accounted for the popularity of the *Autobiography* on this ground. To one, "this is a tale of pluck and luck much more convincing than any found in the pages of Horatio Alger."[7] Others have regarded it as "a typical American success story: the first of that species, and still by all odds the best";[8] and as "an unsurpassed story of how a printer and shopkeeper in Philadelphia rose to be one of the world's great figures, and the most complete representative of his century that any nation can point to."[9]

Related to this idea of the *Autobiography* as the great American success story is Sanford's interpretation. To him the *Autobiography* embodies a folk myth, a kind of parallel to Bunyan's *Pilgrim's Progress* as an "allegory of American middle-class superiority."[10] Noting the serious intent of both the *Autobiography* and *Poor Richard's Almanack* to "impart moral instruction to the public," he concludes that the former is "a great moral fable pursuing on a secular level the theme of John Bunyan's *Pilgrim's Progress*."[11] He conceives Franklin's purpose as having been to give "to this secular 'rise' a moral and spiritual meaning discoverable in the special blessings of God. The boy entering Philadelphia with three loaves under his arm is obviously the prototype of Bunyan's Christian beginning his toilsome ascent to the Heavenly City."[12] Sanford refers to the three loaves of bread as "symbolic rolls," but he cagily refuses to commit himself on *what* they symbolize.[13] As a healthy antidote to Sanford's far-fetched interpretation, we can do no better than cite what Mark Twain said about Franklin's entry into Philadelphia: "He was . . . proud of telling how he entered Philadelphia for the first time, with nothing in the world but two shillings in his pocket and four [*sic*] rolls of bread under his arm. But really, when you come to examine it critically, it was nothing. Anybody could have done it."[14]

Besides Mark Twain's jibe at this facet of the Franklin myth, a few serious objections have been made to the success aspect of the *Autobiography*—to the stress upon it by other strong devotees of the American dream. Paul Elmer More wishes that Franklin had not made the *Autobiography* "so singular a document in petty prudence and economy."[15] Professor Nye writes: "Unfortunately, Parson Weems, Noah Webster's school-books, McGuffey's readers, and a thousand inspirational orators and copywriters have fixed Franklin in the popular mind as the first apostle of frugality and the patron saint of savings accounts."[16]

In our opinion, Franklin is not entirely guiltless. A recurring theme song of the *Autobiography* runs as follows: "My business was now continually augmenting and my circumstances growing daily easier. . . ."[17] When he was elected to the Pennsylvania Assembly after having served previously in several other elective offices, he felt flattered and wrote: "For considering my low beginning they [these promotions] were great things to me."[18]

The technique of Franklin's rise in the society of his time may need more clarification than he has given it in the *Autobiography*. Gladys Meyer believes that it consisted of a combination of elements: "Good repute, the strength of association, the threat of adverse publicity, the use of patronage, the accumulation of wealth, the interest in civic improvement." These, she thinks, "interplayed continually to promote his rise. It is interesting to ask at what personal cost this technique was perfected."[19] She also suggests that Franklin achieved this rise by being "discreet and always aware of the public to whom he spoke."[20] Noting that many things are omitted from the *Autobiography*, she says: "His biography, seemingly so candid, is a masterpiece of discretion. . . . He had no intimate friends, letters to whom might give any direct clue to his inner spirit."[21] This concluding sentence is unwarranted, as the reader will see when he comes to our chapter on Franklin as a writer of personal letters.

II *The Writing of a Masterpiece*

Franklin began his *Memoirs* during a two-week stay at "Chilbolton," Bishop Jonathan Shipley's home near Twyford in Hampshire, England. The time was August, 1771, and Franklin had reached what today would be retirement age, sixty-five. It is likely that during what he calls a "week's uninterrupted leisure" he had thought of his earlier life and the far distance he had come from it.

By far the most famous man in the American colonies, he was also known throughout the world for his experiments in electricity. In London "Dr. Franklin," as he was called, occupied an honored place in the Royal Society. He was a busy public figure in other ways, too, representing at one time four colonies —Pennsylvania, Georgia, New Jersey, and Massachusetts—in the dispute over the tax-exempt status of proprietary lands. He was an active lobbyist in the London newspapers and elsewhere against the Stamp Tax.

His retreat to Twyford therefore has all the earmarks of a "breather" for a man heavily loaded with great affairs of empire. Franklin must have relished his visit, for some four years later he remembered it pleasantly when he wrote a letter from Philadelphia to the bishop: "How happy I was in the sweet retirement of Twyford, where my only business was a little scribbling in the garden study, and my pleasure your conversation, with that of your family!"[22] As Van Doren remarks, "The scribbling through a week or so produced the best-known part of the most famous autobiography in the world."[23]

Franklin's process of composing this book deserves careful attention. He made a three-page list of topics as a guide, for plan or formal design, as we have seen, was very important in his theory of writing. In the actual manuscript he left one half (one side) of the page open for additions and corrections.[24]

The first part, which included some eighty-six manuscript pages, recorded his life to 1730. Intended for his son and for Franklin's immediate family, it covered about a third of his list of topics.[25] This section, in which (says Russel B. Nye) Franklin "wrote with quiet satisfaction of his upward climb from runaway apprentice to man of fortune,"[26] is generally regarded as Franklin at his best.[27] He wrote approximately two thousand words a day—no mean stint, considering that he was on vacation.[28] But possibly his great speed accounted for the "many lapses in style and some obscure sentences" that Farrand finds in this section.[29] Later, when Franklin returned to Philadelphia after the Revolutionary War, Abel James restored this first part to him, and Franklin then made some "improvements in style, largely for the purpose of simplifying and clarifying sentences or passages."[30]

Thirteen years elapsed between the writing of the first and the second parts of the manuscript. When he departed for France at the start of the Revolutionary War, Franklin left papers including the Twyford manuscript in the hands of Joseph Galloway, his colleague in the proprietary dispute.[31] In February, 1782, this Twyford manuscript fell into the hands of Abel James, the executor of Mrs. Galloway's estate.[32] Seconded by Franklin's close friends Benjamin Vaughan and Guillaume Le Veillard (the mayor of Passy, the suburb of Paris in which Franklin lived), Abel James persuaded Franklin to continue the manuscript.[33] Accordingly, in 1784 at Passy, Franklin undertook the second part. He included the letters of Vaughan and James at the beginning of this part, thus making a "disconcerting break in the flow of the narrative. . . ."[34] Evidently he put in these documents to "justify the resumption of the story and to emphasize the change in the character of the memoirs."

By 1784 Franklin's status had changed, as Nye points out, to that of "one of the world's most honored men" as a result of the American victory.[35] Now, therefore, he was writing "not only the story of his life for his son and family but a much more formal account for posterity of how he attained virtue, eminence, knowledge, and wealth."[36] In this section (says Nye) Franklin—writing almost twenty-six pages about his business, civic, and scientific careers—stresses the public record rather than his inner personal development.[37] But Nye's statement is misleading, for almost the entire section deals with Franklin's "Art of Virtue." Max Farrand more accurately states that the second part was "intended for the public"—the first had not been[38]—and that Franklin was "consciously preaching virtue, as exemplified in his own practices and experiences; he was writing to instruct youth."[39]

He had planned to finish the work during his voyage home in 1785, but he wrote three essays instead—on navigation, on smoky chimneys, and on his "smoke-consuming stove."[40] Four years later on July 17, 1788, when he was eighty-three years old and suffering from the gout and a kidney stone, he made out his will and completed a hundred pages more—probably sometime between this date and October 24, the day he wrote the following in a letter to Le Veillard:

I have lately made great progress in the work you so urgently
demand, and have come as far as my fiftieth year. Being now
free from public business, as my term in the Presidentship
[Council of Penna.] is expired and resolving to engage in no other
public employment, I expect to have it finished in about two
months, if illness or some unforeseen interruption does not prevent. I therefore do not send a part at this time, thinking it better
to retain the whole till I can view it all together and make the
proper corrections.[41]

On the same day, he wrote to his friend Vaughan in England,
indicating that he had progressed as far as the year 1756 in
covering his life. Van Doren assumes, therefore, that the third
part of the *Autobiography* was nearly completed since it ends
by bringing Franklin's life to July, 1757. He also thinks that
"it is obvious that he did not make much more use of his papers
than he had at Twyford or at Passy, but still wrote largely out
of his memory."[42] Nye believes that this third part exhibits less
"zest and energy" than the earlier parts, but he also notes that
it still possesses "remarkable force and swiftness."[43] According
to Farrand, Franklin at this time was "an old man and his story
shows the effects of age."[44] Farrand considers the third part
as better than the second but not so good as the first.[45] Having
studied the manuscript in great detail, he sees in this third section a certain shakiness in the handwriting.[46] He describes the
contents of this part as "the emergence of a tradesman into a
man of affairs, the growth of a citizen of local importance into
a person of consequence throughout the colonies, and into a
scientist of reputation not only in England but also on the
Continent."[47]

The fourth and last part of the manuscript, some seven and
one-half pages, Franklin apparently wrote sometime between
November 13, 1789, and April 17, 1790, the time of his death.[48]
These pages were not sent to Vaughan and Le Veillard along
with the fair copies of the original manuscript.[49]

III *Critical Reactions*

The great interruptions during the composition of the *Autobiography* have led Farrand to remark that Franklin was "not
possessed by the genius that forces men to write whether
they will or not, and is necessary to produce great literature."[50]
Furthermore, the so-called fragmentary nature of the *Autobiography* has tended to focus attention on the fact that much is

omitted and that what appears in it carries the reader only to that period of Franklin's life when he "stood really but on the threshold of greatness."[51]

However this may be, the book shows a conspicuous dearth of the scientific interests that absorbed him before 1757. It also shows little of his family or social life and little of his political career to this time. In general, it tends to oversimplify Franklin as a "shrewd tradesman of homely apothegms and a full pocketbook."[52] Considered as pure history, the *Autobiography* needs Franklin's letters, diplomatic papers, scientific writings, and other private records to make it complete.[53] Van Doren believes that three important "chapters" of Franklin's life were actually written separately and "would no doubt have been incorporated in the narrative, in whole or in part," if it had been carried beyond 1757.[54] These three chapters include Franklin's writings on the Hutchinson letters (February-March, 1774), the negotiations to prevent the war (March-May, 1775), and the negotiations for peace (March-July, 1782). These three, according to Van Doren, should be regarded as "further fragments of a work which is itself a fragment."[55] William Temple Franklin thought that his grandfather intended to describe his tour of Scotland in the *Autobiography*.[56] Notwithstanding these numerous points of incompleteness or suggestions about what the work might have contained, this book remains "probably the richest autobiography in the world," especially if judged by the "influences and circumstances, the process of growth" that formed the man.[57]

Certainly, one weakness of the *Autobiography* is its factual inaccuracy, and one or two examples make this defect clear. As an unknown young man of nineteen Franklin wrote a letter to a famous old man, Sir Hans Sloane, president of the Royal College of Physicians and Secretary of the Royal Society and later the president of the Royal Society who succeeded Sir Isaac Newton. In a brief letter now in the British Museum, Franklin claimed to have in his possession a purse made of stone asbestos, a scientific curiosity. If Sloane was interested in buying it or a piece of wood called Salamander Cotton, Franklin would "wait upon" him.[58] In the first part of the *Autobiography*, written nearly fifty years later, Franklin stated that Sloane had called on him, had taken him home to see "all his curiosities, and persuaded me to let him add that [the purse] to the number, for which he paid me handsomely."[59]

Franklin also stretched the truth slightly, although conceivably in a good cause, in his statement that the "New Building" in which George Whitefield preached in Philadelphia was "expressly for the Use of any Preacher of any religious Persuasion . . . so that even if the Mufti of Constantinople were to send a missionary to preach Mahometanism to us, he would find a pulpit at his service."[60] According to Labaree and Bell, the non-sectarianism of this combination school for poor children and preaching place for Whitefield was actually limited to various Protestant ministers.[61]

Worth remembering, too, when reading the *Autobiography* is the fact that it is "a late and retouched self-portrait."[62] The picture of Franklin that emerges from the first part of this book, according to one writer, is that of a "rather stuffy young man."[63] This same writer concedes, however, that the general or total effect of the *Autobiography* upon the reader is the desire to make Franklin his personal friend.[64] The picture certainly presents a Franklin who treats himself as objectively as a scientist—much more so, for example, than Henry Adams. This disinterested quality sometimes takes the form of humor. One instance of his unselfish ability to see himself in a humorous light is the comment on the occasion when, mainly by the power of his pamphlet *Plain Truth* (1747), he organized a group of about twelve hundred volunteer soldiers for the defense of the state. It was a large meeting, and Franklin admits that "the house was pretty full." "I harangued them a little on the subject," he remarks with dry humor.[65]

The image of Franklin in the *Autobiography*, according to the late Dixon Wecter, was that of "a homely and unpretending" man who met "the exactions of life without haste or tension but always with quiet mastery, humorous and a trifle cynical, yet in the truest sense a man of good will and of serene wisdom. . . ."[66] Although many other traits have been noted as shaping the image of Benjamin Franklin presented in the *Autobiography*, there is a consensus as to his clarity, his sanity, his humor, his greatly varied interests, his "bountiful affection," and his "broad humanness." "Perhaps it is not too much to say," writes Oral S. Coad, "that of the great men America has so far produced Benjamin Franklin is the most broadly human."[67]

Less flattering reactions to the character of Franklin in the *Autobiography* are also extant. One writer of 1880 vintage writes that the picture of Franklin both in the *Autobiography* and in his correspondence "resembles a little too much the portrait of a self-sufficient, self-made, pompous tradesman. Vice is represented as want of practical wisdom, not as something to arouse moral indignation."[68] This is a common charge but not, it seems, a well-founded one, for the critic has exaggerated badly. Furthermore, Franklin did not remain aloof or cold to vicious practices of the British empire; in fact, he warmed to the blistering point about them in numerous satires and other writings. Franklin himself was also keenly aware that he had made mistakes, or *errata*, during his life, and he clearly expresses his remorse for these in the *Autobiography*. Moreover, his remark to La Rochefoucauld, that by dwelling so long upon his green years he had intended an exemplum of prudent and imprudent conduct for his son and for other young readers, merits consideration.[69]

Addressing himself to the problem of significant omissions from the *Autobiography*, Van Doren discounts another charge commonly leveled against Franklin: that he overemphasized his own importance and minimized that of others in the life of his era. According to Van Doren, Franklin "left out things [in the *Autobiography*] he had done more often than he even seemed to claim to have done things he had not."[70] But quite frankly, Franklin admits his vanity (*Autobiography*, p. 2). "He knew he had led a great life," writes Van Doren, "in the midst of great affairs. He had a story to tell and he enjoyed telling it. So many of his friends had enjoyed it that he could assume the world would enjoy it too."[71] However, the significant aspect of Franklin's character that appeals to Farrand is humility: the *Memoirs* "tell the story of a printer and shopkeeper who was infinitely bigger than his job but was not above it; of a tradesman who had risen to greatness but was not ashamed of his origin nor of his station."[72]

Apropos of a discussion of the main character in the *Auto-biography*, E. A. and G. L. Duyckinck call attention to three other excellently written character sketches in the book.[73] The first of these is of Franklin's brother—"irascible, jealous, and mortified on the return of the successful adventurer, who is playing off his prosperity before the workmen." According to the Duyckincks, this is "an artist's picture of life, drawn in a few conclusive touches." The second is that of Keimer eating the roast pig on the occasion of the breakdown of his vegetable diet. This sketch is "as happily hit off as any personage in *Gil Blas.*" The portrait of the gloomy Philadelphia croaker, Samuel Mickle, is the third.

Incomplete, fragmentary, and oversimplified in its presentation of the real Franklin (and perhaps of some of the other characters), the *Autobiography* yet resembles others of its kind. Some of the greatest autobiographies have been fragments—those of Leigh Hunt, Edward Gibbon, and Benvenuto Cellini, for example.[74] Smyth likens it not only to Cellini's *Autobiography* but also to Rousseau's *Confessions:* "It conceals nothing. It reveals with perfect candor the most secret passages in the author's life."[75] Van Doren credits Franklin with helping to establish the autobiography as a literary form. "Before him," he writes, "the autobiography as a literary form hardly existed. Rousseau and he at almost the same time took the first steps toward creating it."[76] But here the similarity ends, for Rousseau and Franklin differed greatly as writers—the one "passionate and romantic," the other, "realistic and honest." "Rousseau was primarily a writer," says Van Doren. "He could turn inward and pour his total self into his *Confessions.* Franklin could not stop making history long enough to write it."[77] The latest editors of Franklin's works have nonetheless attributed to him mastery of the autobiography as a literary form.[78]

Critics and scholars alike have made many strained efforts to describe the style of the *Autobiography.* One calls it "bold and joyous"; another, "almost matter-of-fact."[79] One thinks it "simple and charming"; one characterizes it as "inimitable."[80] It is above all a *clear* style, Nye insists; but he uses many other epithets to describe it—vivid, economical, uncluttered, plain, easy, graceful, forceful, flexible, charming, sensible, honest, witty, and orderly.[81] Finally, he quotes Franklin's own statement to the effect that the norm of style in writing should be that of informed and intelligent conversation.[82] Another critic states that the style is clear and vigorous and "moves forward easily and rapidly."[83] Yet another calls it limpid and racy.[84]

Detailed study of the *Autobiography* shows that Franklin possessed great skill in moving from one topic to another, effecting imperceptibly smooth transitions and at the same time maintaining interest by variety of the topics treated, especially in the first part. This movement gives the book, in the words of one writer, "an indescribable freshness and fascination. Unlike many autobiographies, there is no posing for effect; it is the

direct and simple record of a remarkable and wonderfully useful life. . . ."[85] Smyth compares it to the simple, direct idiom
of Bunyan in *Pilgrim's Progress;* Duyckinck, to the charming
humorous touches of Goldsmith in *The Vicar of Wakefield.*[86]
Wecter aptly labels it "serene homespun . . . disarming, wholly
relaxed and delightful."[87] It is never prim or pompous, he goes
on, never passionate or prejudiced. "Instead it appears shrewd,
whimsical, or ironic, skeptical of rhetoric and smug conven-
tions, and curiously detached . . . as if able to bring a cool
scientific appraisal to bear upon himself and his neighbors."[88]
But John Bigelow probably outdoes all others with this description: it is a "limpid narrative, gemmed all over, like a cloud-
less firmament at night, with anecdotes, curious observations,
and sage reflections."[89] (He obviously was trying diligently
to sell his own edition of 1868.) Even the staid William Dean
Howells took exception to this statement of Bigelow's, calling
it an interesting "instance of critical prodigality."[90]

Not all the comments are uncritical. Farrand has tried to
account for what he regards as a change from the colloquial
tone of the first part to the more genteel tone in later parts
by reason of Franklin's residence in France.[91] Possibly, too, he
adds, young Benjamin Bache may have made some of the
changes toward a more genteel style when copying the manuscript, either on his own or on the authority of his grandfather.[92] This writer also observes that Franklin was perfectly
capable of writing "in a first attempt, an awkward sentence of
eighty words, with no punctuation except for commas."[93]

Critics are generally agreed that the first part contains the
most superior writing in the entire book.[94] Van Doren believes
that Franklin read this part to Bishop and Mrs. Shipley and
their children when he first composed it.[95] And his listeners
must have been fascinated, for the first part of the *Autobiography* reads like a picaresque novel. Smollett, the author of several of such eighteenth-century novels, comes to mind. The
second part of the *Autobiography* lacks the spontaneity of
this first part, an effect that makes it seem "written at a heat."[96]

IV *Organic Unity*

As a literary work the *Autobiography* has a certain degree
of unity—more than meets the eye of the casual reader. This
unity of the four parts, considered collectively and separately,

consists in a rather carefully patterned long and short design. Parts one and three are long and of approximately the same length; parts two and four are short, and part four is about a third as long as part two. Thus, whatever Franklin's intentions may have been, either purposeful or not, the quantitative and exterior aspect of the book exhibits a formal design *with variety*. That this formal design is not merely exterior but essentially organic may be easily seen as we try to clarify both the *variety* and the *continuity* of the main parts.

Part one consists of four divisions—an explanation why he wrote the book, remarks on his family (remote and immediate), his apprenticeship on the *Courant*, and his attempts at becoming an independent printer in Philadelphia. It ends with his marriage to Deborah Read and the start of his public projects such as the Junto and the Library Company; it includes, of course, his trips to London and Boston. This part deals chiefly with his achievement of status, his growth from poor apprentice to master printer with his own shop.

Part two, on the other hand, rivets attention on what he considered the causes for the attainment not only of his success up to this point but also of his success in later life—his bourgeois virtues of industry and frugality, his religious principles, and his experiment in achieving moral perfection (The Art of Virtue). Appropriately, this second part points both ways; it bridges the gap between the first and third parts.

In part three, as we have already seen, Franklin continues three previous elements—the extension of virtue from an individual to a world-wide basis (by means of his projected Society of the Free and Easy), the further growth of his public projects, and the more personal record of his life (such things as his study of foreign languages, a trip to Boston, the death of his son, etc.). The component divisions of part three, however, are probably best seen as: (1) the large division of nine miscellaneous topics, the first three proceeding logically from the Art of Virtue of part two and the second six proceeding chronologically without as much as the barest of transition devices; (2) the record of his public projects, by far the largest and the most important division; and (3) the progress of his political career, including his part in the disastrous Braddock expedition. On the whole, the record of public projects receives the stress; this is the distinguishing element of part three and may be said to give it a rough kind of organic unity, just as the experiment in the Art of Virtue characterizes, in the main, part two. He provides continuity between parts two and three by his implicit premise that the attainment of individual virtue was inseparable from projects designed for the benefit of his fellow inhabitants of the globe, either in small local groups or large international ones.

The organic unity of part four centers on the dispute between the Proprietaries and the Pennsylvania Assembly and the successful petition of the latter to the king to abolish the tax exemptions of these original grantees of land from the crown. Short as this section is, about four pages in the Nye edition, it consists of three topics or divisions—Franklin's meeting and disagreement with Lord Grenville on the proposition that "THE KING IS THE LEGISLATOR OF THE COLONIES" [sic], the meeting with the Proprietaries at Thomas Penn's house in Spring Garden (arranged by Dr. Fothergill), and the debate and eventual resolution of the dispute in favor of the Pennsylvania Assembly with the help of Lord Mansfield. The order of these three divisions is that of trial and error, proceeding climactically to the successful resolution and following, of course, the time sequence which has served as a broad frame throughout the book.

Moreover, the fourth part is climactic with respect to the third part because it concentrates on one large project (the dispute with the proprietaries) and dramatizes it as a kind of stepping stone to other issues that were to be fought out during the next twenty-six years. We can see, therefore, that the *Autobiography* is far less chaotic and fragmentary than it seems to be. Studied carefully, it exhibits a surprising degree of *method* and *order*, two elements that Franklin strongly prized in all good writing.

The question has often been raised as to why Franklin ended the book in 1757. The usual answer is that death cut him short. But after 1757, the time of the successful resolution of the dispute with the proprietaries, Franklin was to gain worldwide acclaim, so that he was justified in thinking that the rest of his story was sufficiently well known to all—an integral part of history, in fact.[97] His touching so strongly on his difference with Lord Grenville on the above-mentioned proposition might be cited as evidence supporting this conclusion. It is as though, having brought the reader to the brink of the Revolution, he concluded that he had done his duty. And, indeed, he had.

CHAPTER *3*

Poor Richard's Almanack

W RITING in much the same utilitarian tone and speaking with the same puritanical voice which he had used
in producing the *Autobiography*, Franklin shaped his second
great contribution to the art of writing—the sayings in the
Poor Richard's Almanacks.[1] Although one writer has objected
to the "mercenary and worldly" ring of *Poor Richard's Almanacks*,[2] these proverbial sayings have nevertheless passed into
the "general language of mankind."[3] *The Way to Wealth*,
a collection of these sayings gleaned from *Poor Richard*, is
probably the most printed and translated work in all American
literature.[4] As one writer observes, "*Poor Richard's Almanac*
. . . is probably the most famous example of the unambitious
class of writing to which it belongs."[5] No other almanac has
ever been so famous or so influential.[6]

I *The Nature and Popularity of Almanacs*

There were, of course, other almanacs besides *Poor Richard*.
One of them enjoyed an "enormous popularity." It was published in Dedham, Massachusetts, by Nathaniel Ames under
the title of *Astronomical Diary and Almanac* (1726-1764). Tyler
thought it superior to Franklin's *Poor Richard*.[7] But Ames's
title certainly had less human appeal than Franklin's. Almost
one hundred years earlier William Price's *Almanac for New
England for the Year 1639* had appeared. James Franklin's
Poor Robin's Almanack (1728) had preceded his brother's *Poor
Richard* by some five years. Titan Leeds's *The American Almanac* (1705-1732) had led the field in Pennsylvania before
Franklin appeared on the scene. Almanacs were lucrative for
eighteenth-century printers.[8] As early as 1728, Franklin's rival

Bradford was publishing four of them. Keimer, another of his rivals, also had an almanac. Godfrey's *Pennsylvania Almanac* (1729-1732) and Jerman's *Quaker Almanac* (1731-1732) were printed by Franklin and his partner Hugh Meredith. Thus Franklin had extensive acquaintance with the craft of almanac-making long before he wrote and printed *Poor Richard*.[9] After he entered the heavy competition in Pennsylvania, some of the above-cited almanacs continued—Jerman's and Godfrey's, for example. And there were others, too, like Taylor's, Birkett's, *Poor Robin's*, Mathew Boucher's, and (in nearby Annapolis) Grew's. Still others followed in the wake of Franklin's success: Thomas More's, *Poor Will's*, *Andrew Aguecheek's*, and one featuring a certain A. Weatherwise, Gent., sometimes called Father Abraham.[10] Philadelphia was teeming with almanacs.

Most of these followed a common pattern. Franklin's title page, for example, was "hardly distinguishable from John Jerman's."[11] To give some idea of what the almanacs of this time were like, we can do no better than to quote this excellent description from Newcomb:

> First of all, almanacs were calendars. Secondly, they forecast the weather and, with an astrological flourish, many of them pretended to forecast events—generally in ridiculous and meaningless jargon. They listed remarkable days and interlined them with proverbs and prophecies. They contained sacred and profane—sometimes very profane—poems at the heads of the months or in separate columns for the purpose. They contained advertisements, recipes, want-ads, essays on practical subjects, such as the cure of boils, snake bite, and the dry gripe. Almanacs listed court sessions, gave tables of kings, and noted convenient roads and waterways. They were frequently prefaced by a nude "Anatomy of Man's Body," followed by the benevolent greetings of the philomath. Nothing, indeed, had a more miscellaneous character than a typical eighteenth-century almanac. . . . Almanacs served other functions besides the above more or less traditional ones. If their margins were wide enough, almanacs could be made to double as account books or diaries. In many households, where the only other reading matter was the Bible, children were even taught to read from almanacs.[12]

In 1732 when Godfrey and Jerman took the printing of their almanacs away from Franklin and gave it to Franklin's competitor, Andrew Bradford, Franklin formed his own almanac, advertising it in the *Pennsylvania Gazette* for December 28,

1732, as "JUST PUBLISHED, FOR 1733."[13] But six or eight years before this and as early as his first voyage to London between 1724 and 1726, Franklin had apparently toyed with the idea of publishing one or more almanacs, for he had ordered sent to Philadelphia appropriate printing type for weather and astronomical figures such as were commonly used in almanacs.[14]

The first edition of *Poor Richard* was entirely sold in one month. Franklin, who brought out two other editions during the first year, sold it as far north as Rhode Island and as far south as the Carolinas.[15] Thereafter for many years this particular almanac sold over ten thousand copies annually and was much imitated in England as well as in the American colonies.[16] It was Franklin's first great success. Not only did it put his printing house on a sound financial basis but it also made him known as a writer throughout the colonies.[17]

One theory of the origin of *Poor Richard* as a name is that it comes from a certain Richard Saunders, a seventeenth-century English astrologer and almanac maker. Saunders was the author of an almanac entitled *Apollo Anglicanus*, and Franklin undoubtedly imitated this work.[18] The format of *Poor Richard* resembles that of *Apollo Anglicanus*.[19] Also, James Franklin's *Poor Robin's Almanack* may well have suggested *Poor Richard's Almanack* as a title.[20]

The character of Richard Saunders (Poor Richard) apparently owes something to the character of John Partridge in Swift's *Bickerstaff Papers*. It is quite clear that the Saunderses (Richard and Bridget) and the Partridges (John and his "widow") are close relatives. Comparing Richard Saunders and John Partridge, John Ross finds many points in common: "Both are poor, needy men, frankly preparing their almanacs not so much for the honor of the stars as for their livelihoods. . . . Both are favored with wives who must be supported; and the wives are much of the same type—Bridget's practicality, talkativeness, vigor, and determination are decidedly reminiscent of Mrs. Partridge's 'pretty distinguishable voice' and handiness with the cudgel, and both wives seem to be more practically energetic and forceful than their husbands." As we shall see in the next chapter, Franklin was indebted to Swift for much more than the Titan Leeds hoax.

The Richard Saunders of the early almanacs, originally a comic character, eventually yielded to a character not too unlike Franklin himself, an interesting instance of comedy being transmuted into utility. Ross refers to this change as "the first example in American literature of a tendency common much later—the blurring of a popular comic character through identification with its creator."[22] He cites the later comic character, Artemus Ward, and his "blurring" with Charles Farrar Browne, his creator, as an example. As Newcomb puts it, "The comic Richard became the instructive Richard, a character in pedagogical inclination not too unlike Franklin himself."[23]

As for the contents of *Poor Richard,* the following advertisement from the December 28, 1732, issue of the *Pennsylvania Gazette* announces them as follows:

> JUST PUBLISHED, FOR 1733: POOR RICHARD: AN ALMANACK containing the Lunations, Eclipses, Planets Motions and Aspects, Weather, Sun and Moon's rising and setting, Highwater, &c. besides many pleasant and witty Verses, Jests and Sayings, Author's Motive of Writing, Prediction of the Death of his friend Mr. Titan Leeds, Moon no Cuckold, Batchelor's Folly, Parson's Wine and Baker's Pudding, Short Visits, Kings and Bears, New Fashions, Game for Kisses, Katherine's Love, Different Sentiments, Signs of a Tempest, Death of a Fisherman, Conjugal Debate, Men and Melons, H. the Prodigal, Breakfast in Bed, Oyster Lawsuit, &c. by RICHARD SAUNDERS, Philomat. [*sic*] Printed and sold by B. Franklin, Price 3 *s.* 6 *d.* per Dozen. Of whom also may be had Sheet Almanacks at 2 *s.* 6 *d.*[24]

Many of these phrases referred to actual sayings or verses—for example, "Kings and Bears often worry their keepers" and "Men and Melons are hard to know."[25]

The contents and their order as presented actually differed greatly from the advertisement. In this first almanac, after the title page, which carried a brief advertisement of the lunations, eclipses, weather, and other contents and made a point of their applicability not only to "the Latitude of Forty Degrees" but also to "all the adjacent Places, even from *Newfoundland to South-Carolina,*" there followed in this order: (1) an address to the reader, including the above-mentioned Titan Leeds hoax; (2) an explanation of astrological signs in conjunction with the anatomy of the human body as governed by the twelve constellations; (3) a table calculating the motions of the planets for the first, eighth, fifteenth, and twenty-second days of each month in the entire year; (4) an explanation of the format; (5) a table of English kings and their reigns from Egbert to George II; (6) the almanac proper, one month per page and each headed by a six- or eight-line verse, followed by astronomical signs, weather predictions and short sayings all intermingled; (7) a short table of eclipses, followed by a "Chronology of Things remarkable," which included historical events of interest to Franklin's readers (such as "The Post-Office erected in *America*") and the number of years since each event; (8) the dates of courts, both supreme and provincial, and prefixed by the "Oyster Lawsuit"; (9) a calendar of the "General Meetings" of Quakers and Baptists and of some sixteen town or city fairs; (10) "A Catalogue of the principal Kings and Princes in *Europe*, with the Time of their Births and Ages"; (11) a table of distances between various towns.[26]

Generally speaking, custom and format tended to hold back originality in almanacs, "but what scope there was Franklin exploited fully. . . . He retained the public's interest and won its support by printing a great number of verses [some by major poets such as Dryden and Pope], proverbs, and aphorisms, more pointed, humorous, and memorable than those in any other almanac."[27] These won him an edge in competition with other printers, and in these sayings lay some of his most distinctive qualities as a writer.

Poor Richard abounds with witty insights into human nature. To give some notion of these homely, and often earthy sayings, we offer the following random samples:

(1) A traveller should have a hog's nose, deer's legs and an ass's back.
(2) He that scatters thorns, let him not go barefoot.
(3) Wars bring scars.
(4) God heals, and the doctor takes the fee.
(5) Great talkers, little doers.
(6) The noblest question in the world is, What good may I do in it?

Newcomb, who has studied these sayings more carefully than anyone we know, finds that they underwent a shift from humor in the early years to a more instructive tone during the later ones.

Possibly because it treated many controversial issues and a wide range of heterogeneous material, *Poor Richard* rarely lapsed into dullness. Often, in fact, it was satiric in its use of proverbs, prefaces, and other fillers.[28] Too, we should remember that it was being published during a period of great versatility so far as Franklin's career as a writer affected it. During the period 1732-1758 he was writing such various kinds of material as religious polemic (his lengthy defenses of the Rev. Mr. Samuel Hemphill in 1735), popular science (*An Account of the New Invented Pennsylvania Fire-Places* in 1744), higher education (*Proposals Relating to the Education of Youth in Pennsylvania* in 1749), and advanced or pioneer science (*Experiments and Observations on Electricity* in 1751).[29] In addition, he was corresponding with the principal scientists and men of letters in England and America on a wide variety of subjects, from botany to international politics.

Poor Richard made him famous as a scientist and a Deist in yet another way, for his written tributes to Newton, Locke, Bacon, and Boyle seemed to contradict holy writ. The Christian Bible was becoming less significant than Nature itself; the telescope was capturing the imagination of the Enlightenment. People were finding the stars more interesting than the scriptures. As a writer, Franklin defended in his almanac certain theories of astronomy that seemed to some people utterly contradictory to the teaching of the Bible.[30] We must remember that this intellectual ferment was taking place in a time when the common people in the colonies bought scarcely any books *but* almanacs.[31] Franklin's almanac operated as a kind of descending funicular railway; it carried scientific and philosophical instruction from the heights of lofty minds and disseminated it among common people. He kept this "railway" in operation largely by the vigor and simplicity of his pen.

II *The Sayings—Sources and Revisions*

The *saying* is a kind of catchall for any one of the following overlapping terms—epigram, proverb, aphorism, or maxim. During Franklin's time, writes Newcomb, the *epigram* was understood to be any short poem with a witty ending. Usually its author employed "a method of conveying a single conceit [figure of speech] fully and strongly to the reader, in a narrow compass."[32] Its distinguishing features were wit and humor and compactness, extreme brevity. The *proverb* is usually thought of as a folk saying, the wisdom of the many in a capsule. Significant about it seem to be its popular origin, its quality as a self-evident truth, and its wide folk appeal.[33] In the *Autobiography* Franklin himself specifically relates the word *proverb* to the phrase "the wisdom of many ages and nations."[34] The *aphorism* differs from the proverb in that it can be assigned to a known author. Sometimes, however, as Newcomb reminds us, an aphorism can become proverbial by being picked up and repeated enough times by people.[35] The saying is often identified with the *maxim*, which puts special stress on rules of conduct. The bulk of Franklin's *Way to Wealth*, for example, is a collection of sayings or maxims, according to Gallacher, which require the reader to reflect on them and are therefore lacking in the self-evident quality that genuine proverbs have.[36]

The question of Franklin's original sources for the sayings of *Poor Richard* has been recently illuminated by the excellent research work of Robert Newcomb at the University of Maryland under the able direction of Professor A. O. Aldridge. Newcomb has located sources for approximately two-thirds of all the sayings and for about half of the verses Franklin uses in *Poor Richard* or *The Way to Wealth*.[37] Among the sources Franklin used are the following: James Howell's *Lexicon Tetraglotton*, (1659-1660); Thomas Fuller's *Gnomologia* (1732), *Introductio ad Prudentiam* (1726-1727), and *Introductio ad Sapientiam* (1731); George Herbert's *Outlandish Proverbs* (1640); George Savile, Lord Halifax's *A Character of King Charles II* (1750); Samuel Richardson's "Moral and Instructive Sentiments," an appendix to *Clarissa* (1750-1751); Charles Palmer's *A Collection of Select Aphorisms and Maxims* (1748); Sir John Mennes and Rev. James Smith's *Wit's Recreations* (1640); and an anonymous *Collection of Epigrams* (1735-1737). All these collections were published in London.[38]

The chief of the above sources are Howell's *Lexicon Tetraglotton*, which he says Franklin used for "almost two hundred" sayings in *Poor Richard;* Fuller's *Gnomologia*, from which Newcomb believes Franklin borrowed approximately an equal number; and Herbert's *Outlandish Proverbs*, from which he thinks Franklin took about fifty sayings.[39] The greatest extent of borrowing from Howell occurred during the years 1733-1742; from Fuller, 1745-1751; from Herbert, 1733, 1754, and 1757.[40] It appears that Franklin, as well as his reading audience, liked these works so well that they became serviceable over a number of years.

In the *Autobiography* Franklin tells of how in the year 1733 he took up the study of French, Italian, and Spanish. It is quite plausible that Franklin may have used Howell's *Lexicon Tetraglotton* (which means dictionary of four languages), especially since the first half of this book contained an English-Spanish, French, and Italian dictionary.[41] Also noteworthy in *Poor Richard* are certain untranslatable proverbs in French, Spanish, and Welsh, thought to derive from this *Lexicon*.[42] Many of Howell's sayings were literal translations from foreign sources, and Franklin in many cases lopped from them excess verbiage. Newcomb lists eighteen foreign sayings in *Poor Richard*, nine of which he says may be found in the *Lexicon* (six in Welsh or Gaelic, three in Spanish and French).[43] The well-known saying "There is no little enemy," which appeared in *Poor Richard* in 1733, has a French source in Howell, according to Newcomb, although Franklin in a letter to David Hartley many years later referred to it as an *Italian* adage.[44]

Newcomb traces twenty-one sayings to Thomas Fuller's *Introductio ad Sapientiam* (Introduction to Wisdom), two of which reappeared in *The Way to Wealth*.[45] The other work by Fuller, his *Introductio ad Prudentiam* (Introduction to Prudence), contained sayings rewritten from "Seneca, Cicero, Addison, Taylor, Burton, Quarles, and others."[46] One of these Franklin took verbatim: "Write with the learned, and pronounce with the vulgar."[47] Newcomb says Franklin used twelve sayings from this work alone. Although he did not draw so frequently from the *Prudentiam* and the *Sapientiam* as from the *Gnomologia*, Franklin still used these first two sufficiently for Newcomb to regard them as "a principal source of Poor Richard's sayings."[48]

Franklin copied a "comparatively large percentage of sayings . . . verbatim" from Herbert's *Outlandish Proverbs*.[49] Many of the *Poor Richard* sayings that seem to point to Franklin's borrowing from John Ray's *A Collection of English Proverbs* (1670 and 1676) have slightly different versions in the earlier collections of Herbert and Howell or in the later ones of Fuller. This difference makes exact attribution difficult in some cases. Newcomb thinks the evidence points to Franklin's having used both of the editions of Ray mentioned, but he cannot discover any consistent pattern of borrowings for certain years.[50]

Still another principal source of Franklin's sayings is George Savile's *A Character of King Charles the Second*. By use of concrete terms or metaphors, Franklin improved the sayings of

Savile and made them "less diffuse and abstract."[51] Franklin also drew on Savile's *Thoughts and Reflections* for "more than thirty sayings" in the almanacs of 1753, 1754, 1757, and 1758.[52] Newcomb suggests that "although *Poor Richard's Almanack* is sometimes considered to reflect a pollyana attitude toward life, many of its sayings are drawn from cynical and skeptical authors."[53] One such author was surely George Savile, Marquess of Halifax, who had something of a name as a "trimmer" —that is, one who goes the way the wind is blowing in politics or in other matters of principle. Savile, who had written a work entitled *Character of a Trimmer* (1688), was not at all disturbed by his reputation.[54]

Charles Palmer's *A Collection of Select Aphorisms and Maxims* (1748) is the source for at least eleven sayings, not to mention the nearly verbatim borrowing for three of Franklin's short essays—"The Wit of Conversation," "Mean Employments," and "The Man of Honour"—in *Poor Richard* (1756). "The entry of these relatively long verbatim and near-verbatim entries suggests that other extended prose entries in the *almanack* are not original and that the greatest caution should be used in attributing them as part of the Franklin canon."[55]

Franklin must have admired the satires, as well as other works, of Edward Young and Alexander Pope. For the years 1734, 1746, 1747, and 1750, he used in *Poor Richard* some twenty-eight entries from Young's *Love of Fame: The Universal Passion*, a work excellent for its satiric portraits.[56] From 1736 on, Newcomb notes more than two dozen quotations from the works of Pope in *Poor Richard*.[57]

Turning for a moment to the French authors who served as sources, we see about twenty-four entries from La Rochefoucauld's *Maxims* (1665).[58] Since numerous collections by other authors during the late seventeenth and eighteenth centuries also contained La Rochefoucauld's sayings, Newcomb believes that Franklin took them from different sources at different times because of their "scattered dating" in the almanacs.[59] As an example, he cites "There are no fools troublesome as those that have wit," which he says Franklin took verbatim, along with nearly a dozen other sayings, from the 1706 English translation of the *Maxims*.[60]

Although some of the sayings are definitely known to come from such authors as Rabelais, Cervantes, and Montaigne, the channels whereby they came into *Poor Richard* are often difficult to trace.[61] Six sayings for *Poor Richard* (1737) are attributable to the third book of Montaigne's *Essays*.[62] Of all Franklin's early debts to individual authors, that to Montaigne is most convincing, says Newcomb, who gives these interesting examples among others: "He that can take rest is greater than he that can take cities." "The nearest way to come at glory, is to do that for conscience that we do for glory." "The greatest monarch on the proudest throne, is obliged to sit upon his own arse."[63] As for Rabelais and Cervantes, Newcomb finds no convincing evidence that Franklin drew upon either directly.[64]

Among English authors not previously discussed, but from whom Franklin still borrowed a substantial number of entries, we must list John Gay and Samuel Richardson. Starting in 1740, Franklin took twenty-one sayings from Gay's *Fables* (1727) and a total of about forty from Gay's poems.[65] From Richardson's "Moral and Instructive Sentiments," an appendix to *Clarissa*, Franklin obtained over twenty sayings in 1752.[66]

Newcomb sees Franklin's debt to Quarles's *Enchiridion* (1641) as "substantial."[67] This work was exceedingly popular in its day, and Franklin used it for about a dozen sayings in *Poor Richard* and for at least three in *The Way to Wealth*. The sayings which Franklin took and revised from this source represent in Newcomb's opinion, Franklin's best work as an aphorist.[68] "Act uprightly, and despite Calumny. Dirt may stick to a Mud Wall, but not to polish'd Marble." This saying, which has a source in the *Enchiridion* (Book 4, No. v), appeared in *Poor Richard* for 1757 and also in a letter of Franklin to Joseph Galloway (London, November 8, 1766).[69]

Other sources include James Kelley's *Complete Collection of Scottish Proverbs*, from which Franklin may have gotten several 1733 sayings. One of these, "A light purse makes a heavy heart," Franklin tightened up still further to "Light purse, heavy heart."[70] Other writers borrowed from are Francis Bacon (*Essays*, 1625), a possible source of about six sayings, although some of these probably came from intermediate sources; Dryden (his translation of Virgil's first book of the *Georgics*); Swift; Goldsmith; and Ambrose Philips.[71] Robert Cotgrave's *French Dictionary* may be the source of several sayings.[72] Using the Bible for at least one of his sources, Franklin rewrote the commandment "Honor thy father and thy mother, etc." to read "Honor thy Father and Mother, *i.e.*, Live so as to be an honor to them tho' they are dead."[73] On the occasion of the death of Franklin's four-year-old son, Francis Folger Franklin, *Poor Richard* carried some obituary verses entitled "The Thracian Infant." These verses were taken verbatim from *A Collection of Epigrams* (see above), "A Thracian Custom," No. 240.[74]

From 1733 to 1742 Franklin borrowed about thirty epigrammatic couplets for *Poor Richard,* most of them verbatim.[75] He made a run on *Wit's Recreation* for the period 1733-1736 and on *A Collection of Epigrams* for the period 1737-1740.[76] Other sources of epigrams in Franklin's almanacs include the works of Edward Young, John Gay, Richard Savage, Alexander Pope, Jonathan Swift, John Hughes, Thomas Paget, and others.[77] Several of the longer epigrammatic verses (four to eight lines) came from the *Wit's Recreation* of Reverend James Smith and Sir John Mennes.[78] Newcomb could not find any *Poor Richard* sayings in the collections of epigrams compiled by John Heywood and John Davies.[79]

Although he borrowed from a great variety of sources and often revised what he borrowed, Franklin did not borrow from other almanacs, either English or American, of his time.[80] Newcomb points out that most of the early sayings in *Poor Richard* represent the kind of interests a character like Richard Saunders would have had. Franklin's object of making the almanac a vehicle for serious instruction does not always seem to have been followed very closely. Proverbs, epigrams, couplets such as one finds in Gay's *Fables*—these preponderate in the early almanacs. In the late almanacs, on the other hand, we find more frequently such aphorisms as Savile's and Savage's; and generally these praise a utilitarian public spirit like that Franklin himself exhibited.[81]

Sometimes the sayings themselves served as sources for some of the sentences in his other written works.[82] One such example of a revised *Poor Richard* saying occurs at the end of his *Dissertation on Liberty and Necessity:* "Our *Geese* are but *Geese,* tho' we think 'em Swans; and Truth will be Truth tho' it sometimes prove mortifying and distasteful." In the original 1734 almanac this saying read: "A new Truth is a Truth, an old error is an error,/Tho' Clodpate won't allow either."[83]

The ability to invent "sententious and lucid sayings" as well as to revise unoriginal source material of this kind certainly constituted a prerequisite for young philomaths in the early 1730's in Philadelphia.[84] A study of the changes Franklin made in such revisions adds to our knowledge of his practice as a writer.

In the early years of the *Almanack* his alterations often consisted only of some slight change in the verb or subject of the sentence along with a "general effort for economy."[85] Almost always he improved "both the flavor and the cadence."[86] His improvement of the cadence "added as much to them as his change of words," according to Van Doren.[87] As an example of such improvements, Labaree and Bell cite Howell's "The greatest Talkers are the least doers," which Franklin changed to "Great Talkers, little Doers."

Important as *economy* was as a principle in Franklin's habits of revising the sayings, he did not rely wholly on it. Balance, clarity, and variety were other characteristics he aimed at in making revisions, frequently using such rhetorical devices as metaphor, anticlimax, pun, and racy diction. Often he achieved his effects by virtue of material added, personified, or put into rhymed verse.[88] Newcomb gives this illustration of an Italian proverb "He is a greater Liar than an epitaph," which he says Franklin expanded and personified into the following form: "Here comes Glib-tongue; who can outflatter a Dedication; and lie like ten Epitaphs."[89] Also involved in the skillful revisions of the *Poor Richard* sayings were such artistic procedures as careful selection, "smoothing and balancing awkward phrases, replacing vague and meaningless generalities with . . . specific, sharp, and homely terms."[90]

Newcomb lists ten ways (with examples) in which Franklin revised the original sayings from Fuller's *Gnomologia* to suit his purposes: (1) He heightened the "sense of immediacy and directness" by changing "Wealth and Content do not always live together" to "Wealth and Content are not always good Bedfellows." (2) He substituted *you* for *we*, changing "What is the Use of Patience, if we cannot find it when we want it?" to "What signifies your patience, if you can't find it when you want it?" (3) He added an introductory phrase by changing "A small Leak will sink a great Ship" to "Beware of Little Expenses; a small Leak will sink a great Ship." (4) He used the couplet as an envelope for the proverb, changing "More malice than matter" to "When there's more Malice shown than Matter:/On the Writer falls the Satyr." (5) He replaced abstractions with personifications, changing "It is a Sin against hospitality to open your doors and shut up your countenance" to "Half-Hos-

pitality opens his Doors and shuts up his Countenance." (6)
He injected a dash of internal rhyme here and there, changing
"Pride is scarce ever cured" to "Pride and the Gout, are seldom
cur'd throughout." (7) He employed ironic and sarcastic names,
changing "He had a Mouth for every Matter" to "Henry Smat-
ter has a Mouth for every Matter." (8) He eliminated excessive
pronouns, changing "A Man in Passion rides a horse that runs
away with him" to "A Man in a Passion rides a mad Horse."
(9) He struck out clumsy relative clauses, changing " 'T is
Plenty, that makes you dainty" to "Too much Plenty makes
Mouth dainty." (10) He achieved the tone of the proverb by
the use of balance, changing "Half-witted Fellows speak much,
and say little" to "Half Wits talk much but say little."[91] As a
footnote to the above, we should add that sometimes Franklin
made no changes whatever.

In revising his borrowed epigrams, Franklin often took great
liberties, although after the year 1736, according to Newcomb,
he made progressively fewer changes.[92] Most of the epigrams
he took from collections like the *Wit's Recreation* originally
had only four lines, and it required from six to eight lines
to fill the space at the head of each month in his almanac.
"It is almost certain," Newcomb tells us," "that Franklin himself wrote the additional lines as a preface or moral tag—just
as he similarly wrote prefaces on a smaller scale for many
proverbs and aphorisms."[93] Again, in borrowing a Latin epigram
from Martial, he changed the Latin names to English.[94] The
idea was to make the dish palatable to the colonists. But his
more radical revisions tapered off as he gained experience. After
1750 he increasingly followed the practice of borrowing epigrammatic verse without change.[95]

Franklin's revisions did not always improve the original sayings. This is especially true of some of the reworkings to be
found in *The Way to Wealth*, according to Gallacher.[96] Newcomb also gives an example of a Franklin revision which fails.
The original, "Imitate a good Man, but do not counterfeit him,"
is hardly improved by Franklin's "There is much difference
between imitating a good man, and counterfeiting him."[97]

The following quotation sums up Franklin's revisionary practices in *Poor Richard:* His "method was to retain the general
syntax and basic thought of received sayings but to heighten
their point by judicious abstractions and clarifications. Franklin's revisions, therefore, were predominantly ones of method

rather than of meaning . . . a constant reflection of the lucid
and orderly mind which adapted them."[98] The ingenious revisions Franklin frequently made in borrowed sayings helped
very greatly to promote the success of *Poor Richard.*

III *The Way to Wealth*

Strictly speaking, *The Way to Wealth* is a work entirely separate from *Poor Richard,* for not all of its ninety sayings came
from this almanac.[99] Furthermore, in Newcomb's considered
opinion *The Way to Wealth* represents neither the whole nor
the so-called best of *Poor Richard,* as many editors have erro-
neously advertised it.[100] The best of *Poor Richard,* as he sees it,
comes from the almanacs for the years 1752-1758 and is "largely
unknown" to the general public.[101]

The Way to Wealth probably was not Franklin's title, nor
was its pattern original. For the text which has been most
often printed is not Franklin's text at all, writes Livingston, but
a "garbled and abridged version prepared by some unknown
English editor or publisher."[102] Franklin did use the phrase
"the way to wealth" in his *Advice to a Young Tradesman,* but
he did not use "The Way to Wealth" as an actual title, argues
Livingston.[103] Newcomb compares it to such works as Defoe's
The Complete English Tradesman, Steele's *The Religious Tradesman,* John Sowter's *The Way to Be Wise and Wealthy,* and the
anonymous *Pleasant Art of Money Catching,* all of which
enjoyed great popularity during the time.[104] Although Franklin's
collection was unique in form and content, it fit the pattern of
the day in its economic philosophy.

However this may be, one of Franklin's problems as a writer
in this document was how, in the process of repeating some
ninety proverbs and aphorisms, to avoid monotony. The problem was solved, in Newcomb's opinion, by alternating the
devices of a brief preface and an after comment—an elaboration
on his old technique of "sententious restatement."[105] According
to Newcomb's analysis, the whole divides into three main
parts: the introduction to the character of Richard Saunders,
Father Abraham's speech, and Poor Richard's summary conclusion. The middle or long part, he sees as "organized by
sections which relate to *time, industry, care, frugality, pride,
debt,* and *experience*—in that order."[106]

At first glance it is a little difficult to see any order whatever in this list. *Time* means making the most of time, however, and *care* means overseeing the work of servants carefully. At the end of his discussion of these first three—time, industry, and care—Franklin uses the following transition: "So much for Industry my Friends, and Attention to one's own Business; but to these we must add *Frugality*, if we would make our *Industry* more certainly successful." For practical purposes, then, *time, industry,* and *care* all proceed in a logical fashion (finding time to do work, doing the actual work, and overseeing it with care when you don't do it yourself) and all concern the one topic of *industry*. Similarly, *frugality*, the second large term in *The Way to Wealth,* involves questions of *pride* and *debt,* these last two being arranged in order, from the less important to the more important disastrous consequences ensuing from the lack of frugality.

The third large term is *Prudence*. One paragraph from the end of Father Abraham's speech, we read a summary of the terms "*Industry,* and *Frugality,* and *Prudence.*" Father Abraham has not, however, discussed *Prudence* and only does so in the last paragraph of his speech under the topic of *Experience.* *Prudence,* apparently, is the result of experience. Looked at in this way, the list makes more sense, the order is more obvious than as Newcomb presents it. There is even an order in the presentation of the three large terms—industry, frugality, and prudence—all being necessary in the acquisition of wealth, as Franklin saw it, and following logically from one another.

We have considered this matter of *order* in *The Way to Wealth,* because there, as in the *Autobiography,* it occupies so important a position in the hierarchy of virtues Franklin regarded as necessary to the art of writing. Despite the topical arrangement, the paragraph is nevertheless the "basic structural unit" in *The Way to Wealth.*[107] Further, Newcomb notes a "roughly chronological" date sequence in the sayings drawn from the *Almanack.* "The order of dates suggests that after Franklin decided which of the practical virtues to illustrate, he searched the *Almanack,* or perhaps a working list abstracted from it, for appropriate illustrations."[108]

IV   *Franklin's Use of the Sayings*

As a writer of sayings, Franklin possessed an uncanny ability to adapt means to ends. Often his sayings, or gnomic literature, combined practical means with ethical or didactic ends. Such examples as " 'Tis hard for an empty bag to stand upright" and "Great estates may venture more,/ But little boats should keep near shore" show this fusion of the practical and the didactic.[109] This combination according to one writer, gave the sayings an assured "firm grounding in the folk mind."[110]

Besides their didactic or ethical function the sayings of Franklin frequently were put to an important rhetorical function in controversial literature. "Controversy is likely to produce proverbial literature," writes Meister, because the opposing parties try to "enlist the wisdom of previous ages on their respective sides."[111] In Franklin's hand the proverb became an extremely effective rhetorical weapon.

He frequently used a proverb to present a kind of visual aid to an argument or to an ideal of social behavior. As an example of the use of a proverb to refute an opponent's argument, Meister presents the case of the pacifist who said he did not believe in fighting to save those who would not fight to save themselves. Franklin replied, "You won't pump ship, because 't will save the rats, as well as yourself."[112] In the great debate on British violations of justice in dealing with the colonies, Franklin frequently used proverbs to make his points vividly pictorial for his readers. "What you get from us in taxes," he wrote to the British ministry, "you must lose in Trade; the cat can yield but her skin."[113]

Franklin was not above trickery and expediency in his rhetoric. When recalling what an Englishman had once said about the ends Great Britain would go to in order to win the war, Franklin wrote, "Such Menaces were besides an Encouragement with me, remembering the Adage, that *they who threaten are afraid.*"[114] Meister calls our attention to the fact that earlier Franklin himself had used threats against England and concludes that "even in the rhetorical use of proverbs, one of Franklin's ultimate criteria . . . [was] expediency."[115]

Sometimes Franklin would let the proverb carry the whole burden of his proof, as in the following attack on religious hypocrites: "a little religion, and a little honesty, goes a great way in courts." Sometimes he would state the proverb, present his argument, and then restate the proverb. In his capable hands the proverb was usually set in such a position that it carried the maximum weight of persuasion.

CHAPTER 4

Political Journalism

F RANKLIN'S third great contribution to the art of writing is a large body of heterogeneous works, which for the lack of a better name we shall call "political journalism," since most of them appeared in the newspapers of the day and are ordinarily concerned with political affairs. These took the form of letters to the press, essays, satires, fables, hoaxes, entire pamphlets in some cases—all of them works of persuasion exemplifying what the Greeks meant by the art of rhetoric.

In mid-eighteenth-century America and England the gentle art of persuasion often warmed into the hot war of propaganda. The fires of argument naturally blazed brighter as time went on, until the cracks of muskets and cannonading announced the Revolution in full progress. Chief among the colonial propaganda writers who fed these fires were Tom Paine, Philip Freneau, and Benjamin Franklin. Every American boy knows of Tom Paine's *Crisis* papers and their part in restoring morale to Washington's battered and well-nigh beaten troops at Valley Forge and elsewhere. And many students know of Freneau's biting satire which persuaded the colonists that King George III was trembling like an arrant coward at the prospect of the destruction of his empire. But not so many know of Franklin's part in this great war of nerves. Writing in England, fragmenting British public opinion and ridiculing the policies of the proprietaries and the ministers, Franklin's powerful pen won considerable British support for the American cause.

I Developing Propagandist

Curiously enough, one of the most eloquent defenders of the British up to the year 1760 was Franklin himself. His imagination had caught fire at the "limitless prospect of power and grandeur opening before the British empire" in the decade beginning with the year 1751.[1] "What an Accession of Power to the British Empire by Sea as well as Land! What Increase of Trade and Navigation! What Numbers of Ships and Seamen!"[2] were exclamations that might have been spewed forth by any very faithful subject of the king (or queen) during any one of the great periods of British nationalism—the Elizabethan period or the era of nineteenth-century colonial expansion, for example. Actually, they were written by a very loyal servant of the king, Benjamin Franklin, the Deputy Post-Master of the American Colonies of His Royal Majesty King George II.

Crane startles us when he states that "among the patriot leaders of the American Revolution the last great imperialist was Benjamin Franklin."[3] It was a new kind of imperialism, and Franklin was imbued with it because it strongly reflected his own social observations, observations which he adapted to the changing circumstances of politics up to the very eve of the Revolution. Generally speaking, these social and political theories had flowered in his thinking during the decade of 1750-1760[4].

Weighed against this view of Franklin as a garden variety of British imperialist, we must not fail, however, to note what he refers to in the *Autobiography* as certain "spirited Remarks of my Writings" on the dispute between the royal Governor of Massachusetts and the popular Massachusetts Assembly. These "spirited Remarks" possessed the virtue of increasing the circulation of his paper, the *Pennsylvania Gazette;* and they appeared in an article in the *Gazette* of October 9, 1729. It shows that as early as this year Franklin had taken up the pen in behalf of popular rights and liberty and against the heavy-handed British colonial rule with reference to unnecessary taxes. The spirit of Franklin's "Remarks" may be gathered from the last sentence of this article, which reads: "Their happy Mother Country will perhaps observe with Pleasure, that tho' her gallant Cocks and matchless Dogs [royal governors] abate their native Fire and Intrepidity when transported to a Foreign Clime (as the common Notion is) yet her SONS [the colonists] in the remotest Part of the Earth, and even to the third and fourth Descent, still retain that ardent Spirit of Liberty, and that undaunted Courage in the Defence of it, which has in every Age so gloriously distinguished BRITONS and ENGLISHMEN from all the Rest of Mankind."[5]

The allusion to the abatement of the native fire of the royal governor, William Burnet, probably concerns his death, which occurred shortly before this article appeared. There was certainly no abatement of his insistence that the people pay his salary according to fixed royal demand rather than "according to their Sense of his Merit and Services," as had been the custom, Franklin says, "for these Hundred Years past." For Burnet, despite great opposition, fought to the day of his death to adhere to royal commands regarding the fixing of his extremely fat salary. The allusion to the abatement of Burnet's native fire undoubtedly, therefore, is a trick of rhetoric on Franklin's part.[6]

As his "Remarks" of 1729 indicate, it is possible to trace Franklin's political writings for the years 1757-1776—the period we are primarily concerned with—back to his early journalism. As Crane says, "He drew upon talents for journalism that he had developed long since as a provincial printer and newspaper proprietor."[7]

As chief engineer of the American propaganda machine in London for the periods 1757-1762 and 1764-1775, he industriously worked behind the scenes as agent for Pennsylvania, New Jersey, Georgia, and Massachusetts, secretly churning out countless arguments against the Stamp Act, the Townshend Acts, the Tea Act, and the Punitive Acts.[8] One of Franklin's busiest periods as a writer of propaganda came during the winter of 1765-1766.[9] Literally night and day he was busily answering letters in the public papers. This feverish activity he continued with special vigor until 1770.[10] Throughout this period he printed important documents previously published only in America; he encouraged writing in England on behalf of the colonies; he wrote new pamphlets persuading English readers to the American point of view; and he deluged the newspapers with anonymous essays and letters to the editor, using a variety of forms (fable, hoax, allegory, satire, Socratic dialogue, etc.) and employing a great variety of pseudonyms (approximately forty) to give the effect of great interest by numerous individuals and pressure groups.[11] "It now appears," writes Crane, "that his English political journalism was the largest body of his contemporaneously published writings."[12]

To give some idea of the range and the impact of this propaganda activity on the public, we can cite definitely some thirty-three essays in the *Public Advertiser*, thirty-two in the *London Chronicle*, eighteen in the *Gazeteer*.[13] The *Public Adver-*

tiser had a circulation of about three thousand; the *Gazeteer*, of about five thousand. But these papers were read far more widely than their circulations might indicate. Moreover, when his works gained popularity in these daily papers, they were reprinted in the monthlies. His productions were well timed, for most of them appeared during the months when parliament was in session or when important elections impended. It is no exaggeration to say that Franklin's audience included English and American readers and possibly a few French spies. The former printer's devil of Boston was now writing for the world; and, although he did not know it (since he was interested usually in the accomplishment of only immediate, practical ends), he was writing for all time.

The opposition lost no time in replying to the man they dubbed "Old Doubleface," "Old Traitor F.," and "The Judas of Craven St.,"—the street where Franklin lived.[14] Their names for Franklin were almost as numerous as his pseudonyms for himself. When during the war they called him "the paymaster of the Revolution,"[15] they indicated that his efforts at complete anonymity were not entirely successful. By 1774, in fact, rival writers, employed by the British ministry to produce counter-propaganda, were attributing all propaganda for the American cause, some of which Franklin had not written, to what one of their ranks called "Judas's office in Craven Street."[16]

Sometimes, too, the counterattack took the form of malicious, partisan publishing. When William Goddard reprinted for back-home consumption in the *Pennsylvania Chronicle* a whole batch of Franklin's papers from the London press, he arranged them to give the effect that Franklin was bungling affairs in connection with the Stamp Act.[17] Resistance to this kind of opposition taught Franklin how to fence—a particularly useful skill when he later underwent heavy and prolonged cross-examination on the Stamp Act before the House of Commons. Most often Franklin's letters during this period aimed at correcting letters of English and American writers who had either misstated or misrepresented the facts or the public opinion of the American colonies.[18]

As a political journalist Franklin possessed genuine style in the presentation of his arguments, excelling in what Davy calls the "arts of the exordium [the beginning of a rhetorical work], grace and charm for winning a hearing."[19] This is certainly true, for Franklin's persuasive works invariably exhibit

ingratiating beginnings; and the beginning is where the first
and often lasting impression is made. Certainly his twenty-five
years of carefully disciplined writing and rewriting in connection with *Poor Richard* did much to weed all irrelevancies from
his style.

As a writer of political journalism, Franklin's apprenticeship
was long and arduous but also highly rewarding. His provincial work with *Poor Richard* and the *Pennsylvania Gazette*
prepared him stylistically for what Davy calls the "larger the-
atre."[20] Indeed, it is possible to trace his rhetorical style in
his great works of the period 1758-1775 all the way back to the
New England Courant, his early but excellent school in the
use of satire. Techniques learned so early which stood him in
good stead as an agent of the colonies consisted of such devices
as the following: the use of fable to achieve satire, the letter
to the editor to avoid a direct attack, the pose of puzzled
observer to introduce an open assault, the use of scripture
and proverbs to serve as premises in proof, the use of dialogue
to attain an effect of being fair to an opponent, the use of
innuendo to convey what could not be openly asserted, the
use of burlesque to ridicule an opponent's argument, and the
use of an innocent and generalized approach before an attack
on a specific issue.[21] But Franklin's bag of tricks did not end
here. As a subtle dialectician he could have outfoxed Reynard
himself; and this ability was not accidental.

As we have noted earlier, Franklin had had opportunity to
read the Port-Royal *Art of Thinking* and *Art of Speaking*, which
were considered among the best rhetorics of his age, in the
Courant library. Apparently he thought rhetoric a highly useful branch of learning, for he insisted on its importance in his
Proposals Relating to the Education of Youth in Pensilvania
and also in his *Idea of the English School,* two works embody-
ing his ideas on right education. Knowledge of the art of rhetoric, possibly more than any single thing, contributed to his
success as a journalist, for he employed it constantly from the
smallest saying in *Poor Richard* to his lengthiest pamphlet in
the international arena.

Satire has been called "the most rhetorical of all the kinds
of literature."[22] The era of Franklin was an age of satire; and
some of it—as in Dryden, Pope, and Swift—was very great. The
age demanded satire, for men and manners, not to mention
political institutions, needed radical improvement. As a writer

of eighteenth-century satire, Franklin did not quite adequately assess his power if we can go by a letter written to his sister Jane Mecom, dated December 24, 1767. In this letter he speaks of some of his writings for the London public press, saying, "They were most of them written occasionally for transient Purposes, and having done their Business, they die and are forgotten. I could have easily made a Collection for you of all the past Parings of my Nails." One wishes he had. Fortunately for us, Crane has recovered many of these superior works. Today they stand as monuments of history.

Briefly summing up Franklin's career as a satirist, we may say that it covered a great emotional range, from the gentle graces of the *bagatelles*, which chapter five deals with, to the savage hoaxes of satires like the *Supplement to the Boston Independent Chronicle*. In terms of his own life, his career as a satirist covered a similarly great range of time, extending from the age of sixteen to within three weeks of his death at the age of eighty-four. It covered, as well, a great range of space, from the early days on the *Courant* in provincial Boston to the later periods in the great capitals of the world—London and Paris. Apart from these broad considerations of space and time, however, his best and most prolific period of satire was the decade preceding the outbreak of the war.[23] As probably the strongest influence on his work in this genre, we may note the influence of Swift, especially during the 1730's, according to Davy, but never far removed. A whole collection of Franklin's satires would show marked parallels to the work of Swift, Davy continues, and might well be named "modest proposals." But unlike Swift, Franklin "never wished to attack mankind in general nor, like Pope, to make individuals the target of his wit. His satire served causes."[24] His use of masks as a principal device in satire, his capacity to amuse in a way that always advanced his purpose, his skill in handling humor, the fertile imagination of his comparisons and parallels, his excellent conclusions, careful choice of diction, his detachment, his graceful charm and wit—in all these he was a good follower of Quintillian, that greatest of all teachers of rhetoric.

Davy interprets Franklin's idea of *order* in satire as akin to Quintillian's concepts on *partition* and *arrangement*. Partition means the enumeration in a rigid outline early in the composition of propositions to be discussed. But although Franklin actually avoids this kind of explicit stating of such propositions,

Davy nevertheless concludes that Franklin "certainly worked from outlines carefully planned and revised."[25] And although Quintillian (in the *Institutes of Oratory*) advised answering the strongest charges of the opposition first, he also stated that this order might be reversed, a procedure which Franklin frequently followed.

Davy compares Franklin's advice to Vaughan on *order* with a statement of Aristotle's in the *Rhetoric* regarding arguments most generally applauded. Such arguments are those "of which we foresee the conclusions from the beginning, so long as they are not obvious from first sight—for part of the pleasure we feel is at our own intelligent anticipation; or those we follow well enough to see the point of them as soon as the last word has been uttered."

According to McMahon, the satires alone of all Franklin's political journalism have real worth. In his opinion "they possess a literary polish which is absent in his other political writings."[26] Only the satires he finds "worthy to stand beside the famous *Autobiography* and incomparable *Poor Richard's Almanack*."[27]

II   *The Influence of Swift*

In his battles with British propagandists Franklin (as we have already suggested) sometimes resorted to a rhetorical method employed by Jonathan Swift, the greatest of all satirists. In such satires as the *Rules by which a Great Empire May Be Reduced to a Small One, The Sale of the Hessians,* the *Exporting of Felons to the Colonies,* and others, Franklin's use of Swiftian irony is quite obvious. The following passage from a letter to the printer of the *Public Advertiser,* entitled *Pax Quaeritur Bello* (Peace Sought by War) appeared on January 26, 1766, over the signature of "Pacificus" in connection with extremely bitter controversy over the Stamp Act. Anyone familiar with Swift's *A Modest Proposal* will immediately perceive that Franklin was using his ironic method, and in a very similar way. Franklin was saying the opposite of what he really meant in order to present strongly his intellectually controlled, but fierce, indignation at injustice.

> Now in order to bring these People to a proper Temper, I have a Plan to propose, which I think cannot fail, and which will be entirely consistent with the Oeconomy at present so much in Vogue. It is so cheap a Way of going to work, that

even Mr. G——G——[George Grenville, the British minister]
that great Oeconomist, could have no reasonable Objection to it.

Let Directions be given, that Two Thousand Highlanders
be immediately raised, under proper Officers of their own. . . .
Transport them early in the Spring to Quebec: They with the
Canadians, natural Enemies to our Colonists, who would volun-
tarily engage, might make a Body of Five or Six Thousand
Men; and I doubt not, by artful Management, and the Value
of two or three Thousand Pounds in Presents, with the Hopes
of Plunder, as likewise a Gratuity for every Scalp, the Savages
on the Frontiers might be engaged to join, at least they would
make a Diversion, which could not fail of being useful. I could
point out a very proper General to command the Expedition;
he is of a very sanguine Disposition, [a play on the two mean-
ings of the word *sanguine—bloody* and *optimistic*] and has an
inordinate Thirst for Fame, and besides has the Hearts of the
Canadians. He might march from Canada, cross the Lakes, and
fall upon these People without their expecting or being prepared
for him, and with very little Difficulty over-run the whole
Country.

The Business might be done without employing any of the
Regular Troops quartered in the Country, and I think it would
be best they should remain neuter, as it is to be feared they
would be rather backward in embruing their Hands in the
Blood of their Brethren and Fellow Subjects.

I would propose, that all the Capitals of the several Provinces
should be burnt to the Ground, and that they cut the Throats of
all the Inhabitants, Men, Women, and Children, and scalp them,
to serve as an Example; that all the Shipping should be
destroyed, which will effectually prevent Smuggling, and save
the Expence of Guarda Costas.

No Man in his Wits, after such terrible Military Execution,
will refuse to purchase stamp'd Paper. If any one should hesi-
tate, five or six Hundred Lashes in a cold frosty Morning would
soon bring him to Reason.

If the Massacre should be objected to, as it would too much
depopulate the Country, it may be replied, that the Interruption
this Method would occasion to Commerce, would cause so many
Bankruptcies, such Numbers of Manufacturers and Labourers
would be unemployed, that together with the Felons from our
Gaols, we should soon be enabled to transport such Numbers
to repeople the Colonies, as to make up for any Deficiency
which Example made it Necessary to sacrifice for the Public
Good. Great Britain might then reign over a loyal and submis-
sive People, and be morally certain, that no Act of Parliament
would ever after be disputed.[28]

The irony of Jonathan Swift, then, was one source of Franklin's satire.

Occasionally British injustice so violently stirred Franklin's indignation that he mixed earthy humor with his irony. A letter to the *Public Advertiser,* dated May 21, 1774, shows this quality in the form—again, as in Swift—of a humble proposal. This particular strong satire was provoked by a certain General Clarke who had boasted in Franklin's presence that he would march with a thousand grenadiers from one end to the other of America and geld all the males among the colonists, either by force or by a little coaxing. Franklin adopted this point of view and ultimately turned the tables on Clarke by the use of irony. He suggested that General Gage take an army and proceed with the castration. "Let a company of Sow-Gelders, consisting of 100 Men, accompany the Army. On their Arrival at any Town or Village, let Orders be given that on the blowing of the Horn all the Males be assembled in the Market Place. If the Corps are Men of Skill and Ability in their Profession, they will Make great Dispatch and retard but very little the Progress of the Army." The more notorious ringleaders of the rebellion, like Adams and Hancock, Franklin suggests, "should be shaved quite close." All the males in the town of Boston, as a matter of fact, "should be shaved quite close" in accordance with the principle of the British "that it is better that ten innocent Persons should suffer than that one guilty should escape." A little blood would certainly be spilled by possible conscientious objectors among the colonists, but "Bleeding to a certain Degree is salutary. The English, whose humanity is celebrated by all the World, but particularly by themselves, do not desire the Death of the Delinquent, but his Reformation."

Four advantages, says Franklin, would result from this project: (1) in fifty years there would not remain one rebellious vassal in all North America; (2) the British opera would be saved the great expense of importing Italian tenors (and sopranos), for the castrated Americans with their fine voices could take their place; (3) commerce with the Levant (Middle East) would be greatly enhanced by sending the Americans who had undergone this operation there to serve as eunuch guards for the Moslem harems; (4) the plan "would effectually put a Stop to the emigrations [particularly of males] from this Country [England] now grown so very fashionable."[29]

Among the noblest of Franklin's monuments of satire, besides the popular favorites, the *Rules* and the *Edict,* we must certainly count *The Sale of the Hessians* (1777). It takes the form of a letter from a certain Count de Schaumbergh in Rome to Baron Hohendorf, commander of the hired Hessian troops in America, the former complaining that not enough Hessians are being killed in America. Since he supplies these mercenaries at so much a head, the more killed, the greater his income. In *The Sale* Franklin assumes the role of a moral monster, trafficking in human flesh:

> I do not mean by this that you should assassinate them [the Hessians]; we should be humane, my dear Baron, but you may insinuate to the surgeons with entire propriety that a crippled man is a reproach to their profession, and that there is no wiser course than to let every one of them die when he ceases to be fit to fight.
>
> I am about to send you some new recruits. Don't economize them. Remember glory before all things. Glory is true wealth. There is nothing degrades the soldier like the love of money. He must care only for honour and reputation, but this reputation must be acquired in the midst of dangers. A battle gained without costing the conqueror any blood is an inglorious success, while the conquered cover themselves with glory by perishing with their arms in their hands. Do you remember that of the 300 Lacedaemonians who defended the defile of Thermopylae, not one returned? How happy should I be could I say the same of my brave Hessians!
>
> It is true that their king, Leonidas, perished with them: but things have changed, and it is no longer the custom for princes of the empire to go and fight in America for a cause with which they have no concern.

The effect, of course, was to heap obloquy on the British as cowards who hired other men to do their fighting. To the French and other Europeans, who already had cause to hate British mercantilism, this satire must have had the effect of oil poured on fire. It is certainly the bitterest and most Swiftian of Franklin's satires, especially in its final earthy injunctions and sanctimonious close:

> You did right to send back to Europe that Dr. Crumerus who was so successful in curing dysentery. Don't bother with a man who is subject to looseness of the bowels. That disease makes bad soldiers. One coward will do more mischief in an

engagement than ten brave men will do good. Better that they burst in their barracks than fly in a battle, and tarnish the glory of our arms. Besides, you know that they pay me as killed for all who die from disease, and I don't get a farthing for runaways. My trip to Italy, which has cost me enormously, makes it desirable that there should be a great mortality among them. You will therefore promise promotion to all who expose themselves; you will exhort them to seek glory in the midst of dangers; you will say to Major Maundorf that I am not at all content with his saving the 345 men who escaped the massacre of Trenton. Through the whole campaign he has not had ten men killed in consequence of his orders. Finally, let it be your principal object to prolong the war and avoid a decisive engagement on either side, for I have made arrangements for a grand Italian opera, and I do not wish to be obliged to give it up. Meantime I pray God, my dear Baron Hohendorf, to have you in his holy and gracious keeping.[30]

III *Verbal Irony*

Franklin's use of irony took many forms. In his excellent study Davy divides Franklinian irony into two general categories—situational and verbal.[31] (Both forms are of course often simultaneously present in a given work.) Situational irony is illustrated in the "modest proposals" already discussed. As an example of verbal irony, let us consider two of Franklin's italicized words in his statement about the case of Jonathan Belcher, who had represented the Massachusetts Assembly in England in their dispute about fat salaries against the royal governor of that state, Burnet. Quite ironically (situational) Belcher, who succeeded Burnet as Governor of Massachusetts, was even worse on the salary dispute than Burnet. When the dispute broke out again, Franklin wrote the following about Belcher in the *Pennsylvania Gazette* for September 24, 1730: ". . . by being at Court, it seems, he has had the *Advantage* of seeing Things in another Light, and those Instructions do now appear to him highly consistent with the Privileges and Interest of the People, which before, as a *Patriot,* he had very different Notions of."[32]

Verbal irony, as Franklin employed it, sometimes carried with it a deep sarcasm, as in this example (my italics): "*Pleasant,* surely it is, to hear the Proprietary Partizans, of all Men, bawling for the Constitution, and affecting a *terrible* concern for our Liberties."[33] In the *Supplement to the Boston Inde-*

pendent Chronicle, a hoax dated Boston, March 12, 1782, for the purpose of protesting British use of hired Indians against the colonists, Franklin used understatement as a form of verbal irony to achieve an effect of increasingly greater cruelty and horror. This occurs in Franklin's reference to a description of the scalps of the colonists as "painted, with all the Indian triumphal *Marks*" and in his reference to the scalps as a "Present" to the governor of Canada.

The irony of seeming to praise but actually blaming was another of his tricks of verbal irony. One of his non-political *Dogood* papers provides a good example. In writing of the very bad, sentimental verse that often made up the New England elegies, Franklin praises what he calls one particular form of it, the Kitellic elegy, as "the most extraordinary Peice" [*sic*] ever produced in New England and in many ways "almost beyond Comparison."[34] Although he seems to praise the Kitellic elegy, he is actually saying that it is so extraordinarily bad as to be beyond comparison.

Like a fleet halfback in a football game, he could reverse his field with the greatest of ease. In a passage written in 1767 for the *Gazeteer,* we discern, instead of seeming praise and actual blame, the irony of seeming blame but actual praise. "It is *wrong,* O ye Americans! for you to expect hereafter, any protection or countenance from us, in return for the loyalty and zeal you manifested, and the blood and treasure you have expended in our cause during the war; or that we will make any acts of parliament relating to you, from the time we, the Gentle Shepherd, and his flock, get into power, 'but such as are calculated for impoverishing you and enriching us.' "[35] Obviously Franklin's blame of the Americans is an ironical pose, assumed only to show the stupidity of the British commercial policies promoted by the (ironical) "Gentle Shepherd" George Grenville. In reality Franklin praises the Americans for their generous conduct.

IV *Masks of Neutrality*

Franklin donned various masks to give the effect of numerous different writers interested in colonial questions. Almost always these had the effect of enhancing the rhetoric; in short, they, too, were part of his bag of tricks—and had been for a long time. "From the beginning to the end of his career as a writer Franklin employed ironic masks," says Davy, who recalls Franklin's first disguise as a young widow (Silence Dogood) and his last as a Moslem (Sidi Mehemet).[36]

Franklin's first instinct in controversy during the period 1758-1775 was to seize a mask not only because of political reasons ("his richly double character as colonial agent and Crown officer"), but also because a disguise gave him a better chance of a fair hearing. In an age hot with political debate, a mask made a good impression of neutrality;[37] and the mask of the neutral or detached observer was one of Franklin's favorite methods of persuasion. In the controversy over the Stamp Act, for example, he often wrote in the character of an objective reporter—a native of England—who was coolly presenting the views and principles of the overseas colonists in America. In this fashion Franklin kept his own views, writes Crane, "prudently in reserve, even in his correspondence, until, around 1768, [when] he began to communicate them in strict confidence to a few of his American friends."[38] Davy points out an exception to this habit, however; during the years 1765-1766 Franklin changed his pseudonym from "N.N." to "Homespun" in order to speak out "more tartly and more directly" than he could in the neutral British character he had first assumed.[39]

Further examples show how his various masks of detached observer protected him. In Boston, as Silence Dogood, he immediately gained immunity from local and foreign political and religious dangers—both American and British—in his role as a young widow. (It was even a little more complicated than that, however, for he was actually using excerpts from the London press—see *Dogood* papers, Nos. 8 and 9—in making war on the local politicos and clergymen). Later, in Philadelphia as Richard Saunders, he avoided the disadvantages of an ambitious young man by pretending to be a wise old man. Still later, in London, Franklin, who signed himself "F.B.," presented himself as perfectly neutral—as a Britisher who had "lived many years in that country [America]," "but [who] changes his tone to one of sharp attack when he finds his opponent," Tom Hint, "wrong."[40]

Another favorite mask was that of the humble inquirer. By giving the appearance of humility, he confuses the opposition as to his own true position while he systematically plants dynamite behind the enemy lines. In one instance when he is wearing this mask, he explains that he has read in the London papers (1758) of certain bills passed by the Assembly in Mary-

land but vetoed by the proprietor because he refuses to bear his
fair share of the taxes to defray expenses of the expedition
against Fort Duquesne. The facts, of course, were that the Proprietor did have strenuous objections to paying his taxes, was
not paying them, and did not intend to do so. All these facts
Franklin well knew. But he pretended not to know them in
order to draw the attention of the English public to this unjust
condition in the colonies which permitted the wealthy land-
owner to go scott free of the heavy taxes imposed on the poor
small landowners, the farmer-colonists. This cannot possibly be
true, Franklin, the uninformed, exclaims, for "it is well known
the Proprietary Estates are already taxed equally with the Estates
of any of the Inhabitants in Maryland; and that the Proprietor
has no objection thereto."[41] Franklin then proceeds to take a
careful second look at this accusation of the proprietary interest
and to ask a few questions—twenty-nine, to be exact. Every one
of them is carefully loaded with Franklin's highly charged anti-
proprietary propaganda. But throughout the tract he carefully
"preserves the fiction of an innocent bystander perplexed about
the real facts in the face of contradictory reports" in the newspapers.[42]

This pattern of the innocent, confused inquirer appears again
in The Speech of Polly Baker (1747), probably the most famous
of Franklin's hoaxes. An existing law prohibited sexual inter-
course outside wedlock, but the law was difficult to enforce
for lack of evidence. One sure evidence, however, was the
birth of an illegitimate child, for which the mother was usually
fined or imprisoned. The father, on the other hand, often went
entirely free. Franklin protests this unjust law by having Polly
ask several highly rhetorical questions of the court when she is
dragged there because of the birth of her fifth illegitimate
child, and her questions concern more important matters of
injustice not punished at the time by the law. So effectively
does Polly convince the judge of her innocence and good sense
that he marries her the next day; and whether or not he had
anything to do with the birth of Polly's latest child is left to
the reader's imagination. Polly is a sympathetic character, however, because of her innocence; and, deserted by men she would
willingly marry, she is more sinned against than sinning. Thus
Franklin effectually protests a double standard of sexual morality in his mask of Polly Baker, a person innocent but confused
by the injustice of the official system of punishment.

In *On the Price of Corn, and the Management of the Poor*
(1766) he dons the same mask, this time of a confused country
bumpkin who signs himself *Arator* (ploughman). But the well-
elaborated thirteen arguments that compose this protest against
the corn, or grain, laws reveal a subtle dialectician at work—
certainly not a bumpkin. This is one of Franklin's good though
less well-known rhetorical works.

Most of the masks Franklin created for the benefit of his
British readers represent the speaker as English.[43] When, for
example, the hack writers hired by the British ministry argued
that manufactures should not be set up in factories in the colonies because "their Sheep have but little Wool, not in the
whole sufficient for a Pair of Stockings a Year to each Inhabi-
tant,"[44] Franklin quickly answered in a letter to the *Public
Advertiser* (May 22, 1765) taking the viewpoint of a gullible
British newswriter in order to make fun of such hack writers'
mistaken notions about America. The last part of his argument is:

> It is objected by superficial Readers, who yet pretend to some
> Knowledge of those Countries [the colonies], that such Estab-
> lishments are not only improbable but impossible; for that their
> Sheep have but little Wool, not in the whole sufficient for a
> Pair of Stockings a Year to each Inhabitant; and that, from
> the universal Dearness of Labour among them, the working
> of Iron and other Materials, except in some few coarse Instances,
> is impracticable to any Advantage. Dear Sir, do not let us suffer
> ourselves to be amused with such groundless Objections. The
> very Tails of the American Sheep are so laden with Wool, that
> each has a Car or Waggon on four little Wheels to support
> and keep it from trailing on the Ground. Would they caulk their
> Ships? would they fill their Beds? would they even litter their
> Horses with Wool, if it was not both plenty and cheap?[45]

A little further on in the same article Franklin makes fun
of the crazy idea of some other misinformed British writer
(*Public Advertiser*, March 20 and May 15, 1765) to the effect
that domestication of the whale on the inland lakes, particularly
Lake Ontario, was scheduled to take place that summer. Once
again he employs the same method of pretending to defend
the truth of an obviously foolish statement in order to show
its utter absurdity. And, of course, the demonstration backfires
on the stupidity of the British writers, exactly as Franklin
intended.

. . . all this is as certainly true as the Account, said to be from Quebec, in the Papers of last Week, that the inhabitants of Canada are making Preparations for a Cod and Whale Fishery this Summer in the Upper Lakes. Ignorant People may object that the Upper Lakes are fresh, that Cod and Whale are Salt-water Fish: But let them know, Sir, that Cod, like other Fish, when attacked by their Enemies, fly into any water where they can be safest; that Whales, when they have a mind to eat Cod, pursue them wherever they fly; and that the grand Leap of the Whale in that Chace [sic] up the Fall of Niagara is esteemed by all who have seen it, as one of the finest Spectacles in Nature!—Really, Sir, the World is grown too incredulous.[46]

V *Mask of the Good Man and the Hoax*

In Aristotle's *Rhetoric* the point is made that in matters of doubt we tend to trust good men; they win our confidence. Franklin's rhetorical practice was often to present himself as a character with a calm and gentle disposition—in short, a good man;[47] and his ability to so project himself was one of his strongest features as a writer of persuasion or propaganda. Davy puts it very well: "Pleasant, polite, amiable, and attractive, he [Franklin] recommends himself by constantly evoking in the reader a conviction that truth and virtue are with him and in his words."[48] In evoking this image of the good man, Franklin followed the tradition in satire of Alexander Pope—just as he used two other already-mentioned satiric masks of Pope, those of the humble inquirer and of the public defender.[49]

If truth and virtue were his strong points in his satiric masks of the good man, the tall tale and the hoax figured no less strongly in his character of the man of common sense. In this category belong some of his most excellent satires and hoaxes: *Rules By Which A Great Empire May Be Made Into a Small One*, *An Edict of the King of Prussia*, *The Sale of the Hessians*, and the article written in 1790 entitled *On the Slave-Trade*.

The *Rules*, which Franklin preferred "for the quantity and variety of the matter contained, and a kind of spirited ending of each paragraph," listed twenty arguments or rules by which the British Empire first might be diminished, like a cake, at it edges, and then ultimately reduced to a very small empire indeed.[50] The arguments pertain to injustices visited upon the colonists by the British secretary of state for the colonies, the Earl of Hillsborough; but Franklin assumed as a "modern simpleton" that the intention of this ministry was actually to reduce the size of the mighty British Empire. To illustrate what Franklin called "the spirited ending of each paragraph," we quote the opening address and one or two of the rules:

> An ancient Sage boasted, that, tho' he could not fiddle, he knew how to make a *great city* of a *little one*. The science that I, a modern simpleton, am about to communicate is the very reverse.
>
> I address myself to all ministers who have the management of extensive dominions, which from their very greatness are become troublesome to govern, because the multiplicity of their affairs leaves no time for *fiddling*.
>
> I. In the first place, gentlemen, you are to consider that a great empire, like a great cake, is most easily diminished at the edges. Turn your attention, therefore, first to your remotest provinces; that, as you get rid of them, the next may follow in order.
>
> II. That the possibility of this separation may always exist, take special care the provinces are never incorporated with the mother country; that they do not enjoy the same common rights, the same privileges in commerce; and that they are governed by *severer* laws, all of *your enacting*, without allowing them any share in the choice of legislators. By carefully making and preserving such distinctions, you will (to keep to my simile of the cake) act like a wise gingerbread baker, who, to facilitate a division, cuts his dough half through in those places, where, when baked, he would have it *broken to pieces*. . . .
>
> . . . .
>
> VII. When . . . Governors have crammed their coffers and made themselves so odious to the people that they can no longer remain among them in safety to their persons, recall and *reward* them with pensions. You may make them *Baronets*, too, if that respectable order should not think fit to resent it. All will contribute to encourage new governors in the same practices, and make the supreme government *detestable*. . . .
>
> . . . .
>
> XV. Convert the brave, honest officers of your navy into pimping tide-waiters and colony officers of the customs. Let those who, in time of war, fought gallantly in defence of the commerce of their countrymen, in peace be taught to prey upon it. Let them learn to be corrupted by great and real smugglers; but (to shew their diligence) scour with armed boats every bay, harbour, river, creek, cove, or nook, throughout the coast of your colonies; stop and detain every coaster, every wood-boat, every fisherman, tumble their cargoes, and even their ballast, inside

out, and upside down; and, if a penn'orth of pins is found un-entered, let the whole be seized and confiscated. Thus shall the trade of your colonists suffer more from their friends in time of peace, than it did from their enemies in war. Then let these boat crews land upon every farm in their way, rob the orchards, steal the pigs and poultry, and insult the inhabitants. If the injured and exasperated farmers, unable to procure other justice, should attack the aggressors, drub them and burn their boats; you are to call this *high treason* and *rebellion,* order fleets and armies into their country, and threaten to carry all the offenders three thousand miles to be hanged, drawn, and quartered. *O! this will work admirably!*

The *Rules* is possibly Franklin's finest satire, considered from the standpoint of the great "quantity and variety" it contains. The arguments roughly follow a general-to-specific order, but they also bubble along not only to a boil but to overflowing indignation at the injustice of Hillsborough's ministry. They are, therefore, also arranged in order of intensity to provide a climax of resentment. Within the individual complaints, or rules, too, the material becomes increasingly specific as the emotion develops. In the *Rules,* as in the *Autobiography* and *Poor Richard,* we can observe, therefore, Franklin's great care with the problem of order in writing. To give just one little instance of it, we cite the large-to-small sequence in "bay, harbour, river, creek, cove, or nook." We should notice also how within the paragraph the material follows a climactic order; how he drives home his point by use of irony, italics, and exclamation points at the end of rule fifteen.

The paragraph structure of this satire is worth careful study by all interested in the art of writing. Practically every paragraph ends with a surprise or a sudden turn which is made doubly emphatic by its position at the end of a periodic sentence and by judicious use of italics. To pull this trick nineteen successive times, as Franklin does—the first rule has no surprise—makes great demands upon a writer's sense of variety. Franklin's success is due in part to his making the reader attend carefully to the argument while he also entertains him with his playfully ironic advice on how to disintegrate the gigantic cake-like structure called the British Empire. But at the end of every rule he suddenly reverses the tone and shows his deadly seriousness by means of a strong warning or threat.

Another remarkable characteristic of the paragraph structure is his use of a reversal or turn within paragraphs three, four, and ten considered as wholes. This turn usually comes at the point after he finishes describing the specific situation in the colonies and then tells the minister what he should do about it —always, of course, by way of reducing the great empire to a small one. Usually the turn comes just where he begins employing irony with a vengeance. In paragraph four the turn comes after the word *grievances:* "IV. However peaceably your colonies have submitted to your government, shewn their affection to your interests, and patiently borne their grievances; you are to *suppose* them always inclined to revolt, and treat them accordingly. Quarter troops among them, who by their insolence may *provoke* the rising of mobs, and by bullets and bayonets *suppress* them. By this means, like the husband who uses his wife ill *from suspicion,* you may in time convert your *suspicions* into *realities.*"

The effect of such turns is to pose the excellent and commendable action of the colonies against the stupid and unjust action of the ministers. This kind of weighing the two sides, as on a balance of justice, also gives the effect of judgment against the ministers, particularly since what Franklin advises the fictitious minister to do is an actual record of what the real minister (Hillsborough) had in fact already done in his inefficient and unjust administration of the colonies. Considered as a whole, this satire contains a wealth of grievances and injustices, an enormous amount of specific detail. In our opinion, it amounts to a summary justification of the American Revolution. It is impossible to read it without feeling that the colonists were absolutely right in revolting against Great Britain. Surely it must have affected many of Franklin's British readers in this way. And that is precisely what he had intended it to do. Beneath its playful exterior it is an ultimatum.

Another satire in the form of a hoax that marked the beginning of Franklin's final break with the British government was *An Edict of the King of Prussia.* Franklin preferred the *Rules,* but the *Edict* at first attracted a greater audience; the *Rules,* however, later became more popular, judging from Franklin's letter to his son William (London, November 3, 1773).[51] In the form of a fictitious royal proclamation of the "King of Prussia," one of the principal German states, it ordered the British in a very high-handed tone to do practically everything the British government was then arbitrarily ordering the

American colonies to do. The "King" considered Great Britain to be a kind of colony of Prussia since the original settlers of Britain had been Germanic tribes that had never officially declared their separation from the so-called mother country. The satire, a masterpiece of irony, protested the *Ad Valorem* taxes and the prohibition of manufacturing in the colonies of such goods as iron and other metals; the restrictions on exporting wool, hats, and other items; and the British dumping of criminals in the colonies. Presented in the tone of a capricious and arbitrary ruler who pretends to be granting favors to his subjects—actually the favors were tyrannical trade impositions —it ridicules the British commercial practices from the first to the last sentences. The opening and the ending read:

> We have long wondered here at the supineness of the English nation, under the Prussian impositions upon its trade entering our port. . . .

. . . .

> Some take this Edict to be merely one of the King's Jeux d'Esprit: others suppose it serious, and that he means a quarrel with England; but all here [Dantzig] think the assertion it concludes with, "that these regulations are copied from acts of the English parliament respecting their colonies," a very injurious one; it being impossible to believe that a people distinguished for their love of liberty, a nation so wise, so liberal in sentiments, so just and equitable toward its neighbours, would, from mean and injudicious views of petty immediate profit, treat its own children in a manner so arbitrary and tyrannical!

Here, too, at the beginning and end of the composition, he once more takes up his mask as detached observer, a common citizen writing from the neutral city of Dantzig, a self-governing port near Prussia. The beginning and ending form a frame for the king's edict, which is presented from a different point of view, the mask of the king himself.

One of Franklin's friends, an author named Paul Whitehead, was so fooled by this hoax that he thought the Prussian King actually intended an invasion of England. But he did not stand alone in this respect, as Franklin makes clear in the above-mentioned letter to his son:

> What made it [*the Edict*] the more noticed here was that people in reading it were, as the phrase is, *taken in*, till they had got half through it, and imagined it a real edict, to which mis-

take I suppose the king of Prussia's *character* [Frederick the Great was known for his military feats] must have contributed. I was down at Lord Le Despencer's when the post brought that day's papers. Mr. Whitehead was there, too (Paul Whitehead, the author of *Manners*), who runs early through all the papers and tells the company what he finds remarkable. He had them in another room, and we were chatting in the breakfast parlour, when he came running in to us out of breath, with the paper in his hand. "Here!" says he, "here's news for ye! Here's the king of Prussia claiming a right to this kingdom!" All stared, and I as much as anybody; and he went on to read it. When he had read two or three paragraphs, a gentleman present said: "Damn his impudence; I dare say we shall hear by next post that he is upon his march with one hundred thousand men to back this." Whitehead, who is very shrewd, soon after began to smoke it, and looking in my face said: "I'll be hanged if this is not some of your American jokes upon us." The reading went on, and ended with abundance of laughing and a general verdict that it was a fair hit.

In reality the *Edict*, a parody of British mercantile regulations, closely mimicked the form and gravity of an actual act of Parliament. Like every such act, it contained as its constituents the following parts: introduction, precedent, causes, regulation, and penalty. Accordingly, it commences with what one writer has called a "moralizing invocation to peace, progress, and prosperity."[52] "FREDERICK, by the grace of God, King of Prussia, &c. &c. &c. to all present and to come, Health. The peace now enjoyed throughout our dominions, having afforded us leisure to apply ourselves to the regulation of commerce, the improvement of our finances, and at the same time the easing our domestic subjects in their taxes. . . ." Then follows an historical justification for the proclamation—the ancient connection of Germany and Britain. After this come the five restrictive articles of the edict: the regulations concerning commerce; the manufacture of iron and steel products; the export of wool; the manufacture of hats; and the expatriation of convicts. Each of these articles follows closely in style (hence parodies) a part of the actual act of Parliament it satirizes.[53] Simson demonstrates that Franklin not only used certain statutes of the British Parliamentary Acts as sources but also copied out nearly the exact wording of these statutes; for part of his rhetorical purpose was to identify the unjust statutes for his reading public.[54] Simson regards the *Edict* as Franklin's most successful political satire.[55]

The publication of the *Edict* was undertaken with special care. A letter of Franklin to the publisher H. S. Woodfall of the *Public Advertiser*, advised him to "observe strictly the Italicking, Capitalling and Pointing [Punctuation]."[56] Woodfall himself gave the hoax the following "buildup" in its first appearance (*Public Advertiser*, September 22, 1773):

> *For the* Public Advertiser.
> The Subject of the following Article of
> FOREIGN INTELLIGENCE
> being exceedingly EXTRAORDINARY, is the
> Reason of its being separated from the usual
> Articles of *Foreign News.*

Davy sees both the *Edict* and the *Rules* as "an epitome and sharp iteration of nearly all of Franklin's contributions to a decade of Anglo-American dispute."[57] The *Supplement to the Boston Independent Chronicle*, although of later date (1782), again shows Franklin working with the hoax. It protested the British hiring of Indians to fight against the colonists. Rendered as an inventory of eight packages of scalps sent in return for paper money to the governor of Canada, the scalps to be transmitted by him to England, this hoax proceeds to a brilliant and systematic climax, describing in great detail the scalps of the various murdered people—the aged, the women, boys, girls, and the unborn. "No. 8. This Package is a Mixture of all the Varieties above-mentioned; to the number of 122; with a Box of Birch Bark, containing 29 little Infants' Scalps of various Sizes; small white Hoops; white Ground; no Tears; and only a little black Knife in the Middle, to show they were ript out of their Mothers' Bellies." We might suppose that a description of such an atrocity would have to be the end of the matter. But Franklin's power as a satirist went farther:

> It was at first proposed to bury these Scalps; but Lieutenant Fitzgerald, who, you know, has got Leave of Absence to go to Ireland on his private Affairs, said he thought it better they should proceed to their Destination; and if they were given to him, he would undertake to carry them to England, and hang them all up in some dark Night on the Trees in St. James's Park, where they could be seen from the King and Queen's Palaces in the Morning; for that the Sight of them might perhaps

strike Muley Ishmael [King George III] (as he called him) with some Compunction of Conscience. . . .

Monday last arrived here Lieutenant Fitzgerald above mentioned, and Yesterday the Waggon with the Scalps. Thousands of People are flocking to see them this Morning, and all Mouths are full of Execrations. Fixing them to the Trees is not approved. It is now proposed to make them up in decent little Packets, seal and direct them; one to the King, containing a Sample of every Sort for his Museum; one to the Queen, with some of the Women and little Children; the Rest to be distributed among both Houses of Parliament; a double Quantity to the Bishops.

The tone of the *Supplement* results from its grotesque combination of gruesome satire and hoax. In a letter to the Countess of Ossory, no less a literary person than Horace Walpole commented upon the anonymity of this work: "Dr. Franklin himself, I should think was the author. It is certainly written by a first-class pen, and not by a common man-of-war."[58] (Walpole's allusion to a man-of-war refers to the additional but fictitious letters of John Paul Jones, which Franklin appended to the second edition.) The *Supplement* appeared in 1782 and was printed on Franklin's own private press at Passy in France. His purpose in writing the *Supplement*, according to some scholars, was to improve his bargaining position with the British in the peace negotiations of that year.[59]

Eight years later, after he had returned for the last time from France and had completed his *Autobiography*, Franklin reverted to his use of the hoax. Just three weeks before his death he composed a clever parody of a speech on the slavery question made in Congress by James Jackson of Georgia. In this satire, entitled *On the Slave-Trade*, Franklin put on, for the last time, a mask—that of a Moslem, a certain Sidi Mehemet—in order to parody the so-called religious arguments of the slaveholding faction. The hoax convinced many readers, sending them to search libraries and bookstores for "Martin's Account of his Consulship," which Franklin mentioned in the satire.[60]

VI *Rhetorical Tricks*

In addition to the mask and the hoax, Franklin's repertoire of rhetorical tricks included many other ingenious devices—the use of parallels, maxims, anecdotes, examples, lists, queries, ledger accounts, intentionally bad logic, personifications, understatement, and unusual diction.

He especially favored the device of *parallelism* as a broad form for his satire. In his well-known *Exporting of Felons to the Colonies,* which he had printed in his *Pennsylvania Gazette* for May 9, 1751, he used this trick of parallelism, or analogy, to turn the tables on the British government. The latter had been using the colonies as a dumping ground for convicts and had recently considered passing a measure to make it illegal for the various colonial assemblies to pass laws discouraging the importation of such convicts. Franklin proposed returning the favor: the British dump convicts on America; very well, let Americans send them in return our rattlesnakes. These were to be distributed in St. James's Park, in Spring-Gardens, and in other of the most fashionable spots of London, "in the Gardens of all the Nobility and Gentry; but particularly in the Gardens of the *Prime Ministers,* the *Lords of Trade* and *Members of Parliament;* for to them we are *most particularly* obliged." By this kind of parallel, or analogy, Franklin demonstrated the folly of the British policy respecting felons.

A similar anonymous satire, which uses parallelism, appeared in a London paper shortly after the repeal of the Stamp Act. At this time the British were raising a great hullabaloo about not being paid by the Americans for the costs of printing the unused paper stamps. In Franklin's satire the British demands were likened to a certain Frenchman who "used to accost English and other Strangers on the Pont-Neuf, with many Compliments, and a red hot Iron in his Hand; *Pray Monsieur Anglois,* says he, *Do me the Favour to let me have the honour of thrusting this hot Iron into your Backside?* Zoons, what does the Fellow mean! Begone with your Iron or I'll break your Head! *Nay Monsieur,* replies he, *if you do not chuse it, I do not insist upon it. But at least, you will in Justice have the goodness to pay me something for the heating of my Iron.*" The parallel between this story and the unjust British demands is obvious. It is a splendid example of Franklin's uncanny ability to simplify and clarify—of his never losing sight of the central issue in the argument.

The *maxim,* or saying, often carries great force in rhetoric, particularly when handled by a masterful writer like Franklin. Many of his arguments incorporate maxims as premises. But it is wise to remember, as Davy warns us, that rhetoric supported by maxims may fall into a certain logical vulnerability, especially if the maxim is presented without a factual basis.[61]

In argumentation, therefore, a maxim may be really no better than its logical opposite if there is no accompanying support of facts.

Sometimes Franklin followed his old technique in *The Way to Wealth* of piling one saying upon another. The third paragraph of the letter to the *Public Advertiser* (September 14, 1773) illustrates this method of achieving rhetorical intensity: "To be sensible of Error is one Step towards Amendment;— no man is infallible; and MINISTERS are but *Men;—*'tis never too late to mend, nor is it any Impeachment of our Understanding to confess that we have been mistaken; for it implies *that we are wiser Today than we were the Day before;* and surely *Individuals* need not be ashamed publicly to retract an Error, since the LEGISLATURE itself does it every Time that it repeals one of its own Acts."[62] It is difficult to disagree with the conclusion that Franklin's "arguments rely in great part upon maxims, upon historical or imaginary examples, upon parallels, and upon his countless anecdotes."[63]

The *list* figures prominently as a form in Franklin's rhetorical works. We have seen examples of it in the *Rules* and in the twenty-nine "Queries Addressed to a Friend of Lord Baltimore." A further example occurs in a letter to the *London Chronicle* (December 27, 1759), where Franklin lists eleven ironical reasons why Canada should be restored to the French, among them the following:

2. We should restore it, lest, thro' a greater plenty of beaver, broad-brimmed hats become cheaper to that unmannerly sect, the Quakers.
3. We should restore Canada, that we may *soon* have a new war, and another opportunity of spending two or three millions a year in America; there being great danger of our growing too rich, our European expences not being sufficient to drain our immense treasures. . . .

. . . .

8. Should we not restore Canada, it would look as if our statesmen had *courage* as well as our soldiers; but what have statesmen to do with *courage?* Their proper character is *wisdom.*[64]

The use of *queries* in the form of rhetorical questions we have already commented upon. Suffice it to say that the query as well as the list were two of Franklin's favorite strategems.

On at least one occasion he shaped his arguments into the form of an *account*. The letter to the *Public Advertiser* (January 17, 1769) itemizes such an account for the losses incurred from the American troubles and the much greater ones to be expected if war ensued. The accounts (really two of them) were between "The Right Hon. G. G. [George Grenville] Esq.; and Co. [Lord Hillsborough and the Duke of Bedford] . . . with the Stockholders of Great Britain." In the first, Franklin, under his mask as "Another London Manufacturer," proves that Lord Grenville owes the British people some 7,250,000 pounds for his bungling; in the second, he shows that the pursuance of war would add about 108,500,000 pounds to the figure in the first account. Under the various headings in the second account Franklin lists "For the Blood spilt on both Sides," no charge; for "The Honour and Glory of having made slaves of Three Millions of Freemen," no charge. He concludes: "Thus stand the Accounts; and yet this G. G. the Root of the Whole Evil, sets up for an OEconomist."[65]

With this same satire we may illustrate a typical Franklinian *personification*. At the beginning of the letter Franklin had argued that peace and lucrative commerce had existed between England and America, and would have continued to exist, "had not the evil Genius of England whispered in the Ear of a certain Gentleman [George Grenville] 'George! be a Financier.'" By making the abstract evil of Grenville concrete in the form of a temptation by the devil, Franklin heightens the ridicule of the minister's policies, which pretended to be for the good of all concerned.

Franklin often used *bad logic* to ridicule the stupidity of his opposition.[66] But he was quick to spot fallacies when others employed them, as in the case of Congressman Jackson's defense of the slave trade. To the Georgia congressman Franklin retaliated sharply in kind, using the bad logic of Jackson's actual proslavery arguments in his own attack upon the institution of slavery as a political and economic interest. Instead of white plantation owners enriching themselves from the labor of Negro slaves, however, he reversed the situation by supplying an equal or analogous, condition: the Moslems' pirating of Christian white people along the African coast and elsewhere and selling them into slavery. Thus Sidi Mehemet, a Moslem speaker in this satire, becomes a "straw man," a character made use of to show the folly of an argument. The usual procedure in such arguments was to set up the character and then knock him down, or have him knock himself down. Sidi's defense of slavery really brings about his own downfall because he is incapable of rational thinking:

Have these *Erika* [*] considered the Consequences of grant-ing their Petition? If we cease our Cruises against the Christians, how shall we be furnished with the Commodities their Coun-tries produce, and which are so necessary for us? If we forbear to make Slaves of their People, who in this hot Climate are to cultivate our Lands? Who are to perform the common Labours of our City, and in our Families? Must we not then be our own Slaves? And is there not more Compassion and more Favour due to us as Mussulmen, than to these Christian Dogs? . . . If we cease then taking and plundering the Infidel Ships, and making Slaves of the Seamen and Passengers, our Lands will become of no Value for want of Cultivation; the Rents of Houses in the City will sink one half; and the Revenues of Government arising from its Share of Prizes be totally destroyed! And for what? To gratify the whims of a whimsical Sect [the Erika], who would have us, not only forbear making more Slaves, but even to manumit those we have.[67] [*The Erika had petitioned and prayed for the "Abolition of Piracy and Slavery as being unjust."]

The bad logic here is self-evident. It rests on a whole series of false premises that are easily translatable into terms of Negro slavery in the then newly created American states and, in fact, in the entire ante-bellum South later: that in a warm country (like the South) manual labor could be done by no other people except colored slaves, that the owners of slaves were the chosen people of God, and that Negroes were ene-mies of "Christianity incorporated," that to do honest labor was to risk the opprobrium of being called "slave," that Negro slavery was essential for the economic and political survival of the South as a whole (an argument later used by Calhoun, which time has proved false). By using such intentionally bad logic, Franklin ridiculed Jackson's stupid defense of slavery.

A common form of argument proceeds by attempting to reduce an opponent's ideas to absurdity. In a letter to Joseph Priestley, dated Philadelphia, July 7, 1775, Franklin carries this technique to an *ultima Thule* by reducing the British position to *madness*. The English had been burning American towns; Franklin calmly conceded that they might burn them all. In a letter to the *Pub-*

lic Ledger (1774) he had raised the question, in rather homely terms, as to whether John Bull, an honest farmer, would "be long satisfied with Servants [the ministers] that before his Face attempt to kill his *Plow Horses* [the hard-working American Colonists]?" But in his letter to Priestley he uses a different figure of speech, comparing the ministry to an insane female shopkeeper: "She must certainly be distracted; for no trades-man out of Bedlam ever thought of increasing the number of his customers, by knocking them on the head; or of enabling them to pay their debts, by burning their houses."[68]

A good instance of *understatement* occurs in *Exporting of the Felons,* where Franklin refers to the rattlesnakes as "mis-chievous" creatures. He repeats this epithet "mischievous" for effect and mentions it a third time in his ending, where he protests British commercial policy, saying, "In this . . . as in every other Branch of Trade, she [Britain] will have the Advan-tage of us. She will reap *equal* Benefits without equal Risque of the Inconveniences and Dangers. For the Rattle-Snake gives Warning before he attempts his *Mischief* [my italics]; which the Convict does not."

Considering his handling of *diction* (word choice) in rhe-toric, we see that Franklin was hardly a novice. "Scarcely any-thing is more commonly found in Franklin's work," writes Davy, "than manoeuvers to possess the sanctifying term or to pin the damning label upon the opponent."[69] We should note, for example, Franklin's scorn of the euphemism "check" to cover the massacre of the colonists by the French and the Indians in his reply entitled *The Interest of Great Britain Considered with Regard to her Colonies, and the Acquisitions of Canada and Guadaloupe:* "'T is a modest word, this *check,* for massacring men, women and children." Then, in the best Swiftian manner, he proposes the Egyptian method of stifling children in their sleep.

Many commentators on Franklin have noted his care with words. His own assiduity with respect to the niceties of satiric diction receives expression in a letter to his son William (Jan-uary 9, 1768) in which he grumbles that the editor of the *London Chronicle* must be either a Grenville man or "very cautious." For the editor had entirely changed in the *Causes of the American Discontents* certain words Franklin had intended to stress; and, by his omissions and corrections, he had, according to Franklin, "drawn the teeth and pared the nails of my paper, so that it can neither scratch nor bite. It seems only to paw and mumble."[70]

VII *Miscellaneous Rhetorical Forms*

Two forms of Franklin's rhetorical writings—the fable and the pamphlet—need special attention; and, since the fable was a form he particularly enjoyed, we shall discuss it first.

One of Franklin's most interesting fables appeared at the end of his *Apology for Printers,* printed in the *Pennsylvania Gazette* for June 10, 1731. It takes the form of a request directed to readers who might be displeased with him for printing "things they don't like." After ably building up his credit as a man of sense and understanding in two lists—one general, the other in reference to a particular complaint—he draws his remarks to a close with the following fable about the difficulty, and the folly, of attempting to please everybody.

A certain well-meaning Man and his Son, were travelling towards a Market Town, with an Ass which they had to sell. The Road was bad; and the Old Man therefore rid, but the Son went a-foot. The first Passenger they met, asked the Father if he was not ashamed to ride by himself, and suffer the poor Lad to wade along thro' the Mire; this induced him to take up his Son behind him: He had not travelled far, when he met others, who said, they were two unmerciful Lubbers to get both on the Back of that poor Ass, in such a deep Road. Upon this the old man gets [*sic*] off, and let his Son ride alone. The next they met called the Lad a graceless, rascally young Jackanapes, to ride in that Manner thro' the Dirt, while his aged Father, trudged along on Foot; and they said the old Man was a Fool, for suffering it. He then bid his Son come down, and walk with him, and they travell'd on leading the Ass by the Halter; 'till they met another Company, who called them a Couple of senseless Blockheads, for going both on Foot in such a dirty Way, when they had an empty Ass with them, which they might ride upon. The old Man could bear no longer; My Son, said he, it grieves me much that we cannot please all these People: Let us throw the Ass over the next Bridge, and be no farther troubled with him.

Franklin then says that "Had the old Man been seen acting this last Resolution, he would probably have been call'd a Fool for troubling himself about the different Opinions of all that were pleas'd to find Fault with him."[71]

Many years later, in the period which is our main concern (1757-1776), Franklin made use of three other fables. As the reader will see, the herd of cows in the first stands for the colonists and the avaricious farmer represents Lord Hillsborough; the eagle symbolizes Great Britain, and the cat, the colonies in the second; the lion kitten in the third represents the colonies, and the mastiff, Great Britain. These fables appeared in the *Public Advertiser* (January 2, 1770) "humbly inscribed" to the Secretary of State for the American Department (Lord Hillsborough).

I.

A Herd of Cows had long afforded Plenty of Milk, Butter and Cheese to an avaritious Farmer, who grudged them the Grass they subsisted on, and at length mowed it to make Money of the Hay, leaving them to *shift for Food* as they could, and yet still expected to *milk them* as before; but the Cows, offended with his Unreasonableness, resolved for the future *to suckle one another.*

II.

An Eagle, King of Birds, sailing on his Wings aloft over a Farmer's Yard, saw a Cat there basking in the Sun, *mistook it for a Rabbit,* stoop'd, seized it, and carried it up into the Air, *intending to prey on it.* The Cat turning, set her Claws into the Eagle's Breast; who, finding his Mistake, opened his Talons, and would have let her drop; but Puss, unwilling to fall so far, held faster; and the Eagle, to get rid of the Inconvenience, found it necessary to *set her down where he took her up.*

III.

A Lion's Whelp was put on board a Guinea Ship bound to America as a Present to a Friend in that Country: It was tame and harmless as a Kitten, and therefore not confined, but suffered to walk about the Ship at Pleasure. A stately, full-grown English Mastiff, belonging to the Captain, despising the Weakness of the young Lion, frequently took it's *Food* by Force, and often turned it out of its Lodging Box, when he had a Mind to repose therein himself. The young Lion nevertheless grew daily in Size and Strength, and the Voyage being long, he became at last a more equal Match for the Mastiff; who continuing his Insults, received a stunning Blow from the Lion's Paw that fetched his Skin over his Ears, and deterred him from any future Contest with such growing Strength; regretting that he had not rather secured it's Friendship than provoked it's Enmity.[72]

John Adams used to tell a story to the effect that Franklin had dashed off the fable of the cat and the eagle within the space of a few minutes. But Crane refutes this idea with the opinion that Franklin "even in his later years, usually worked slowly and carefully as literary craftsman" and that he was "exceedingly economical of his ideas and materials."[73] These three fables, or political allegories, certainly show their author as a very careful writer, for they are very tightly written. Nothing is wasted. Each one is a story shortly told.

Other Franklin fables bearing on political subjects, but not always journalistic in nature, include such bagatelles as *The Conte, The Harrow, The Levée*, and *The Apologue*. A complete list of Franklin's political fables would, of course, number many more, among them the *Proposed New Version of the Bible*. We must remember, too, that Franklin delighted in using this particular form in oral as well as in written discourse.

Many of Franklin's writings during the period he represented the cause of the colonies against the proprietaries, and earlier, were printed separately as pamphlets. As a form the pamphlet required special skill in rhetoric. It addressed itself to an immediate purpose, tried to influence public opinion or win votes on a particular question, appealed largely to the man in the street, and depended for its success on a large and rapid circulation. According to McMahon, Franklin's pamphlets, a large part of his political writings, conformed to these requirements.[74] In the eighteenth century—an age of prolific pamphleteering in politics—Franklin's mastery of invective and satire, Smyth states rather categorically, placed him "easily first in the giant race of revolutionary pamphleteers."[75] It is well to recall that Tom Paine was also a pamphleteer.

Among the more noteworthy of Franklin's political pamphlets belong the following: *A Modest Enquiry into the Nature and Necessity of a Paper Currency* (1729); *Plain Truth* (1747); *The Interest of Great Britain* (1760); *Narrative of the Late Massacre* (1764); *Cool Thoughts* (1764), dealing with the proprietary dispute; the famous *Examination Before the House of Commons on the Stamp Act* (1766); and *The Retort Courteous* (1786).

The titles of the first and third pamphlets are self-explanatory.[76] *Plain Truth*, the second, was a proposal for a militia to protect the colonists against the French and Spanish, whose ships were harassing the Americans. Of this pamphlet Mc-

Mahon writes: "His appeals were such as would find ready response in the minds of his readers: the protection of life and property, the horrors of invading armies, the prospects of financial loss."[77] The matter was complicated by the Quakers' refusal to fight on religious principles and by their having to be handled tactfully.

The Interest of Great Britain, according to Crane, represents the climax of Franklin's political writing for the period 1758-1761.[78] In this pamphlet Franklin argued that the interest of Great Britain concerned more the security of Canada and the West rather than the islands of the West Indies. He had carefully prepared the way for this pamphlet by a letter in the *London Chronicle* (December 27, 1759) signed "A. Z." The letter is a preliminary sketch of the later pamphlet. Of the pamphlet itself the great Edmund Burke had this to say: "He [Franklin] is clearly the ablest, most ingenious, and the most dexterous of those who have written upon the question, and we may therefore conclude that he had said everything in the best manner that the case would bear.[79] The authorship of this pamphlet has undergone questioning. At one time Richard Jackson, a British lawyer and friend of Franklin, was thought to have had a hand in it. Although he did not deny that Franklin may have conferred with Jackson, I. Minis Hayes attributed the writing of the pamphlet wholly to Franklin on grounds of a Franklin manuscript in the American Philosophical Society collection.[80]

A Narrative of the Late Massacres in Lancaster County of a Number of Indians, Friends of this Province, By Persons Unknown (1764) contains some of Franklin's greatest rhetoric, and it is directed, ironically enough, at his fellow Americans. This work is also unique for its eloquent attack on the brutal, white murderers of some innocent and friendly Indians of the Six Nations, a group which had a record of nearly a century for friendliness and faithfulness to the English. Jorgenson says that the prophet Jeremiah and the Gothic writer Mrs. Radcliffe together could hardly write with more terrifying effect than Franklin in this attack directed at the "Paxton boys," as they were called.[81] According to Allan Nevins, this uprising of the "Paxton boys" virtually "threatened a civil war, which Franklin and others averted."[82]

O, ye unhappy Perpetrators of this horrid Wickedness! reflect a Moment on the Mischief ye have done, the Disgrace ye have brought on your Country, on your Religion, and your Bible, on your Families and Children! Think on the Destruction of your captivated Country-folks (now among the wild *Indians*) which probably may follow, in Resentment of your Barbarity! Think on the Wrath of the United *Five Nations,* hitherto our Friends, but now provoked by your murdering one of their Tribes, in Danger of becoming our bitter Enemies. Think of the mild and good Government you have so audaciously insulted; the Laws of your King, your Country, and your God, that you have broken; the infamous Death that hangs over your Heads; for Justice, though slow, will come at last. All good People everywhere detest your Actions. You have imbrued your Hands in innocent Blood; how will you make them clean? The dying Shrieks and Groans of the Murdered, will often sound in your Ears: Their Spectres will sometimes attend you, and affright even your innocent Children! Fly where you will, your Consciences will go with you. Talking in your Sleep shall betray you, in the Delirium of a Fever you yourselves shall make your own Wickedness known.

.   .   .   .

Let us rouze ourselves, for Shame, and redeem the Honour of our province from the Contempt of its Neighbours; let all good Men join heartily and unanimously in Support of the Laws, and in strengthening the Hands of Government; that Justice may be done, the Wicked punished, and the Innocent protected; otherwise we can, as a People, expect no Blessing from Heaven; there will be no Security for our Persons or Properties; Anarchy and Confusion will prevail over all; and Violence without Judgment, dispose of every Thing.

The Retort Courteous deals with England's complaints that she did not have to give up frontier posts after the Revolution because Americans were not paying their debts, which the treaty obligated them to do. It contains well-varied refrains at the end of each of the arguments, the gist of which is "These Americans *don't pay their Debts!"*

The Examination Before the House of Commons on the Stamp Act sold rapidly. The colonists, according to McMahon, believed that Franklin's spoken words on that famous occasion had carried weight in the repeal of the Stamp Act.[83] No doubt they had. But his printing of the pamphlet also helped formulate public opinion in England, not to mention France, for it circulated widely and was translated into French. At least one writer regards it as "a most consummate piece of political and editorial craftmanship on the part of Franklin himself."[84]

Crane believes that Franklin wrote pamphlets about the Stamp Act dispute other than *The Examination,* possibly during the year 1765, when he was charged by an anonymous writer in the *Pennsylvania Journal* with keeping silent on the threat to American liberties.[85] Then, too, in connection with the Stamp Act and other subjects, some of Franklin's letters to the London press were almost small pamphlets. Crane, who refers to these letters as "pamphlets *in parvo,*" states that they reflected Franklin's extensive work as a pamphleteer in America between 1729 and 1764.[86]

Closely allied to Franklin's work in satire and political pamphleteering is the body of editorials he wrote to promote innumerable civic projects in Philadelphia. While it may be questioned as to just how *political* these were, at least one writer believes that "Franklin stands in the American tradition for the proposition that reflections about society should produce useful institutions for the improvement of the conditions of life."[87] Quite often in past history the means whereby such institutions have been innovated have been political.

An illustration will clarify this statement. When Franklin was credited with the original idea for the Pennsylvania Hospital—a hospital that was to receive and cure poor sick persons—he denied it and said the hospital had sprung from the thinking of Dr. Thomas Bond, one of his good friends.[88] While this was true, the fact remains that without the aid of Franklin's pen this project would not have succeeded. He laid the groundwork for the entire institution through his writings in his newspaper, which prepared the minds of his fellow citizens for the idea. This "was my usual custom in such cases," he said.[89] Later, when the subscriptions began to flag, it was Franklin again, acting through the political arena of the Pennsylvania Assembly, who saved the hospital.[90]

As a member of the Assembly, too, his ability to write helped him to further such projects as the formation of a state militia for the common defense. In the latter instance the regular Secretary of the Council had had no experience in drawing up official political proclamations. Franklin drafted the proclamation, relying on his experience with church announcements of public fasts in New England, where politics and petitions for divine aid frequently went hand in hand on the same poster.

Franklin's proclamation was translated into German and read widely in the different congregations of the province.[91] Thus, ironically, the clergy encouraged the forming of the state militia in Pennsylvania.

In a similar way he wrote (with the assistance of a Mr. Francis, then attorney general) a pamphlet entitled *Proposals Relating to the Education of Youth in Pennsylvania* (1749), which he offered as the act of some "public-spirited gentlemen."[92] This, he says, was his regular procedure. And although it sounds rather conceited as he describes it in the *Autobiography*, it is true that he was avoiding as much as he could, according to his usual rule, the presentation of himself to the public as the author of a scheme for its benefit.

One other branch of Franklin's career as a writer of political works, although it could hardly be called *journalistic*, covers his activities as a participating author in important state documents. The Albany Plan for Union, the Declaration of Independence, the Treaty of Alliance with France, the Peace Treaty with Great Britain (or Treaty of Paris), the Constitution itself —in all these Franklin played his part, writing with a trace of the senatorial, "the dignity of antique Rome."[93] While it is true that his was only one of several plans submitted at Albany, his plan was nevertheless the preferred one.[94]

Professor I. Bernard Cohen gives the following interesting example of a Franklin improvement over Jefferson—no mean writer himself—in the Declaration of Independence. Jefferson's original rough draft contained the statement that all men were created equal. According to Jefferson, says Cohen, this statement was "sacred and inviolable." In the manuscript these words are changed in Franklin's handwriting to read: "We hold these principles to be self-evident." "Historians usually interpret this alteration simply as a literary improvement and certainly Franklin's cadence has a wonderful ring to it and is much more effective than Jefferson's," writes Cohen.

> But the difference between the two phrases is much more profound than mere literary quality. Jefferson implied that the principles in question were holy, of divine origin, and were to be respected and guarded with reverence for that reason: to deny them would be sacrilege. But 'self-evident' was a technical or scientific term applied to axioms, as John Harris' popular eighteenth-century *Dictionary of Arts and Sciences* defined it, and was exemplified in such propositions as: "That nothing

can act where it is not; That a thing cannot be and not be at the same time; That the whole is greater than a part; That where there is no law, there is no transgression; etc."[95]

"Franklin's revisions . . . placed the principle that all men are created equal in the category of an axiom, self-evident; like the laws of motion, it was a principle 'deduced' from experience."[96]

As we consider Franklin as a writer involved deeply with public causes, we see clearly that he stood for "the equality of all men despite their color or their creed."[97] Cohen calls attention to the attack on race prejudice in *A Narrative of the Late Massacre*, a work already cited. We may do well to attend to Franklin's argument: "The only Crime of these poor Wretches [the Indians slaughtered by the "Paxton boys"] seems to have been, that they had a reddish-brown Skin, and black Hair; and some People of that Sort, it seems, had murdered some of our Relations. If it be right to kill Men for such a Reason, then should any Man, with a freckled Face and red Hair, kill a Wife or Child of mine, it would be right for me to revenge it, by killing all the freckled red-haired Men, Women, and Children, I could afterwards anywhere meet with." The folly of such stupid vindictiveness is obvious; the blood of such slaughters of innocent Indians—and Negroes—cries aloud for justice.

It may interest persons arguing for racial discrimination on the ground that the Negro is less intelligent than the white man to know that Franklin along with the famous Dr. Samuel Johnson was a member "of a society [Dr. Bray's Associates] dedicated to improving the lot of the Negro" through the founding of schools in America.[98] In a letter to this organization in London (dated Philadelphia, December 17, 1763) Franklin tells of visiting a Negro school in Philadelphia. "I am on the whole pleased," he says, "& from what I there saw have conceived a higher Opinion of the natural capacities of the Black Race than I had ever before entertained. Their apprehension seems as quick, their Memory as strong, and their Docility in every Respect equal to that of white Children."[99]

"To the end Franklin found a cause to champion," writes Davy, "and broken in body though he was, he yet contrived to champion it with the wit and skill of his best years."[100] The reference is to the satire against the slave trade written three weeks before his death. As Davy points out, some of the arguments Franklin ridicules with deliberate irony in this piece anticipate some of the foolish arguments "employed by defenders of slavery for seventy years after Franklin's time."[101] While it is a fact that Congress voted down Franklin's memorandum on behalf of the Pennsylvania Society for Promoting the Abolition of Slavery, refusing either "to prohibit the slave trade until 1808 or to abolish slavery at any time," the defeat was really not a defeat.[102] For we cannot help feeling, as Baender says, that "Franklin was addressing posterity, as he must have known only too well in those few painful weeks before his death."[103]

In summation, Franklin's political writings were historically important for the following reasons: They had an enormous influence in forming and directing public opinion. Together with the works of Tom Paine they roused the colonists to revolt. These writings of Franklin won sympathy for the American cause from Europe and even from England. They won money from France. Following the war, they helped arrange peace terms and strengthen diplomatic bonds between various countries. Finally, they worked for the internal progress and development of the new nation.[104]

CHAPTER *5*

The Essays

SINCE THE HISTORY of the personal essay as a genre is long and complicated, we may sketch it only briefly here. It begins in the late sixteenth century with the *Essais* of Montaigne (1580); but before Montaigne the French had developed a form known as the *leçon morale,* which often resembled a collection of sayings organized around a central topic or moral lesson. Montaigne developed this form into the essay by adding a highly personal element. In the early part of the seventeenth century Francis Bacon contributed elements of practicality and utilitarianism to the essay, stressing the original aphoristic quality in his style. Writers such as Joseph Hall, Thomas Overbury, John Earle, George Savile, and Jean de La Bruyère injected what were known as *Characters,* sketches of typical persons, vices, or virtues. In the eighteenth century Defoe, Steele, and Addison transformed the essay into a vehicle for their periodicals—*A Weekly Review of Affairs in France,* the *Tatler,* and the *Spectator.* Under their hands the essay attempted—under the dual headings of entertainment and instruction—to reform the age, refine the taste of the reader, and provide a wide variety of topics for conversation. *Humor* and *satire* received strong stress in a generally more informal style.[1] This was the state of the essay by the time Franklin came to it in the early 1720's.

Three large groups of Franklin's essays—the *Dogood* papers, the *Busy-Body* papers, and the *Bagatelles*—must be considered. We will also treat some of the hoaxes (those not covered in the previous chapter) and the essay entitled *On Conversation,* which appeared in the *Pennsylvania Gazette* for October 15, 1730. We have selected the latter because it seems representative of the separate essays that Franklin composed and printed from time to time in his paper.

I *The Dogood Papers*

In the *Autobiography* (pp. 16-17) Franklin tells how as a young apprentice he overheard the writers for his brother's *Courant* discussing their work.

> I was excited to try my hand among them. But being still a boy and suspecting that my brother would object to printing anything of mine in his paper if he knew it to be mine, I contrived to disguise my hand; and writing an anonymous paper, I put it one night under the door of the printing house. It was found in the morning and communicated to his writing friends when they called in as usual. They read it, commented on it in my hearing, and I had the exquisite pleasure of finding it met with their approbation, and that in their different guesses at the author, none were named but men of some character among us for learning and ingenuity. . . . Encouraged . . . by this attempt, I wrote and sent in the same way to the press several other pieces, which were equally approved, and I kept my secret till my small fund of sense for such performances was pretty well exhausted, and then I discovered it, when I began to be considered a little more by my brother's acquaintances.

Evidence in possession of the Yale editors of the Franklin papers (I, 8) points to the fact that these writings were the *Dogood* papers, printed from April 2 to October 8 in the year 1722.

As indicated in Chapter I of this book, the *Courant* owed a more than sizeable debt to the *Spectator*. Similarly, it is easy to demonstrate a resemblance between the *Dogood* papers and the periodical essays composing the *Spectator*. In their use of a character mask of an observer at the same time belonging to and yet apart from society, in the characterization of this observer at the beginning of the essay, in their common purpose (to correct the follies of the age), and in their common desire to please, the *Spectator* and the *Dogood* essays agreed. The *Spectator* had his club; Silence Dogood had her lodger (a minister) and her neighbor (Rusticus). Other common techniques were the use of Latin mottoes, lay sermons, allegorical visions, eaves-droppers, street-strollers, and letters from correspondents. They even treated the same subjects: the excess of religious zeal, the extravagance of female fashions, the plight of widows, and alcoholism.[2] In style the *Dogood* papers resembled the colloquial manner of the *Spectator,* but discarded the learned allusions and literary anecdotes, replacing them with homely sayings (*Dogood,* No. V) and with comic, and sometimes earthy, stories (No. XIII).[3] Horner notes many resemblances between the *Spectator* papers of Addison and Steele and the *Dogood* papers of Franklin "in method, purpose, and matter."[4] The bulk of the fourteenth *Dogood* paper, for example, is an extract of *Spectator* No. 185.[5]

But although Franklin's debt to the *Spectator* for style and other matters was large, his more immediate models for the *Dogood* papers lay closer to home in the "homely and unsophisticated satire" of the Couranteers themselves—James Franklin, who is believed to have written under the pseudonyms of Abigail Afterwit and Timothy Turnstone; Mathew Adams, who wrote as Harry Meanwell; and a Mr. Gardner, who disguised himself as Fanny Mournful.[6] The Couranteers, who had domesticated the *Spectator* brand of essay, had also supplied Franklin with a lively and more native humor.[7]

The smallpox and the Indian wars had decimated the male population of Boston in the year 1722. The town abounded with widows. The choice of a young widow as a mouthpiece for the young printer's apprentice was therefore timely. The name "Silence" ill becomes the talkative nature of this young woman and therefore must be ironic. Dogood as a surname properly expressed Franklin's early didactic spirit. But he also may have thought Dogood an appropriate name for the deceased young minister who had married her. As for her character, she best describes it herself in the last paragraph of the second paper (April 16, 1722):

I am an Enemy to Vice, and a Friend to Vertue. I am one of an extensive Charity, and a great Forgiver of *private* Injuries: A hearty Lover of the Clergy and all good Men, and a mortal Enemy to arbitrary Government and unlimited Power. I am naturally very jealous for the Rights and Liberties of my Country; and the least appearance of an Incroachment of those invaluable Priviledges, is apt to make my Blood boil exceedingly. I have likewise a natural Inclination to observe and reprove the Faults of others, at which I have an excellent Faculty. I speak this by Way of Warning to all such whose Offences shall come under my Cognizance, for I never intend to wrap my Talent in a Napkin. To be brief; I am courteous and affable, good humour'd (unless I am first provok'd,) and handsome, and sometimes witty, but always, Sir, Your Friend and Humble Servant, SILENCE DOGOOD.[9]

Silence had her fling at the town of Boston every two weeks, as she had announced in her first letter, with only three exceptions. Two of the exceptions came at three-week intervals, but this was balanced somewhat by the appearance of the third after only one week.[10]

In the first *Dogood* letter Franklin satirizes the tendency of people not to blame or praise anything they read until they know what kind of person the writer is and also their tendency to criticize a literary performance in terms of what they know about the author's circumstances—"whether he be *poor* or *rich, old* or *young,* a *Schollar* or a *Leather Apron Man,* etc." Taking this observation as a cue for a brief satiric character sketch of a typical sentimental heroine, Franklin then describes Silence as a poor girl whose father had been washed overboard from a ship by a "merciless wave" at the very moment he was rejoicing at her birth.

Eventually, because of her mother's poverty, Silence became a bound apprentice to a country minister, who "instructed her in all that Knowledge and Learning which is necessary for our Sex," including needlework, writing, arithmetic, etc. The minister, it seems, owned a library, and so Silence had spent a good deal more time in reading books than had most other girls of her day. Left an orphan by her mother's death, she declared that she really had "no affliction but what was imaginary, and created in my own Fancy; as nothing is more common with us Women, than to be grieving for nothing, when we have nothing else to grieve for."

The second letter tells of how the bachelor minister who had brought her up proposed to her and won her. "Whether it was Love, or Gratitude, or Pride or all Three that made me consent, I know not; but it is certain, he found it no hard Matter, by the help of his Rhetorick to conquer my Heart, and persuade me to marry him." After seven years of happy married life and the birth of three children, her husband passed to his heavenly reward. As a widow of several years she admits she "could be easily persuaded to marry again." But since good husbands are hard to find, she has decided to forego such intentions.

In the third letter she invites correspondence from members

of the female sex. At the age of sixteen Franklin must have thoroughly enjoyed this prank on his female readers, for he tells them that he will look on such correspondence as favors and will acknowledge them "accordingly."

The fourth *Dogood* paper is probably the best known of all. It is the famous one dealing with "The Temple of Learning," a clever satire of Harvard College. It contrasts noticeably with the brevity of the third. Beginning with an appropriate Latin quotation from Cicero to the effect that he was neither talking Greek nor teaching Latin, Franklin shows Silence faced with the problem of whether or not to send her young son to college. She makes discreet inquiries of her "Reverend Boarder," Clericus, but he fails to satisfy her curiosity. Wandering into an orchard while she ruminates this problem, she falls asleep and dreams of the famous Temple of Learning to which every peasant desired to send at least one of his children. "Most of them [the peasants] consulted their own Purses instead of their Childrens Capacities: So that I observed, a great many, yea, the most part of those who were traveling thither, were little better than Dunces and Blockheads. Alas! Alas!"

At the entrance to the temple stand two porters—Riches and Poverty. Poverty refuses to admit anyone who has not gained the favor of Riches, so that many are turned away "for want of this necessary Qualification." Silence is careful to explain that she got in only as a *spectator*.

In the middle of a great hall on a throne raised above "two high and difficult steps sat LEARNING in awful State; she was apparelled wholly in Black, and surrounded almost on every Side with innumerable Volumes in all Languages. She seem'd very busily employ'd in writing something on half a Sheet of Paper, and upon Enquiry, I understood she was preparing a Paper, call'd, *The New-England Courant*." She was surrounded by English, Latin, Greek, and Hebrew. The latter three, who had been veiled by Idleness and Ignorance, only unveiled themselves to "those who have in this Place acquir'd so much Learning as to [be able to] distinguish them from *English*" and who consequently "pretended to an intimate acquaintance with them."

The whole tribe then began to climb the two "high and difficult Steps" to the throne; but most of them, aided by Madam Idleness and her Maid Ignorance, found the ascent too difficult and withdrew, while those who were assisted by "Diligence and a docible Temper" had to be dragged up the steps by those who had already made the ascent. "The usual Ceremonies at an End, every Beetle-Scull seem'd well satisfy'd with his own Portion of Learning, tho' perhaps he was *e'en just* as ignorant as ever."

After graduating from the Temple, some took to merchandising, others to traveling, "some one Thing, some to another, and some to Nothing; and many of them from henceforth, for want of Patrimony, liv'd as poor as Church Mice, being unable to dig, and asham'd to beg, and to live by their Wits it was impossible." The greater part, however, traveled along a well-beaten path to the Temple of Theology. This surprises Silence, until, as she writes, "I spy'd Pecunia [Money] behind a Curtain, beckoning to them." In the Temple of Theology, Silence also sees Plagiarism, "diligently transcribing some eloquent Paragraphs out of Tillotson's *Works*, &c., to embellish his own."

Silence says she cannot help reflecting upon the folly of parents who, "blind to their Children's Dulness, and insensible of the Solidity of their Skulls, because they think their Purses can afford it," persist in sending their children to the Temple of Learning, where they learn little more than "how to carry themselves handsomely, and enter a Room genteely, [*sic*] (which might as well be acquir'd at a Dancing-School,) and from whence they return, after Abundance of Trouble and Charge, as great Blockheads as ever, only more proud and self-conceited."

In the fifth *Dogood*, Silence defends the female sex against a charge that they are "the prime Causes" of a great many vices of men. But in the sixth *Dogood*, Silence attacks women for pride in clothing, particularly the hoop-petticoats then in fashion. "These monstrous topsy-turvy *Mortar Pieces*, are neither fit for the Church, the Hall, or the Kitchen; and if a Number of them were well mounted on Noddles-Island, they would look more like Engines of War for bombarding the Town, than Ornaments of the Fair Sex." She concludes her argument by saying that she has little hope of persuading her sex "utterly to relinquish this extravagant Foolery," but she would at least "desire them to lessen the Circumference of their Hoops, and leave it with them to consider, Whether they who pay no Rates or Taxes, ought to take up more room in the King's High-Way, than the Men, who yearly contribute to the Support of the Government."

The seventh *Dogood* paper is one of the earliest examples of literary criticism in American literature. It parodies the sentimental school of obituary verse rife in Franklin's Boston. Silence marches directly to the front firing line with her first sentence: "It has been the Complaint of many Ingenious Foreigners, who have travell'd amongst us, *That good Poetry is not to be expected in New-England*." She then attacks, in the best tradition of eighteenth-century literary satire, the pious effusions of an elegy composed upon the death of a Mrs. Mehitabell Kitel—an actual person, according to Labaree and Bell.[11] Silence remarks that the author of this elegy has "invented a new Species of Poetry, which wants a Name, and was never before known." Since this kind of poetry cannot in any sense be called either "Epic, Sapphic, Lyric, or Pindaric, nor any other Name yet invented, I presume," she says, "it may be called the Kitellic," in honor of the dead person. Such "Elegies which are of our own Growth (and our Soil seldom produces any other sort of Poetry) are by far the greatest part, wretchedly Dull and Ridiculous." Appropriately she then proceeds with systematic womanly vigor and pungency to offer, in her best household manner, a *recipe* for making a New-England elegy.

For the Title of your Elegy. Of these you may have enough ready made to your Hands; but if you should chuse to make it your self, you must be sure not to omit the words *Aetatis Suae* [Latin for "his age"], which will Beautify it exceedingly.

For the Subject of your Elegy. Take one of your Neighbours who has lately departed this Life; it is no great matter at what Age the Party dy'd, but it will be best if he went away suddenly, being *Kill'd, Drown'd,* or *Froze to Death*.

Having chose the Person, take all his Virtues, Excellencies, &c. and if he have not enough, you may borrow some to make up a sufficient Quantity: To these add his last Words, dying Expressions, &c. if they are to be had; mix all these together, and be sure to *strain* them well. Then season all with a handful or two of Melancholly Expressions, such as *Dreadful, Deadly, cruel, cold Death, unhappy Fate, weeping Eyes,* &c. Hav[ing] mixed all these Ingredients well, put them into the empty Scull of some *young Harvard;* (but in Case you have ne'er a One at Hand, you may use your own,) there let them Ferment for the Space of a Fortnight, and by that Time they will be incorporated into a Body, which take out, and having prepared a sufficient Quantity of double Rhimes, such as *Power, Flower; Quiver, Shiver; Grieve us, Leave us; tell you, excel you; Expeditions, Physicians; Fatigue him, Intrigue him;* &c. you must spread all upon Paper, and if you can procure a Scrap of Latin to put at the End, it will garnish it mightily; then having affixed your Name at the Bottom with a *Moestus Composuit* [composed in a state of melancholy], you will have an Excellent Elegy.

N.B. This Receipt will serve when a Female is the Subject of your Elegy, provided you borrow a greater Quantity of Virtues, Excellencies, &c.

Dogood essays eight and nine were printed while Franklin had sole management of his brother's newspaper, his brother having been jailed for charging that the Massachusetts authorities were not exerting themselves sufficiently to capture a pirate ship said to be off the coast.[12] The serious tone of these two essays contrasts sharply, therefore, with that of the others.

The eighth essay is in its entirety a long but important quotation from the *London Journal* for February 4, 1721. Franklin introduces this quotation by saying, "I prefer the following Abstract from the London Journal to any thing of my own, and therefore shall present it to your Readers this week without any further preface." The "Abstract," which we have further abridged, follows:

Without Freedom of Thought, there can be no such Thing as Wisdom; and no such Thing as publick Liberty, without Freedom of Speech; which is the Right of every Man, as far as by it, he does not hurt or controul the Right of another; and this is the only Check it ought to suffer, and the only Bounds it ought to know.

This sacred Privilege is so essential to free Governments, that the Security of Property, and the Freedom of Speech always go together; and in those wretched Countries where a Man cannot call his Tongue his own, he can scarce call any Thing else his own. Whoever would overthrow the Liberty of a Nation, must begin by subduing the Freeness of Speech; a *Thing* terrible to Publick Traytors.

.   .   .   .

That Men ought to speak well of *their Governours* is true, while *their Governours* deserve to be well spoken of; but to do publick Mischief, without hearing of it, is only the Preroga-

tive and Felicity of Tyranny: A free People will be shewing that
they are *so*, by their Freedom of Speech.

. . . .

Freedom of Speech is ever the Symptom, as well as the
Effect of a good Government. . . .

From reading this particular essay, too, one might judge that
Franklin knew Latin and Roman history rather well, for it contains numerous Latin quotations and historical allusions in support of the argument. Studied as a whole, the *Dogood* papers
reveal interest in such writers as Cicero, Terence, Seneca, Pliny,
and Tacitus, which we might expect in a neoclassical age.

The subject of *Dogood* nine is religious hypocrites and the
harm they do when stationed in government offices; they are
people who "ruin their Country for God's sake," as Franklin
puts it. They skilfully deceive their countrymen in the name
of religion and under pretext of legal procedure. Franklin felt
very strongly against such public deceivers. "This Subject raises
in me an Indignation not to be born," [*sic*] he says. While the
satire is mainly political rather than religious or anticlerical,
it is true that in this letter, as Davy says, Silence forgot that
she had earlier characterized herself as "a Lover of the
Clergy."[13]

Franklin anticipates twentieth-century New Deal social legislation in *Dogood* ten. He makes Silence admit that the idea
of insurance for widows, which she sponsors, is not her own,
for it probably came from Defoe.[14] The next letter goes beyond
even New Frontier legislation; in it Silence advocates similar
insurance for old maids.

In *Dogood* twelve Silence delivers herself of a temperance
lecture. Moderate drinking, she doubts not, tends to be serviceable to those people who "want the Talent of a ready Utterance"
in order to "discover the Conceptions of their Minds in an
entertaining and intelligible Manner." Humorously she concedes that "much Study and Experience, and a little Liquor,
are of absolute Necessity for some Tempers, in order to make
them accomplish'd Orators." "But after all," she says, "it must
be consider'd that no Pleasure can give Satisfaction or prove
advantageous to a reasonable Mind, which is not attended with
the *Restraints* of *Reason*."

The thirteenth *Dogood* concerns what a casual stroller might
see during a night's walk in Boston. Silence, who takes such

a moonlit stroll, hears herself talked about by persons pretending to know her; one says that she is a low character who keeps up a correspondence with a criminal who helps her in her writing. Another guesses that she is actually a man and, at that, a man needing more reforming "in himself, than spending his Wit in satyrizing others."

The last letter in the *Dogood* series concerns the case of Timothy Cutler, the rector of Yale College who was expelled for his Arminian and Anglican views. The Arminians liberalized certain Calvinistic doctrines such as predestination, and they believed that the human will constituted an element in the salvation of the soul. Since Franklin believed strongly in what he called "morality," the necessity of practical deeds in religion—voluntary effort, in short—he sympathized with Cutler and his two colleagues, who left for England to be ordained in the Anglican church. Broadly tolerant of all religions, Franklin censured any kind of "indiscreet Zeal" among Christian denominations.

Although Silence received at least two other invitations to continue her letters (one by James Franklin and another by an unknown assailant who twitted her on the depletion of her wit), the fourteenth *Dogood* marked the end of the series.[15] In all, it was a remarkably original performance for a sixteen-year-old boy. The vernacular style and the use of the Widow Dogood as vehicle for a type of shrewd, middle-class humor distinguished these essays.[16]

The *Dogood* papers were important in Franklin's career as a writer. They led to later *Dogoods*—such characters as his old Janus, the Busy-Body, Poor Richard, etc. Such characters marked the beginnings of the crackerbox tradition which makes up a really sizeable and significant part of American humor.

In terms of Franklin's development as a writer the *Dogood* papers are important because they express the growth of Franklin's ability at satire; for at sixteen Franklin had achieved, as he says in the *Autobiography,* a reputation as "a young genius that had a turn for libelling and satyr."[17] Had he remained in Boston, argues Davy, the growth of Franklin's "reputation for libelling and satire" might have called down upon his head a fate even worse than his brother's.[18] From fear of such a fate he fled Boston, according to Davy. But, whatever the reason for Franklin's departure from Boston, his *Dogood* papers were "among the most literary essays which that period published."[19]

II   *The Busy-Body Papers*

The circumstances of publication of the *Busy-Body* papers are told in the *Autobiography*. There Franklin describes how in the year 1728 he happened to mention to a certain George Webb, who had applied for work, his plan to publish a newspaper in opposition to Bradford's *American Weekly Mercury*. Webb violated Franklin's confidence by relaying this plan to Samuel Keimer, another of Franklin's rivals. Keimer then beat Franklin to the public by immediately announcing that he himself planned to publish a newspaper. Franklin retaliated with the *Busy-Body* papers. A further circumstance of publication in connection with the *Busy-Body* papers includes the fact that Keimer's first issue of his *Universal Instructor in all Arts and Sciences: and Pennsylvania Gazette* appeared December 24, 1728—before Franklin could begin his own paper with his partner, Hugh Meredith.[20] The *Busy-Body* papers themselves, as Franklin explains in the *Autobiography,* he wrote as "Entertainment for Bradford's paper (*The American Weekly Mercury*), under the Title of the Busy Body which Breintnal [a Quaker member of the Junto] continued some Months." These papers stopped with the issue of September 25, 1729, at which time Franklin and Meredith bought out Keimer's bankrupt paper and forthwith abbreviated its title to *Pennsylvania Gazette*. According to a marginal note on the February 18, 1729 issue, possibly by Franklin himself, Franklin wrote only the first four, part of number five, and part of number eight of the *Busy-Body* papers. Labaree and Bell regard this note as true.[21]

Keimer, however, had drawn Franklin's satire upon himself even before this incident because of his bad taste in publishing an article on abortions which he had taken from Chambers' *Cyclopedia*. Keimer's article appeared in the fifth issue of his own *Gazette* (January 21, 1729), and Franklin answered it—according to Labaree and Bell[22]—in Bradford's *American Weekly Mercury* exactly one week later. This reply took the form of three letters under two pseudonyms, Martha Careful and Caelia Shortface. Both ladies objected to Keimer's indignity to their sex. Labaree and Bell think it significant that the *Busy-Body* papers appeared "the next week after Martha and Caelia had voiced their sex's sense of scandal and insult."[23]

Franklin's manner of introducing his three letters from Martha and Caelia foreshadows his later strategy in the London press. "Having had several Letters from the Female Sex, Complaining of S. K.," he writes, "I have thought fit to Publish the Two following."[24] (The "Two" refers to the ladies rather than to the letters, which are short and three in number.) In the first letter Martha Careful, writing in behalf of the rest of her "Agrieved Sex," threatens to take Keimer "by the Beard at the next Place" she and her friends meet him and "make an Example of him for his Immodesty."[25] In Caelia Shortface's two letters to Keimer she, too, speaks for several of her acquaintances, threatening "That if thou proceed any further in that Scandalous manner, we intend very soon to have thy right Ear for it."[26]

The first *Busy-Body* paper lives up to its officious-sounding name. In the form of a letter to Mr. Andrew Bradford, it bluntly tells him what is wrong with his paper. The Busy-Body speaks in the first person: "I have often observ'd with Concern, that your *Mercury* is not always equally entertaining . . . [and is] frequently very dull." He then states his purpose and character: "With more Concern have I continually observ'd the growing Vices and Follies of my Country-Folk. And tho' Reformation is properly the concern of every Man; that is, *Every one ought to mend One;* yet 'tis too true in this Case, that *what is every Body's Business is no Body's Business,* and the Business is done accordingly. I, therefore, upon mature Deliberation, think fit to take *no Body's Business* wholly into my own Hands; and, out of Zeal for the Publick Good, design to erect my Self into a Kind of *Censor Morum* [Censor of Morals]."

He offers a word of encouragement to womankind: "Let the Fair Sex be assur'd, that I shall always treat them and their Affairs with the utmost *Decency* and Respect. I intend now and then to dedicate a Chapter wholly to their Service; and if my Lectures any Way contribute to the Embellishment of their Minds, and Brightening of their Understandings, without offending their *Modesty,* I doubt not of having their Favour and Encouragement."

He explains his aims—entertainment and instruction in morality, philosophy, and politics. "Sometimes I propose to deliver Lectures of Morality or Philosophy, and (because I am naturally enclin'd to be meddling with Things that don't concern me) perhaps I may sometimes talk Politicks. And if I can by any means furnish out a Weekly Entertainment for the Publick, that will give a Rational Diversion, and at the same Time be instructive to the Readers, I shall think my Leisure Hours well employ'd: And if you publish this I hereby invite all ingenious Gentlemen and others, (that approve of such an Undertaking) to my Assistance and Correspondence."

The first *Busy-Body* paper partook of the nature of an announcement. It included a seventeenth-century *character*. And it made some brief comments on the need of the age for correction (its purpose). The second paper, more like modern essays, confined itself to a single subject, *Ridicule*. But, it, too, had its characters—Ridentius, in all his folly; and his opposite, Eugenius, "who never spoke yet but with a Design to divert and please."

The third *Busy-Body* paper continues the same pattern as the second by setting up two characters to personify the subject matter. This time, however, the subject is *Virtue*. And the man representing it is Cato, a humble American farmer, "a man whom Fortune has placed in the most obscure Part of the Country." The other character, Cretico, plays the part of the "sowre Philosopher." He possesses cunning and craft, but he is "far from being Wise." Keimer apparently thought the character of Cretico applied to himself, for in the *Universal Instructor* (February 25, 1729)[27] he warned Franklin against scandal and defamation.

Busy-Body four has a three-part structure. The first part invites correspondence. The second part, an amusing letter from a female shopkeeper, complains that her neighbor's children disrupt the shop on the occasions of the bothersome social visits of their mother. The disruptions take the form of the children's urinating on the "Goods" (dry goods) and mixing up the assortments of nails; the mother takes the attitude that no real damage is done by this kind of play: "Let them play a little," she remarks, "I'll put all to rights my self before I go." But of course things are never put to rights, and the shopkeeper complains that she finds "a great deal of Work to do after they are gone." In the third part Franklin (in his role as Busy-Body) writes a more formal discourse on the regulation of social visits: "It is a nice thing and very difficult, to regulate our Visits in such a Manner, as never to give Offence by coming too seldom, or too often, or departing too abruptly, or staying too long."

He then refers to the Turkish custom of concluding visits by perfuming the beards of the males present when the host wants to bid his visitors good-by. The Busy-Body serves notice on his visitor that after providing French brandy and snuff for the men and citron-water for the ladies, he expects them to retire.

The fifth *Busy-Body* announces its purpose as "a Terror to Evil-Doers as well as a Praise to them that do well." The last part of this essay is a fairly long and serious defense of the Busy-Body against an attack on his character of Cretico (see the third paper) that appeared in Keimer's *Universal Instructor.*

The eighth and final *Busy-Body* that Franklin is known to have participated in calls attention to the fact that someone has written a key to the fourth *Busy-Body,* thereby converting "a gentle Satyr upon tedious and impertinent Visitants into a Libel on some in the Government." It also contains a letter from Titan Pleiades, an astrologer, who hopes to find a fortune buried in the earth. The astrologer proposes a union of Busy-Body, his correspondent who had the supernatural gift (see *Busy-Body,* No. 4), and himself, who with united endeavors might eventually become the three richest men of the province. (Titan Pleiades is obviously a humorous reference to Titan Leeds, the almanac maker whom Franklin later pilloried in *Poor Richard.*) Busy-Body replies to this letter with a general attack on all get-rich-quick schemes (including the romance of digging for buried pirate treasure) and their disastrous results to poor persons taken in by their proponents. He concludes with a characteristic Franklin ending, by relating the story of a father who gave his son a valuable piece of land and assured him that he had found a "considerable Quantity of Gold by Digging there" and that the son might do the same if he carefully observed the rule of never digging "more than Plow-deep."

These five essays comprising Franklin's part in the *Busy-Body* papers have sometimes been likened to commonplace books, because of their rather loose structure, their use of sayings, Latin epigraphs, letters, etc. There is a workday, didactic quality about them, too—an air of the print shop. Davy therefore calls the *Busy-Body* papers "a sort of Silence-Dogood-in-breeches series of essays" for the purpose of destroying the competition of Keimer's *Universal Instructor.*[28] They succeeded in their purpose.

When we examine one of the separate essays Franklin contributed to his *Pennsylvania Gazette,* the successor of Keimer's
paper, we shall see that at times he was certainly capable
of writing a well-organized essay in the nineteenth- and twentieth-century manner. In his essay "On Conversation" (October
15, 1730) he begins with his customary quote from the classics
(Terence's *Andria*).[29] Immediately following this quotation he
announces: "The Bounds and Manner of this Paper will not
allow a regular and methodical Discourse on the Subject, and
therefore I must beg Leave to throw my Thoughts together
as they arise." Nevertheless he develops his essay quite method-
ically. First, he observes that to give pleasure in conversation
is "an Art which all people believe they understand and practice, tho' most are ignorant or deficient in it." Then he analyzes
the art of giving such pleasure into two parts—*"Complaisance*
and *Good Nature."* *Complaisance* he defines as "a seeming
preference of others to ourselves"; *Good Nature,* as "a Readiness to overlook or excuse their Foibles, and do them all the
services we can." Following these definitions, he lists and
explains seven errors of conversation, seven "Things which
cause Dislike," proceeding generally from the most common
as well as the most disagreeable to the less common and the
less disagreeable—at least in the first part of the essay—and
using such adjectives as "common," "disobliging," and "disagreeable" to make this progress clear.

The list includes the following: (1) *"talking overmuch";*
(2) "seeming wholly unconcerned in Conversation, and bearing no other Part in the Discourse than a *No* or *Yes* sometimes,
or an *Hem,* or perhaps a *Nod* only"; (3) "ever speaking of
ourselves and our own Affairs"; (4) *"Story-telling,"* especially
those with "rambling Particulars"; (5) *"Wrangling* and *Disputing";* (6) "Raillery"; (7) and "Scandal." This list constitutes
the middle, or main part, of the composition.

In the short transition paragraph that follows, Franklin
explains in the first sentence that these are only "the most
obvious" mistakes and that "whosoever avoids them carefully
can never much displease." His conclusion recapitulates his
main points. This essay "On Conversation" has the clear-cut
beginning, middle, and end characteristic of Franklin's later
method as a writer of essays.

III *The Bagatelles*

Franklin achieved his highest development as a writer of belles-lettres with a series of approximately fifteen essays known as the *bagatelles*. These essays, most of which were composed as letters to Mmes. Brillon and Helvétius, were with some exceptions printed on his own private press during his residence in France (1776-1785). At the time, he lived in Passy, a suburb of Paris, where he enjoyed the social and intellectual company of a small group of sophisticated French people; among them, besides the two ladies mentioned, were his good friends the Abbé Morellet, the Abbé de la Roche, Cabanis, Le Veillard, and others.

Since we have treated at length both the social background and the excellent artistic quality of these works in our edition of these essays, entitled *Franklin's Wit and Folly: The Bagatelles* (1953), we refer the reader interested in a more detailed discussion of these aspects to this book. We shall say here merely that the bagatelles represent Franklin's brief and only excursion into the domain of belles-lettres. Here, as in no other of his works, we see him as an artist who has momentarily laid aside his constant watchword of *utility*. For once the essay in his hands becomes not a mere means to an end. The *bagatelles* are little classics that must be judged among Franklin's finest creations.

The scholarly textual problems connected with the *bagatelles* are legion and in a state of flux because of new discoveries. For this reason the readers would do well to consult Professor A. O. Aldridge's chapter about this subject in his book *Franklin and his French Contemporaries* (1957) as well as the excellent recent work of Professor Chinard, which we shall discuss below. In our discussion of the *bagatelles* we present only the most representative of them and a few of the major problems that scholars, editors, and critics encounter in reading them. One of these problems concerns definition.

What is a *bagatelle?* As Franklin used the word in his letter to Mme. Brillon (April 8, 1784) it certainly included the "several other little things, of which some samples have been printed here in the house, solely for our friends." These, as Aldridge sees it, were distinct from the *Information to Those Who*

Would Remove to America and the *Remarks Concerning the Savages of North-America* that Franklin alludes to in this same letter.[30]

The *Information* was a serious kind of realistic real-estate brochure to inform French dandies—and others romantically contemplating moving to the New World—that they would have to work for a living in the new country. The *Remarks* satirized the exploitative attitude of the white man toward the American Indian, particularly "the Cheating of Indians in the Price of Beaver." It also pleaded for common courtesy and politeness towards people whose "manners differ from ours."

Franklin also tells Mme. Brillon in this letter that "if you have not lost The Handsome and the Deformed Leg, and The Morals of Chess [two other *bagatelles*], you have with these here [what he was sending enclosed] a complete collection of all my Bagatelles which have been printed at Passy." He talks about the gout, apparently referring to probably the most famous of all the *bagatelles,* the *Dialogue between the Gout and Mr. Franklin,* which he also enclosed. Conceivably Franklin could have written other *bagatelles* elsewhere than at Passy, and conceivably Mme. Brillon may have been in possession of them; but, to the best of our knowledge, he nowhere refers to his other light essays as *bagatelles.* The term *"bagatelles," as he used it,* then, meant the light-hearted or humorous essays which he wrote for the intimate company at Passy, or possibly for a few friends like Priestley in England during this period, and which he usually printed on his own private press.

Aldridge and Davy have hastened to point out that even such a qualified definition has serious shortcomings and that numerous other essays of earlier periods belong to this same genre[31]—such as *The Craven Street Gazette* (written for Polly Stevenson), *The Speech of Polly Baker,* and *Advice on Choosing a Mistress.* The canon of the *bagatelles* should probably be revised to include the following, with the added stipulation that this list is by no means complete or final: *The Dialogue Between Franklin and the Gout, The Whistle, The Ephemera, The Elysian Fields, The Flies, Letter to Mme. La Freté (Bilked for Breakfast), Letter to the Royal Academy, A Tale, The Handsome and the Deformed Leg, The Morals of Chess, Two Extra Commandments (Franklin Papers,* XLIII, 19½), *To the Abbé de la Roche at Auteuil* (containing the drinking song), *Letter from Franklin to the Abbé Morellet* (with drawings by

W. T. Franklin), *The Craven-Street Gazette, On the Death of a Squirrel, The Art of Procuring Pleasant Dreams, On Early Marriages, On the Choice of a Mistress* (Letter to Cadwallader Colden), *The Harrow, A Petition of the Left Hand, An Economical Project, A Letter from China, The Speech of Polly Baker,* and *The Witch Trial at Mount Holly.*

Besides the *bagatelles* already mentioned in the list above there are, of course, numerous other nominations among Franklin's essays and letters: among others, the letter to Mrs. Thompson (February 8, 1777) the letters to Catharine Ray, and the letter to Jacques Barbeu-Duborg (London, April, 1773) about flies drowned in Madeira wine. (Thinking about the drowned flies leads him to speculate on various methods of embalming drowned persons and of reviving them. He says that he himself has "a very ardent desire to see and observe the state of America an hundred years hence," but would prefer an ordinary death and being immersed in a cask of Madeira.)

One should list, too, among the supplementary *bagatelles* some of Franklin's drinking songs. (In this instance, of course, we have *bagatelles* which are in verse, not essay form.) We have Van Doren's word that Franklin "was convivial in taverns"; as a young man, he liked rum "and Madeira, sang songs, and wrote some."[32] His drinking songs, says Van Doren "are probably his best expressions in verse."[33]

The hoaxes—some of them, at least—also fall into the category of *bagatelles. The Proposed New Version of the Bible* and the *Parable Against Persecution,* for example, were both used on numerous social occasions to divert Franklin's guests. According to his friend Priestley, the famous chemist and English clergyman, Franklin would lay the parable loosely in the Bible and read it. He would then read the first chapter of Job. Often the guests mistook the latter for Franklin's own work.[34] In this guessing game he usually gave his auditors the choice of identifying the fifty-first chapter of Genesis (which does not exist) or his own imitation. Since his imitation was very accurate as to style, the guests often failed. The *Proposed New Version of the Bible* led Matthew Arnold far afield.[35] Paul Elmer More thought Franklin intended "a satire on monarchical government" by it under pretext of modernizing the text.[36]

To give the reader some idea of the great emotional range the *bagatelles* cover, we select two, *To the Royal Academy* and *The Elysian Fields;* and in presenting them we reverse the usual order of the sublime and the ridiculous. In order to present Franklin's earthy satire of a certain scientific academy, probably of Brussels, we offer a few excerpts from this less well-known *bagatelle*. It was the custom for this academy to undertake investigation of research projects in mathematics and the natural sciences for a prize. Franklin starts his essay by proposing a rather unusual question for investigation by the academy.

My Prize Question . . . *To discover some Drug wholesome & not disagreeable, to be mix'd with our common Food, or Sauces, that shall render the Natural Discharges, of Wind from our Bodies, not only inoffensive, but agreeable as Perfumes.*

That this is not a chimerical Project, and altogether impossible, may appear from these Considerations. That we already have some knowledge of Means capable of Varying that Smell. He that dines on stale Flesh, especially with much Addition of Onions, shall be able to afford a Stink that no Company can tolerate; while he that has lived for some Time on Vegetables only, shall have that Breath so pure as to be insensible to the most delicate Noses; and if he can manage so as to avoid the Report, he may any where give Vent to his Griefs, unnoticed. But as there are many to whom an entire Vegetable Diet would be inconvenient, and as a little Quick-Lime thrown into a Jakes [outdoor toilet] will correct the amazing quantity of fetid Air arising from the vast Mass of putrid Matter contain'd in such Places, and render it rather pleasing to the smell, who knows but that a little Powder of Lime (or some other thing equivalent) taken in our Food, or perhaps a Glass of Limewater drank at Dinner, may have the same Effect on the Air produc'd in and issuing from our Bowels? This is Worth the experiment. . . .

For the Encouragement of this Enquiry, (from the immortal Honour to be reasonably expected by the Inventor) let it be reasonably considered of how small importance to Mankind, or to how small a Part of Mankind have been useful those Discoveries in Science that have heretofore made Philosophers famous. Are there twenty Men in Europe at this Day, the happier, or even the easier, for any knowledge they have pick'd out of Aristotle? What Comfort can the Vortices of Descartes give to a Man who has Whirlwinds in his Bowels! The Knowledge of Newton's mutual Attraction of the Particles of Matter, can it afford Ease to him who is rack'd by their mutual Repulsion, and the cruel Distensions it occasions? The Pleasure arising to a few Philosophers, from seeing, a few Times in their Life, the Threads of Light untwisted, and separated by the Newtonian

Prism into seven Colours, can it be compared with the Ease and Comfort every Man living might feel seven times a Day, by discharging freely the Wind from his Bowels? Especially if it be converted into a Perfume. . . . And surely such a Liberty of *Ex-pressing* one's *Scent-iments,* and *pleasing one another,* is of infinitely more Importance to human Happiness than that Liberty of the Press, or of *abusing one another,* which the English are so ready to fight & die for.—In short, this Invention, if compleated, would be, as Bacon expresses it, *bringing Philosophy home to Mens Business and Bosoms.* And I cannot but conclude, that in Comparison therewith, for universal and continual *UTILITY,* the Science of the Philosophers abovementioned, even with the Addition, Gentlemen, of your *"Figure quelconque"* and the Figures inscrib'd in it, are, all together, scarcely worth a

FART-HING.[37]

This *bagatelle,* as perhaps no other, is remarkable for both the quality and the quantity of its puns. Franklin was a lover of puns; and the following letter to Dr. Richard Price at Brighthelmstone, England (September 16, 1783), in connection with this letter to the academy and the balloon experiments at Versailles reveals one of his slyest:

All the conversation here at present turns upon the Ballons fill'd with light inflammable Air. . . . Inflammable air puts me in mind of a little jocular paper I wrote some years since in ridicule of a prize Question given out by a certain Academy on this side of the Water, and I enclose it for your Amusement. On second thoughts, as it is a mathematical Question, and perhaps I think it more trifling than it really is, and you are a Mathematician, I am afraid I have judg'd wrong in sending it to you. Our friend Dr. Priestley, however, who is apt to give himself *Airs,* and has a kind of Right to everything his Friends produce upon that Subject, may perhaps like to see it, and you can send it to him without reading it.

Anyone who thinks Dr. Price forwarded this letter to Dr. Priestley "without reading it" should consult a psychiatrist.

The *bagatelle* known as *The Elysian Fields* was written to Mme. Helvétius, a wealthy widow who but a few years before had lost her husband. At the time this letter was written (December 7, 1778), Franklin's wife had been dead nearly four years, and he had proposed to Mme. Helvétius. Like other examples noted, this essay has a clearly discernible beginning, middle, and end. With its elements of surprise and balanced irony it constitutes more of a complete *jeu d'esprit* than some of the other *bagatelles*. In it Franklin tells how he had been so disturbed by her refusal to marry him that he had returned home, fallen on his bed, and, believing himself dead, had found himself in the Elysian Fields. He was asked if he "desired to see anybody in particular." "Lead me to the home of the philosophers," he had replied. Two, Socrates and Helvétius, lived in a nearby garden. Since he could talk no Greek and only a little French, Franklin desired to see Helvétius.

He received me with great courtesy, having known me for some time, he said, by the reputation I had there. He asked me a thousand things about the war, and about the present state of religion, liberty, and the government in France.—You ask nothing of your dear friend Madame H [elvétius]; nevertheless she still loves you excessively and I was at her place but an hour ago. Ah! said he, you make me remember my former felicity.—But it is necessary to forget it in order to be happy here. During several of the early years, I thought only of her. Finally, I am consoled. I have taken another wife. The most like her that I could find. She is not, it is true, so completely beautiful, but she has as much good sense, and a little more of Spirit, and she loves me infinitely. Her continual Study is to please me; and she has actually gone to hunt the best Nectar and the best Ambrosia in order to regale me this evening; remain with me and you will see her. . . . At these words the new Madame H—— entered with the Nectar: at which instant I recognized her to be Madame F[ranklin], my old American friend. I reclaimed her. But she told me coldly, "I have been your good wife forty-nine years and four months, nearly a half century; be content with that. Here I have formed a new connection, which will endure to eternity.

Offended by this refusal of my Eurydice, I suddenly decided to leave these ungrateful spirits, to return to the good earth, to see again the sunshine and you. Here I am! Let us revenge ourselves.

Playfully, more like a father than a wooer, Franklin made love to young Mme. Brillon, one of the great beauties of France, and about thirty-five years his junior. "What highlights the correspondence [between Franklin and Mme. Brillon] is the thrust and parry of verbal courtship," says Granger.[38]

In one of her letters to "Papa" Franklin, as she called him, she wrote: "You combine with the best heart, when you wish, the soundest moral teaching, a lively imagination, and that drole roguishness which shows that the wisest of men allows his wisdom to be perpetually broken against the rocks of femininity."[39] This is an apt description of Franklin's letters to her. In all, they exchanged a correspondence of over one hundred and fifty letters, several bagatelles, and poems between 1777 and 1789.[40] Some of these letters, such as *The Elysian Fields* and *The Ephemera*, served as exercises in French composition for Franklin; and some scholars have had much to say about Franklin's bad French. Professor Chinard, however, takes a different view: "His French [in *The Elysian Fields*] may not be of classical vintage, although it did not shock the purists of the time; but it was distinctly his. He knew exactly what he wanted to say and he said it in his own words, in his own way, in an easy and fluent manner."[41] Like the style of several excellent French writers, Franklin's French style has "a deceptive simplicity."[42]

Of all the *bagatelles, The Ephemera* is undoubtedly the most charming. It is also one of the most philosophic. In it Franklin makes delicate fun of his omnivorous scientific and philosophic interest in the world of nature, his difficulties with the French language, the vivacious disposition of the French people to talk rapidly and "three or four together," and French excitability about matters of art, particularly music. Behind this surface humor, however, he plays skillfully on the transitoriness of life —his theme—and the vanity of human wishes.

In this tender allegory, for that is the form of *The Ephemera*, the old insect philosopher is Franklin himself, aged seventy-two; "the ever-amiable Brillante" is Mme. Brillon. The happy people who live securely under a wise government, equitable and moderate, are the French, who at the time were involved in a hot dispute about the respective merits of the composers Gluck and Picini. (On hearing that Franklin himself preferred Gluck to Picini, Marie Antoinette is reported to have said, "What can a man whose trade is to place [lightning] rods on buildings know of music?") "My Compatriotes, Inhabitants of this Bush," were the Americans in the wilds of a distant continent. The eighteen hours stand for the life of man. Employing his delicate symbolism of the insect world, Franklin touches on such distant and serious matters as the origin of the universe and the end of the world, the true value of time and of life, and the microcosm and the macrocosm.[43]

Structurally considered, the beginning of *The Ephemera* explains the occasion and introduces the subject of the insects. With kind permission of the Cornell University Library, we quote from an original manuscript–a version of *The Ephemera* which Franklin wrote in English:

Passy Sept 20, 1778

You may remember, my dear Friend, that when we lately spent that happy Day in the delightful Garden and sweet society of the Moulin Joli, I stopt a little in one of our Walks, and staid some time behind the Company. We had been shewn numberless Skeletons of a kind of little Fly, called an Ephemere, all whose successive Generations we were told were bred and expired with the Day. I happen'd to see a living Company of them on a Leaf, who appear'd to be engag'd in Conversation. —You know I understand all the inferior Animal Tongues: my too great Application to the Study of them is the best Excuse I can give for the little Progress I have made in your charming Language. I listened thro' Curiosity to the Discourse of these little Creatures, but as they in their national Vivacity spoke three or four together, I could make but little of their Discourse. I found, however, by some broken Expressions that I caught now & then, they were disputing warmly the Merit of two foreign Musicians, one a *Cousin* [a gnat], the other a *Musketo;* in which Dispute they spent their time seemingly as regardless of the Shortness of Life, as if they had been Sure of living a Month. Happy People! thought I, you live certainly under a wise, just and mild Government; since you have no public Grievances to complain of, nor any Subject of Contention but the Perfection or Imperfection of foreign Music.

Franklin then develops the longer middle part of the essay into the form of a soliloquy by an old, white-haired insect.

"It was, says he, the Opinion of learned Philosophers of our Race, who lived and flourished long before my time, that this vast World, the *Moulin Joli*, could not itself subsist more than 18 Hours; and I think there was some Foundation for that Opinion, since by the apparent Motion of that great Luminary that gives Life to all Nature, and which in my Time has evidently declin'd considerably towards the Ocean at the End of our Earth, it must then finish its Course, be extinguish'd in the Waters that surround us, and leave the World in Cold and Darkness, necessarily producing universal Death and Destruction. I have lived seven of these Hours; a great Age; being no less than 420 minutes of Time. How very few of us continue so long!—I have seen Generations born, flourish and expire. My present Friends are the Children and Grandchildren of the Friends of my Youth, who are now, alas, no more! And I must soon follow them; for by the Course of Nature, tho' still in Health, I cannot expect to live above 7 or 8 Minutes longer. What now avails all my Toil and Labour in amassing Honey-Dew on this Leaf, which I cannot live to enjoy! What the political Struggles I have been engag'd in for the Good of my Compatriotes, Inhabitants of this Bush; or my philosophical Studies for the Benefit of our Race in general! For in Politics *what can Laws do without Morals!* our present Race of Ephemeres will in a Course of Minutes, became corrupt like those of other and older Bushes, and consequently as wretched. And in Philosophy how small our Progress! Alas, *Art is long and Life is short!* My Friends would comfort me with the Idea of a Name they say I shall leave behind me; and they tell me I have lived long enough, to Nature and to Glory: But what will Fame be to an Ephemere who no longer exists? And what will become of all History in the 18th Hour, when the World itself, even the whole *Moulin Joli,* shall come to its End, and be buried in universal Ruin?—

The old philosopher insect then closes with this remark which is in the usual gallant style of Franklin's letters to Mme. Brillon: "To me, after all my eager Pursuits, no solid Pleasures now remain, but the Reflection of a long Life spent in meaning well, the sensible Conversation of a few good Lady-Ephemeres, and now and then a kind Smile and a Tune from the ever-amiable BRILLANTE."

The handling of tone during the soliloquy is particularly effective. Seldom has pathos been more "delicately sustained," writes Professor Hornberger.[44] The classical quotations from Horace, Hippocrates, and Caesar in this section suit the discourse of a philosopher, as do Franklin's classical periods. *The Ephemera,* as Professor Chinard points out, is no mere *bagatelle;* it is "a work of art and a literary masterpiece."[45] His recent study of the manuscripts of this work shows that Franklin took special care with style in its composition, that he pursued the exact word through frequent corrections and revisions, and that he made determined efforts to express nuances of thought and feeling. This so-called *bagatelle* is an answer, Chinard goes on, to critics like Sainte-Beuve who had argued that Franklin lacked imagination and was only a utilitarian, a practical experimenter.[46]

Two other *bagatelles* written to Mme. Brillon rank among the more popular of these productions—*The Whistle* and the *Dialogue Between Franklin and the Gout*. Along with the *Ephemera* these enjoyed great popularity in the 1790's, being copied and recopied.[47]

The essay as Franklin used it in the eighteenth century covered a rather broad range of subject matter, in form and in purpose. Some of these essays represent Franklin's most polished work as a writer. All of them are interesting and well worth studying, especially by students of writing. For students of history, too, they are often important as original source material not otherwise generally available. Franklin's essays constitute some of his most important work as a writer. The essay and the letter were the two forms he used more often than any other.

CHAPTER 6

The Letters

THE SINGLE FORM that Franklin used more often than any other in his writing was that of the letter. Most of his writings on science, for example, were personal letters to his learned friends. Many of his anecdotes and *bagatelles* were written as letters. In such areas as politics, economics, religion, morals, and aesthetics, writes Van Doren, his private correspondence is richer than his formal pamphlets. "Even his *Autobiography* began as a long letter to his son."[1]

Franklin had "what may be called a kind of private mind," says Van Doren, attempting to account for the appeal of this form for him. "He liked the sense that what he wrote was being written for some actual definite person, rather than for a general audience." The much-noted quality of variety in Franklin's letters may be explained by the fact that they were addressed to such a great variety of persons.[2]

Franklin's letters are the nearest thing we have to his conversation, argues Van Doren, for very few records of his actual talk have survived. "He seldom wrote a letter in which there was not some graceful or witty turn of language or sentiment."[3] In his letters even more than in his *Autobiography*, the personality of Franklin emerges with typical "broad humanness."[4] An admirable letter-writer, Franklin in his personal correspondence reveals himself to be cheerful and humorous and of a warm, affectionate nature. The *Autobiography* does not disclose some of Franklin's most charming qualities as a man—his delight in children, young persons, and ladies of all ages.[5] But the letters exhibit these qualities to a marked degree.

Although few letters "by or to" Franklin during the first thirty years of his life have been recovered by the current editors of the Franklin *Papers*, such letters become more numerous in the 1740's[6] for his epistolary labors increased as his age advanced. On August 22, 1772, for example, he wrote thirteen letters to different persons on the following subjects: canals, antislavery propaganda, silk culture, business conditions, labor supply for a glass factory, the taking of oaths, the post-office business, books to be selected for the Library Company, the establishment of a factory to make nails, and the investments of the Pennsylvania Hospital in England.[7] Considered as a whole, Franklin's personal correspondence might well be described as voluminous. Had he written nothing else, this alone would have given him claim to a high literary reputation.[8]

The variety of emotional tones in Franklin's letters kept pace with the great variety of the subject matter. Such moods as condescension to a young sister, indignation at the enemies of his country, unruffled confidence in right and truth, urbanity in explaining to his niece the customs of French women—all these we find in the letters.[9] As this statement suggests, his letters were never dull, formal, or stodgy.[10] "Letters to him were a form of art," writes Van Doren.[11] "Among the most delightful letter-writers of our language," "among the supreme writers of familiar letters," "the best of all the letter-writers of the time —these are the judgments of three discriminating literary critics on Franklin's ability in this genre.[12]

I Representative Letters

Although numerous critics have commented upon the excellence of Franklin's style as a writer of letters,[13] few of them, with the exception of Van Doren, have provided, however, any very specific comments about his style. Perhaps the best way of attacking the problem of style is by presenting examples or touchstones—some representative letters. Van Doren gives a sample of what he calls Franklin's "grand style" in the letter to Washington written on March 5, 1780:

> Should peace arrive after another campaign or two, and afford us a little leisure, I should be happy to see your Excellency in Europe and to accompany you, if my age and strength would permit, in visiting some of its ancient and most famous kingdoms. You would, at this side of the sea, enjoy the great reputation you have acquired, pure and free from those little shades that the jealousy of a man's countrymen and contemporaries are ever endeavoring to cast over living merit. Here you would enjoy, and know, what posterity will say of Washington. For a thousand leagues have nearly the same effect as a thousand years; the feeble voice of those grovelling passions can not extend so far in either time or distance. At present I

enjoy that pleasure for you, as I frequently hear the old generals
of this martial country (who study the maps of America and
mark upon them all your operations) speak with sincere appro-
bation and great applause of your conduct; and join in giving
you the character of one of the great captains of the age.

I must soon quit the scene, but you may live to see our country flourish, as it will amazingly and rapidly after the war is
over; like a field of young Indian corn, which long fair weather
and sunshine had enfeebled and discolored, and which in that
weak state, by a thundergust of violent wind, hail, and rain
seemed to be threatened with absolute destruction; yet the
storm being past, it recovers a fresh verdure, shoots up with
double vigor, and delights the eye not of its owner only but
of every observing traveler.

The simile of this second paragraph is obviously modeled after
Homer.

One of the most charming letters Franklin ever wrote is the
one he addressed to Mrs. Jonathan Shipley on the occasion of
his visit to Twyford during the summer of 1771, when, as we
noted in Chapter II, he wrote the first part of the *Autobiography*. The letter, dated August 12, combines his gratitude for
a most enjoyable visit with a report on his escorting young
"Kitty" Shipley (aged eleven) via stagecoach to London, where
she was to attend school.

Dear Madam,

This is just to let you know that we arriv'd safe and well in
Marlborough Street about Six, where I deliver'd up my Charge:

The above seems too short for a Letter; so I will lengthen
it by a little Account of our Journey. The first Stage we were
rather pensive. I tried several Topics of Conversation, but
none of them would hold. But after Breakfast we began to
recover Spirits, and had a good deal of Chat. Will you hear
some of it? We talk'd of her Brother, and she wish'd he was
married. And don't you wish your Sisters married too? Yes.
All but Emily; I would not have her married. Why? Because
I can't spare her. The rest may marry as soon as they please,
so they do but get good Husbands. We then took upon us
to consider for'em what sort of Husbands would be fittest for
every one of them.

As there were five girls in the Shipley family, this took some
time. Georgiana received a "Country Gentleman," Betsey a

"City Merchant," Emily a "Duke," Anna Maria an "Earl," and Kitty herself was to have an old "General" who might leave her a "rich young Widow" when he died. At dinner she revised her choice for Betsey from a "Merchant" to a "Vice Count."

The letter, too long to reproduce in entirety, concludes in the following vein:

> Thus we chatted on, and she was very entertaining quite to Town.
>
> I have now made my Letter as much too long as it was at first too short. The Bishop would think it too trifling, therefore don't show it him. I am afraid too that you will think it so, and have a good mind not to send it. Only it tells you Kitty is well at School and for that I let it go. My Love to the whole amiable Family, best Respects to the Bishop, and 1000 Thanks for all your Kindnesses, and for the happy Days I enjoy'd at Twyford. With the greatest Esteem and Respect, I am,
>
> Madam,
Your most obedient
and humble Servant
B. Franklin

Sometime near the date September 17, 1782, a daughter was born to the Marquis de Lafayette, and Franklin wrote him a short letter, felicitating him on the event.

Dear Sir

> I continue to suffer from this cruel Gout: But in the midst of my Pain the News of Madame de la Fayette's safe Delivery, and your Acquisition of a Daughter gives me Pleasure.
>
> In naming [y]our Children I think you do well to begin with the antient [sic] State. And as we cannot have too many of so good a Race, I hope you and Madame de la Fayette will go thro' the Thirteen. . . .
>
> While you are proceeding, I hope our States will some of them new-name themselves. Miss Virginia, Miss Carolina, and Miss Georgiana will sound prettily enough for the Girls; but Massachusetts and Connecticut, are too harsh for the Boys, unless they were to be Savages.
>
> That God may bless you in the Event of this Day as in every other prays
>
> Your affectionate Friend and Servant
B. Franklin

Franklin's letter to his stepniece Elizabeth Partridge concerning his reception by the French ladies will also bear quoting. A paragraph from this letter, dated Passy, October 11, 1779, reads:

> You mention the Kindness of the French Ladies to me. I must explain that matter. This is the civilest Nation upon Earth. Your first Acquaintances endeavour to find out what you like, and they tell others. If 'tis understood that you like Mutton, dine where you will you find Mutton. Somebody, it seems, gave it out that I lov'd Ladies; and then every body presented me their Ladies (or the Ladies presented themselves) to be embrac'd, that is to have their Necks kiss'd. For as to kissing of Lips or Cheeks, it is not the Mode here: the first is reckon'd rude, and the other may rub off the Paint.

These are only a few of the most representative letters of Franklin. Readers interested in further reading of Franklin's letters would do well to consult Carl Van Doren's *The Letters and Papers of B. Franklin and Richard Jackson, 1753-1785* and *The Letters of B. Franklin and Jane Mecom;* W. G. Roelker's *B. Franklin and Catherine Ray Greene: Their Correspondence, 1755-1790;* J. M. Stifler's *"My Dear Girl": Franklin's Correspondence with Polly Stevenson, Georgiana and Catherine Shipley;* Labaree and Bell's *Mr. Franklin;* and G. Chinard's forthcoming edition of the Franklin-Mme. Brillon correspondence. (See bibliography.) The titles of these works should give the reader some notion of a few of Franklin's principal correspondents.

II *Correspondents*

One of the most learned of Franklin's London correspondents was Richard Jackson, a wealthy lawyer of the Inner Temple. A Member of Parliament and one who owned much land, Jackson was interested in agriculture. He sympathized with the colonies, especially with Connecticut. Yale University gave this man an honorary doctorate.[14] The correspondence between him and Franklin was not very active at first, writes Van Doren, but it burgeoned shortly after the period 1757-62, when they were becoming better friends.[15] Jackson was made agent for Pennsylvania on April 2, 1763, and Franklin was added to the Committee of Correspondence. Thus "the two now were required to correspond as officials. As they were also friends and philosophers, their letters for the two years (1762-64) are full of other things besides official business."[16] But there was a great deal of the latter, too.

> Franklin's letters for these two years 1762-64 are full of Pennsylvania affairs: the conflict between the Assembly and the governor over the taxation of the Proprietary lands; the modes of raising money and the nature of the paper currency to be issued; the trouble caused by the Indian war commonly known as Pontiac's; the Assembly's petition, first drafted by Franklin (no. 32), for a change from Proprietary to Royal government; the shift to graver concerns as the colonists became aware of the threat implied in George Grenville's revenue bills of 1764 and the proposed Stamp Act; Franklin's election as Speaker of the Assembly, his defeat as a member from the City of Philadelphia, and his appointment to return to London as joint agent with Jackson.[17]

Although he was writing "from behind the scenes of Pennsylvania politics," he was also writing from his personal life; and this correspondence covered the period 1753-85 except for the periods when Franklin returned to America and while he resided in France.[18] It is just possible that Jackson may have supplied him with some of the ideas for the pamphlet *The Interest of Great Britain* (1760), although it is believed to have been written by Franklin.[19] Similarly, Franklin is thought to have furnished materials for *An Historical Review of the Constitution and Government of Pennsylvania* which Jackson wrote.[20]

Among Franklin's favorite correspondents in London during this same general period (1758-75, and even as late as 1785) we must include the Shipleys (already discussed) and the Stevensons. For Polly Stevenson he wrote the amusing epitaph on the death of her favorite American squirrel, Mungo, which he had given her, including the observation that the squirrel was well educated, having "traveled far, and seen much of the world." For Mrs. Stevenson he wrote *The Craven-Street Gazette* (1770), a beautiful little example of the mock heroic.

In a letter to Polly Stevenson (Philadelphia, March 25, 1763) Franklin discussed the problem of the fine arts in utilitarian America. "The Arts delight to travel westward," he wrote her. "After the first cares for the necessities of life are over, we shall come to think of the embellishments. Already, some of our young geniuses begin to lisp attempts at painting, poetry, and music."[21] Eight years later in a letter (London, July 4, 1771) to Charles Wilson Peale, the celebrated American painter,

Franklin repeated this observation about the arts and their westward travel. "The Arts have always travelled Westward, and there is no doubt of their flourishing hereafter on our side of the Atlantic, as the Number of wealthy Inhabitants shall increase, who may be able and willing suitably to reward them, since from several Instances it appears that our People are not deficient in Genius."[22] The historian Bridenbaugh points out that Franklin had carried Arcangelo Corelli's sonatas and Francesco Geminiani's concertos for sale in his printing office as early as 1739. Noting that "by temperament and training Franklin was perhaps less qualified to render judgments in aesthetic than in other matters," Bridenbaugh says that Franklin's "universality of interest kept him aware of the advances made by his countrymen in the artistic as well as the practical and scientific aspects of intellectual endeavor."[23] Polly Stevenson apparently liked music. In the above-mentioned letter Franklin asks her if she will intercede in behalf of an American composer with a certain Mr. Stanley, a composer she knew. He also speaks apologetically to her about the generally low state of American music at that time.[24]

During the years 1757-75 Franklin also carried on a correspondence with Joseph Galloway, his old political ally in Pennsylvania in the dispute between the popular and proprietary parties. Galloway's desertion to the British side in 1777 terminated this correspondence.

Throughout the period 1776-85 Franklin wrote many letters, notes, and *bagatelles*, to the French group in and around Passy. Among his correspondents at this time were Mmes. Brillon, Helvétius, and La Freté, the abbé Morellet and the abbé de la Roche, Cabanis, Cerutti, Le Veillard, Mme. Golofkin, Mme. Le Roy, Mme. Boulainvilliers, *et al*. After his return to Philadelphia Franklin apparently received from Mme. Helvétius, Morellet, Cabanis, and one other friend whom he addresses as "Dear Friend" "several Productions of the Academy at Auteuil" which he says gave him great pleasure.[25]

Franklin knew the author of the *Adventures of Baron Munchausen* (1785), Rudolf Erich Raspe, having met him during a brief visit with Sir John Pringle to Germany in the summer of 1766. Their meeting resulted in a brief correspondence during 1766-67. Raspe was a young librarian of the Royal Library of Hanover; he wished to emigrate to America, but was discouraged by Franklin.[26]

Many of the lines of Franklin's numerous interests and activities radiated from his printing establishment. Among the great European printers whom he knew were William Caslon, John Baskerville, William Strahan, Pierre Fournier, and François Didot.[27] But it was Strahan, the outstanding printer of Great Britain and eventually printer to King George III, who became one of Franklin's closest friends. Born of humble Scottish parents and apprenticed at an early age, Strahan's background and rise in the printing business resembles closely that of Franklin in America. Strahan served England as Member of Parliament from 1774 to 1784. He died in 1786. Clary claims that Franklin wrote more letters to Strahan than to any other person.[28]

The correspondence between Strahan and Franklin first developed from "a few casual business letters."[29] This correspondence began on July 10, 1743, according to Clary, with the exchange of a young journeyman printer by the name of David Hall.[30] (When Franklin retired from the printing business in 1748, Hall succeeded him.) Before long, a warm and lasting friendship had grown up between Franklin and Strahan. Their correspondence is important because it throws light on Franklin's printing interests after 1743. Typical of the Franklin-Strahan correspondence is the letter dated February 12, 1744, combining business and personal interests. By 1748 this correspondence had begun to include exchanges between Mrs. Franklin and Mrs. Strahan. (See letter dated Philadelphia, October 19, 1748.) Two years later (June 21, 1750), the marriage of Franklin's daughter to Strahan's son was proposed. But the match did not come off.

Strahan provided Franklin with types from Caslon to found printing offices in such places as New Haven. He also sold him books and scientific instruments. When Franklin arrived in London in 1757, he met Strahan face to face after having corresponded with him for fourteen years; and his friendship with him enabled Franklin to present the American cause to the British public with maximum effectiveness. Franklin's letters to British newspapers were rarely ever excluded, possibly because of his excellent relations with the proprietors or shareholders of the principal newspapers, according to Crane.[31] Caleb Whitefoorde, a wine merchant, a writer himself, and Franklin's "good friend and neighbor in Craven St." was a proprietor of the *Public Advertiser*.[32] But William Strahan was the principal shareholder of the *London Chronicle* as well as a prominent shareholder in the *Public Advertiser,* the *Public Ledger,* and *Lloyd's Evening Post.* According to Crane, Franklin contributed to all of these papers.[33] Little wonder, then, that he thought of his friendship with Strahan as so important. The birth of a nation, the course of an empire, depended on such friendships, on such correspondence.

The degree of mutual understanding between these two men may perhaps be judged by Franklin's familiar reference to him as "Straney" in his letter from Philadelphia, December 19, 1763. But by July 5, 1775, if we judge merely by surface appearance, these two friends had become enemies and had terminated their relations altogether. This famous letter written from Philadelphia is self-explanatory; Strahan had become a member of the British Parliament in 1774.

> Mr. Strahan:
>
> You are a member of Parliament, and one of that majority which has doomed my country to destruction. You have begun to burn our towns and murder our people. Look upon your hands! They are stained with the blood of your relations! You and I were long friends. You are now my enemy, and I am
>
> Yours
> B. Franklin

Although this letter was never sent—according to Van Doren[34] —it expressed the thought and feeling of thousands of colonists towards the British parliament in general, and it is probably no exaggeration to say that a great deal of Franklin's fame as a writer hinges on it. Two days later he wrote a friendly letter to Strahan, to which he had a friendly answer.[35] Although the correspondence was stopped during the war, it was revived again in 1781. And as late as 1784, Strahan was still trying to persuade Franklin to take up permanent residence in London.[36]

In a letter dated Passy, February 16, 1784, Franklin makes use of printer's jargon in advising Strahan how to deal with the British political situation. Similarly in a letter of August 19, 1784, Franklin remembers Strahan's once observing to him, as they sat together in the House of Commons, that no two journeymen printers within his knowledge had ever met with such success. When Strahan died, his friendship with Franklin had extended over forty-three years. Franklin wrote a letter of condolence to the son, Andrew, whose mother was apparently also dead at this time.

Some of Franklin's personal letters bore directly on important political matters. The letter of May, 1751, to Peter Collinson makes clear, for example, Franklin's "diligence" in procuring the post-office appointment for himself.[37] Other of his letters were less personal—his correspondence, for example, with Thomas Cushing, urging a policy of moderation against the colonists. He exchanged diplomatic correspondence with the French Foreign Minister Charles Gravier, Comte de Vergennes. He urged John Adams and the Congress to reduce their almost constant demands on the French for money. He corresponded with Burke on the exchange of Gen. Burgoyne for Henry Laurens.[38] "Franklin's political letters," writes McMahon, "are, in general, concise and business-like, and, naturally, lacking in the charm of his personal letters. However, they reveal fully the wisdom of this great diplomat and his intelligent grasp of the political problems of his day.[39]

Franklin's letters to Governor Shirley of Massachusetts in 1754 would certainly be considered among the more important of his political letters. In these letters he stated the highly important principle of equal justice in the various parts of the British Empire and also summed up, as Van Doren says, "almost all the American arguments of the Revolution."[40] Then there were the letters with French officials during the period 1776-85; those to Deane, Lee, Jay, and Adams; others to the commercial agents of France and Holland; epistles to American naval officers like John Paul Jones; and letters to American Congressmen like Charles Thompson and Robert Morris, and so *ad infinitum*.[41] Franklin's letters to Washington are models of diplomacy, particularly the one dated March 5, 1780, which we have quoted.[42]

As a final interesting example of the way Franklin's social and scientific correspondence sometimes coalesced with political matters in his letters, we offer the specimen he wrote in answer to a suggestion of Edward Bridgen of the Royal Society —a man whom Franklin referred to as "a particular Friend of mine and a zealous one of the American cause."[43] Bridgen had offered to furnish the Americans with copper for pennies and was willing to help by having them stamped in England if Franklin would offer the designs. In a letter dated Passy, October 2, 1779, Franklin suggested that one side of the coin

The Letters

be stamped with mottoes such as he had earlier fashioned for the *Poor Richard Almanacks*—"*Honesty is the best Policy,*" "*A Penny sav'd is a Penny got,*" "*Keep thy Shop and thy Shop will keep thee,*" "*Early to rise, will make a Man healthy, wealthy and Wise,*" etc.[44] On the other side of the coin he planned to engrave "all the different Species of Barbarities with which the English have carry'd on the War in America expressing every abominable Circumstance of their Cruelty and inhumanity, that the figures can express, to make an Impression on the Minds of Posterity as Strong and durable as that on the Copper."[45]

CHAPTER 7

Scientific Papers

"THIS IS AN AGE of experiments," wrote Franklin in the *Autobiography*.[1] He was attempting to discover the causes for the different speeds of ships and was suggesting that a set of experiments ought to be undertaken to ascertain these causes.

Frequently in his scientific letters he followed the same procedure of suggesting a set of experiments to discover facts about the infinitely various natural phenomena that aroused his interest. His correspondence on such matters was very extensive; and, according to one writer, it was carried on in nine languages; for Franklin was a member of "one or more scientific societies in almost every country of Europe."[2] Another writer refers to Franklin's "unflagging correspondence" with scientific investigators and sees the cause of Franklin's broadly human political conceptions as growing out of his scientific interests.[3]

As we have seen in Chapter VI, it was Franklin's custom to intermingle his warm personal feelings in "even scientific communications."[4] A letter to Dr. William Brownrigg, dated London, November 7, 1733, for example, describes in a very human manner his experiment for stilling the waves of a pond by pouring oil on the waters. He says he got this trick from Pliny. But he does not tell us whence he acquired the sense of showmanship he used to carry off this trick; it was his habit to wave his cane over the water and mutter incantations as though performing a great feat of magic.

The most outstanding work Franklin wrote in the field of science, or natural philosophy, as it was then called, began as a series of letters to his Quaker friend Peter Collinson in England. Collinson read these letters on electricity to the Royal Society and published some of them in the *Gentleman's Magazine*. In 1751 they came out in pamphlet form under the title of *Experiments and Observations on Electricity, Made at Phil-*

adelphia in America. This work marked the real beginnings of the science of electricity.

One of these letters to Peter Collinson (October 19, 1752) deals with the famous kite experiment. Franklin first describes the construction of the kite—cedar sticks, a large silk handkerchief as "fitter [than paper] to bear the wet and wind of a thunder gust without tearing," a piece of sharp wire about a foot long fitted to the top of the kite, twine and a short silk ribbon attached to the twine, with a metal key at the point where the silk and the twine join. Then he writes

This kite is to be raised when a thunder-gust appears to be coming on, and the person who holds the string must stand within a door or window, or under some cover, so that the silk ribbon may not be wet; and care must be taken that the twine does not touch the frame of the door or window. As soon as any of the thunder-clouds come over the kite, the pointed wire will draw the electric fire from them, and the kite, with all the twine, will be electrified, and the loose filaments of the twine will stand out every way, and be attracted by an approaching finger. And when the rain has wet the kite and twine, so that it can conduct the electric fire freely, you will find it stream out plentifully from the key on the approach of your knuckle. At this key the phial may be charged; and from electric fire thus obtained, spirits may be kindled, and all the other electric experiments be performed, which are usually done by the help of a rubbed glass globe or tube, and thereby the sameness of the electric matter with that of lightning completely demonstrated.[5]

Experiments such as this one won him the Copley medal for the year 1753, a signal honor. The letter (quoted from the original in the Archives of the Royal Society in London) Franklin wrote on the reception of this award, a gold medal, reads as follows:

Philad[a] May 29, 1754

Gentlemen,

The very great Honour you have done me, in adjudging me your Medal for 1753 demands my grateful Acknowledgements, which I beg you would accept as the only Return at present in my Power.

I know not whether any of your learned Body have attain'd the ancient boasted Art of *multiplying Gold;* but you have certainly found the Art of making it infinitely *more valuable.*

You may easily bestow your Favors on Persons of more Merit; but on none who can have a higher sense of the Honour, or a more perfect Respect for your Society and Esteem of its excellent Institution, than

> Gentlemen
> Your most obliged
> & most obed t. Servant
> B. Franklin[6]

Another letter from the same collection is dated London, November 7, 1773, and addressed to Dr. Brownrigg. Like the one to the Royal Society, it shows Franklin's human touch, his sense of humor, and his ability to mingle sociability with the researches of science. We quote an amusing paragraph from this letter, a letter which Professor I. Bernard Cohen rightly regards as one of the most famous of Franklin's *scientific* letters.

> I suppose Mrs. Brownrigg did not succeed in making the Parmesian Cheese, since we have heard nothing of it. But as a Philosophess, she will not be discouraged by one or two Failures.—Perhaps some Circumstance is omitted in the Receipt, which by a little more Experience she may discover.—The foreign Gentleman, who had learnt in England to boil Plum pudding, and carried home a Receipt for making it, wondered to see it brought to the Table in the Form of a Soup. The Cook declar'd he had exactly followed the Receipt. And when that came to be examined, a small but important Circumstance appeared to have been omitted. There was no Mention of the Bag.[7]

In the course of his travels and researches Franklin made the acquaintance of numerous American and European physicians, some of them great scientists in their own right. Among them were such Philadelphians as Thomas and Phineas Bond, John Redman, Benjamin Rush, William Shippen, John Morgan, Thomas Cadwallader, and John Jones; the New Yorkers Cadwallader Colden and John Bard; the Bostonian Benjamin Waterhouse; the Englishmen Sir John Pringle, Sir William Watson, John Fothergill, William Heberden, Edward Bancroft, William Hewson, John Lettson (who wrote a life of Franklin); the Scottish doctors Alex Monro and William Cullen; the French Jacques Barbeu-Duborg, Joseph Ignace Guillotin (who investigated mesmerism with Franklin), and Félix Vicq-d'Azyr. In

Vienna there was Dr. Jan Ingenhousz, the court physician to Maria Theresa and Joseph II. Ingenhousz was a special friend of Franklin's; they not only corresponded with each other but also traveled together in England and in France.[8] In one letter to Ingenhousz, that of May 4, 1779, from Passy, Franklin conceived of science and learning as transcending in some cases mere national boundaries, political disputes, and even wars. The letter in question discusses the Northern Lights and mentions Dr. Priestley, Benjamin Vaughan, and the Royal Society.[9] Theodore Diller writes that Franklin took a "deep interest in medical matters" during his entire life.[10] This interest found expression in his correspondence with many of these physicians.

One of the earliest essays Franklin wrote on a scientific subject is that on earthquakes (1737). Another, which appeared in pamphlet form, is *An Account of the New-Invented Pennsylvania Fireplaces* (1742). Governor Thomas read this pamphlet and offered Franklin a patent for the "sole vending" of these stoves. But Franklin declined it "from a principle which has ever weighed with me on such occasions; viz., *that as we enjoy great advantages from the inventions of others, we should be glad of an opportunity to serve others by any invention of ours, and this we should do freely and generously.*"[11] A London ironmonger took this same stove, made a few minor changes in it, and reaped a small fortune from it. This same fate befell several of Franklin's inventions, according to his statement in the *Autobiography.*[12]

Readers interested in Franklin's representative scientific writings should see his letter to Ingenhousz *On the Causes and Cure of Smoky Chimneys,* Franklin's description of a new stove for burning pitcoal and consuming all the smoke; his letter to Alphonsus Le Roy on maritime observations; his description of a process to be used in making large sheets of paper in the Chinese manner; his letters of 1749 and 1753 to Cadwallader Colden; his letter to John Perkins on whirlwinds and waterspouts; the one to the Abbé Soulavie on the formation of the earth. He wrote others to a Mr. Bodoin on magnetism and the theory of the earth; to Mr. Naire of London concerning a hygrometer (1786); to David Rittenhouse describing a new theory on light and heat; and to Dr. Kinnersley on electrical experiments (July 17, 1771).[13]

Some of Franklin's scientific writings enjoyed great popularity. From 1753 to 1769 his series of letters on electricity—

which he had sent to Peter Collinson and which had then appeared in pamphlet form in 1751—grew into a book of about five hundred pages. The enormous popularity of this book may be seen not only by its numerous editions but also by its translations—into Latin, Italian, French, and German.[14] The above-mentioned work on smoky chimneys also achieved great popularity during Franklin's own time. Republished in London in 1787, it was reviewed favorably in several different places and frequently reprinted in extract form. According to one authority its popularity arose from three things: the desire of many persons with smoky chimneys for practical information, surprise of others that a great publicist like Franklin should concern himself with such a question, and the attraction for still others of the new method of scientific reasoning (observation and induction) "which made an appeal that very mildly resembled that of the clever reasoning in a detective story."[15]

Numerous writers have commented on Franklin's excellence as a stylist in writing scientific exposition. Simplicity, perspicacity, and frankness are qualities noted by Smyth and Rufus Griswold among older writers: "Every paper is characterized by downright perspicacity of thought and forthright directness of style." "Franklin's style is in all respects admirable. That of his scientific papers, in simplicity, clearness, precision and condensation is unparalleled. Discarding the symbols of geometry, and indeed all technical language, he succeeded in presenting the most difficult problems and abstruse speculations in the shortest space, and so perspicuously that a child could perfectly understand them."[16]

The noted scientist Sir Humphrey Davy delivered the following statement about Franklin's style: "The style and manner of his publication on electricity, are almost as worthy of admiration as the doctrine it contains. He has endeavoured to remove all mystery and obscurity from the subject. He has written equally for the uninitiated and for the philosopher; and he has rendered his details amusing and perspicacious, elegant as well as simple. Science appears in his language, best adapted to display her native loveliness. He has in no instance exhibited that false dignity, by which philosophy is kept aloof from common applications."[17]

Professor I. Bernard Cohen refers to the "splendid style" of Franklin's writing in the work on electricity, suggesting that this book is available for anyone who might prefer to read it and draw his own conclusion instead of taking a hearsay report.[18] In the conclusion of his paper on waterspouts and whirlwinds Franklin himself attacks the bad writing in some scientific papers of his time, saying, "If my hypothesis is not the truth itself it is at least as naked, for I have not, with some of our learned moderns, disguised my nonsense in Greek, clothed it in algebra or adorned it with fluxions. You have it in *puris naturalibus*."[19]

The lucid and precise prose that Franklin wrote throughout his career as scientist, journalist, and statesman owed much to the style upheld by the Royal Society. Although this group was composed of scientists, it exerted a very potent influence on the language of the time; it reacted strongly against what Jorgenson calls the "clogged prose of the seventeenth century."[20] Order, simplicity, and clarity were its ideals. It opposed all forms of fanciness in language.[21] One of its members, Thomas Sprat, "urged writers 'to reject amplifications, digressions, and swellings' in favor of 'clear senses and a native easiness.' "[22] Franklin admired this kind of writing; as MacLaurin puts it, "It appears that Franklin's preference was for writers who wrote a clear, straightforward style; who had something definite to say, and who said it as lucidly as possible; who were, in short, the kind of writers most admired on both sides of the Atlantic by the men and women of the 'Age of Reason.' "[23]

As we have seen in the development of Franklin as a writer, his methods and forms of expression were "laboriously acquired in his youth, developed in all his newspaper writing, sharpened by the sayings he gathered and prepared for 'Poor Richard.' " And the style resulting from this long and assiduous preparation "undoubtedly had much to do with the wide acceptance of the results of his experiments in electricity."[24] In short, his ability to write well helped propagate the scientific ideas which were of vast importance in the history and development of modern science. But in their own right the scientific writings of Franklin also have "high and peculiar literary merit."[25] Here as elsewhere his writings were always lightened by the saving grace of sly wit and humor, as when, for example, he wrote to Cadwallader Colden, "I must own that I am much in the *Dark* about *Light*."[26]

Religious and Philosophical Tracts

IT IS APPROPRIATE that the last chapter of this book on Franklin as a writer should deal with his religious and philosophical works, for his often-stated aim in life was the accomplishment of good for mankind.

If it is true, as one writer says, that only in certain of his philosophical writings can we "see his mind at full stretch," surely we ought to consider, however briefly, a few of these writings.[1] "The total list of Franklin imprints," argues Stifler, "discloses the fact that more than seventy-five per cent were of a religious character though of course the bulk of his work, counting by pages, was of a public nature."[2] This statement may be open to question; but there can be no doubt that problems of religion, particularly of practical morality, come in for frequent mention and discussion in a great number of Franklin's works. In part, the didactic temper of the age contributed to this. Like the Austrian composer Haydn, he was so much a man of his times, so representative of the enlightenment (including its less excellent aspects), that it is impossible to separate him from the eighteenth century as a whole.

Franklin's position in religion has been characterized as similar to that of the Dissenters of his day—to people like Joseph Priestley and Richard Price.[3] Essentially, it was not far removed from modern Unitarianism. Professor V. W. Crane, however, sees Franklin as undergoing a turn from liberal to conservative Deism. "The problem of his conversion from extreme intellectual radicalism to a relatively conservative and comfortable [D]eism is . . . difficult."[4] Crane accounts for this change partly in terms of the unsettling effects Franklin had observed such ideas to have had on the actions of his friends John Collins and James Ralph. (See *Autobiography*.) Too, Franklin's mind quite naturally veered away from metaphysics, because of "his bias towards the concrete, his preference for *practical* ideas."[5] The work that best represents his earlier position—his "intellectual radicalism"—is his *Dissertation on Liberty and Necessity, Pleasure and Pain* (1725), which he wrote when only nineteen and dedicated to his friend Ralph.

One interesting source used in the composition of this dissertation was a copy of Ozell's translation of *Logic, or, the Art of Thinking*, by Arnauld and Nicole of the Port Royal group, which is now in the Philadelphia Library Company and which bears Franklin's signature.[6] The syllogistic form he used in this dissertation no doubt derived from this book; but the dissertation also shows the influence of Locke, Shaftesbury, and Anthony Collins—Deists all.[7] Finally, he quoted from Dryden's play *Oedipus* on its title page.[8]

As a journeyman printer working for Samuel Palmer's large printing establishment in London in 1725, Franklin had set up the third edition of William Wollaston's *The Religion of Nature Delineated*. Not agreeing with some of Wollaston's arguments, Franklin had composed his dissertation as a refutation of some of Wollaston's ideas. This piece won him the respect of his employer Palmer, although he did not agree with him. Franklin printed one hundred copies; distributed some to his friends; but destroyed the rest, thinking they might have a bad effect. Only two copies of the original (Yale University and the Library of Congress) are known to have survived.[9]

The dissertation is in reality an elaborate argument to the effect that justice exists in the universe. Starting with his basic assumptions that *"There is said to be a First Mover, who is called God, Maker of the Universe,"* and that *"He is said to be all-wise, all-good, all-powerful,"* he draws from them the following two axioms: *"If He is all-good, whatsoever He doth must be good"*; *"If He is all-wise, whatsoever He doth must be wise."* Then he presents the really startling conclusion, the first of several, *"If He is all-powerful, there can be nothing existing or acting in the Universe against or without his Consent; and what He consents to must be good, because He is good; therefore Evil doth not exist."*

This was no small feat for a young man of nineteen, to disprove the existence of all the evil in the world. Franklin does not deny that there were things in the world to which we give the *name* of evil, such as "Pain, Sickness, Want, Theft, Murder, etc." But he does demonstrate in the second part of his dissertation that these things to which we give the name of evil might also be accounted for by another principle—that of pleasure and pain, it being a common human tendency to call "evil" anything painful and "good" anything pleasant.

Of course, starting with such assumptions, especially the one concerning the omnipotence of God, it was not too difficult to dispose easily of the much-debated question of his age—that of liberty or necessity, the freedom of the human will. Franklin concluded that since God was all-powerful there could be no such thing as freedom of the will, a slightly different answer from that of Jonathan Edwards, who had argued for limited freedom of choice within the well-bounded destiny mapped out for man by God. Then Franklin—by defining pleasure and pain in relation to each other as balancing effects and by concluding that every creature always received equivalent quantities of each—demonstrated that every one of God's creatures received justice on earth. Therefore a puritanical conception of an after-life in which the wrongs of this life would be righted was really unnecessary. Justice, he concluded, did exist.

For the benefit of readers who might think some of Franklin's youthful reasoning a little rash, we add that at one point in the dissertation—following Wollaston's principle that "Every Action which is done according to *Truth,* is good; and every Action contrary to Truth, is evil"—Franklin defends the stealing of horses, still quoting from Wollaston.

"To act according to Truth is to use and esteem every Thing as what it is, etc. Thus if *A* steals a Horse from *B,* and rides away upon him, he uses him not as what he is in Truth, *viz.* the Property of another, but as his own, which is contrary to Truth, and therefore *evil.*" But, as this Gentleman himself says, (Sect. I. Prop. VI) "In order to judge rightly what any Thing is, it must be consider'd not only what it is in one Respect, but also what it may be in any other Respect; and the whole Description of the Thing ought to be taken in": So in this Case it ought to be consider'd that *A* is naturally a *covetous* Being, feeling an Uneasiness in the want of *B's* Horse, which produces an Inclination for stealing him, stronger than his Fear of Punishment for so doing. This is *Truth* likewise, and *A* acts according to it when he steals the horse. Besides, if it is prov'd to be a *Truth,* that *A* has not Power over his own Actions, it will be indisputable that he acts according to Truth, and impossible he should do otherwise.

But even at the age of nineteen Franklin was clever enough to value common sense more than rigid logicality, for with characteristic humor he adds: "I would not be understood by this to encourage or defend Theft; 'tis only for the sake of the Argument, and will certainly have no *ill Effect*. The Order and Course of Things will not be affected by Reasoning of this Kind; and 'tis as just and necessary, and as much according to Truth, for *B* to dislike and punish the Theft of his Horse, as it is for *A* to steal him."

Years later Franklin felt guilty that this dissertation might have been responsible for disturbing the religious principles of his friend James Ralph. But Ralph's principles were doubtless upset by something else, for previous to the writing of Franklin's dissertation, Ralph had abandoned his wife and child in Philadelphia.[10]

Professor Aldridge refers to the "logical weakness" of Franklin's dissertation, but he is not specific about what that weakness consists of beyond assuming that God should provide us with an excess of pleasure rather than a mere balance of pleasure and pain. This seems not only an unwarranted assumption on Aldridge's part but one not consistent with the basic assumptions and reasonings of Franklin.[11]

Franklin was not through with his pleasure-pain principle. Thirty-one years later in a letter of condolence to Elizabeth Hubbard on the occasion of his brother John's death, he again adverts to it. Also, the editors of the Franklin papers call attention to an essay (the manuscript of which is in the Pennsylvania Historical Society Library) entitled *On the Providence of God in the Government of the World,* which exhibits reasoning reminiscent of that Franklin employed in his dissertation. The presumed date of the manuscript is 1732.[12]

Franklin's position as a traditional Deist rather than a freethinker became strengthened with the passage of time, and he became more conservative with respect to religion. The undated (although later) essay entitled *An Arabian Tale,* for example, is strongly Deistic in its conclusion, with its grand concept of the natural chain of being extending from "an elephant down to an oyster."

Another early document revealing Franklin's religious position is his *Articles of Belief and Acts of Religion,* dated November 20, 1728, and alluded to in the *Autobiography.* The heading of this manuscript states that it is in two parts, but the second part has not been found.[13] The first part begins with a statement of first principles, the belief in one supreme God, "Author and Father of the Gods themselves." Following the aforementioned idea of the chain of being, Franklin posits in it a hierarchy both below and above man. Next, he describes the vast universe and the small place man holds in it: "When I stretch my Imagination thro' and beyond our System of Planets, beyond the visible fix'd Stars themselves into that Space that is every Way infinite, and conceive it fill'd with Suns like ours, each with a Chorus of Worlds for ever moving around him then this little Ball on which we move, seems, even in my narrow Imagination to be almost Nothing, and my self less than nothing, and of no sort of Consequence." Man is therefore vain, argues Franklin, to suppose that God pays attention to him or that He expects or requires praise from man, He being "INFINITELY ABOVE IT." Nevertheless man has within him "something like a natural Principle" that inclines him to worship. Franklin therefore concludes that it seems required of him to "pay Divine Regards to SOMETHING."

Each of the numerous Gods above man may be either (a) immortal or (b) changeable after many years. But each is wise, good, and powerful. Franklin singles out "that particular wise and good God, who is the Author and Owner of our System" as the object of his devotion; and he conceives this God as having passions like ours. He also cares for us, is pleased by our Praise, and offended by our neglect. In addition to praise, this God requires *virtue*, or good deeds. This God also takes pleasure in the *happiness* of his creatures. This God is not offended, argues Franklin, by the "pleasant Exercises and innocent Delights" of his children. But for them to be really happy they must be *virtuous*. Therefore, he concludes, man not only must praise this God continually but also must perform virtuous actions.

It is obvious that Franklin had conceived of a kind of polytheism with a separate God governing each of innumerable systems. This might be thought inconsistent with his statement that he believed in one supreme God. But he explicitly states that this one supreme God was "Author and Father of the Gods themselves." It was apparently to one of these lesser Gods that he addressed his daily liturgy.

In reality, the *Articles of Belief* represented a program for "daily self-examination in the virtues."[14] He described it in the *Autobiography* as "a little Liturgy or Form of Prayer for my own private Use."[15] Disgusted by the lack of "morality" in the sermons of a Presbyterian minister in Philadelphia to whose support he contributed, Franklin had decided to invent his own liturgy and go no more to "the public assemblies."[16] The *Articles of Belief* were his liturgy. By "morality," Franklin meant the very thing that some genteel modern churchgoers sometimes censure in their most courageous preachers—the application of the gospel to the dirty worlds of ward-heeling politics, cut-throat economics, and tradition-sanctioned racism. In religion, as elsewhere, Franklin was eminently practical and eminently rational.

The "Adoration," or first third of Franklin's liturgy, followed the statement of first principles. It required the worshipper first to put himself into a proper state of mind by a brief preliminary prayer for God's favor. Then came the six-point statement praising God, followed by suggestions for reading and meditation. These in turn were followed by the singing of a long hymn taken from Milton's "Paradise Lost" (V, 153-56, 160-204).

The second third, "Petition," was made up of a preliminary petition to God to help the worshipper to avoid vice and to embrace virtue. Appended to this petition were fourteen other short petitions having to do with the acquisition of virtue and each was followed by the refrain, "Help me, O Father."

The last third, "Thanks," took the form of a short prayer, similar in structure to the petitions. Each of the four parts, which were similar in length to the petitions, was followed by the refrain, "Good God, I thank thee."

Rather different from the elaborate religious ritual of *The Articles of Belief* were Franklin's attempts at modernizing and otherwise improving the language of the King James version of the Bible. *The Lord's Prayer* represents such an experiment. In this work (*circa* 1779) he gives reasons for each of his revisions. The revisions tend toward greater conciseness, improved clarity, or better modern idiom. Sometimes he did not especially improve, but merely imitated biblical language. Two works which show this kind of imitation are *A Parable Against Persecution* and *A Parable on Brotherly Love*, both of them heavily didactic. Although the former was printed by Franklin on the Passy press and widely publicized by his friend Joseph Antoine Cerutti in France, it can hardly be called a *bagatelle* because of its unrelieved seriousness. Franklin nevertheless regarded it as one of *his bagatelles*. But it is simply an imitation of biblical language and, as already noted, was frequently used as a kind of guessing game—in short, a parlor hoax. The *Parable Against Persecution,* printed *circa* 1759 in London,[17] has a textual history too long and complicated for present discussion.[18] What it and its companion parable on brotherly love show about Franklin's writing beyond mere imitation, is his already-noted tendency to analogize and to moralize. For the parable against persecution concerns the lack of religious toleration displayed by Abraham in receiving into his tent a stranger and afterward driving him out when he discovers the stranger does not worship the same god as he does. At midnight the Lord appears to Abraham to ask about the stranger and to remind him that since He had tolerated Abraham's rebellious spirit for 198 years, surely Abraham should tolerate the stranger for one night. After Abraham chases after the stranger and rights things, God promises not only to punish Abraham for his sin by forcing upon his children a period of wandering for four hundred years in a strange land but also to reward him for his repentance by showering on his children power, "gladness of heart," and "much substance."

The *Parable on Brotherly Love* concerns the repayment of good for evil in the case of the borrowing of an axe by the sons of Jacob. Reuben had refused to lend his axe to any of his three brothers—Simeon, Levi, or Judah. When Reuben lost his axe and the other three each acquired one, Reuben attempted to borrow from those whom he had refused to help with these results: "Simeon answered him, saying, 'Thou woudest not lend me thine axe, therefore I will not lend thee mine.' . . . And Levi reproached him, saying, 'Thou woudest not lend me thine axe when I desired it, but I will be better than thou, and will lend thee mine.'" Shamed, Reuben refused to accept the loan under these conditions. Only Judah loaned his axe with a fine, generous, and forgiving spirit. When Reuben thanked him and said that Judah was indeed his true brother whom he would always love, Judah responded, "Let us also love our other brethren; behold, are we not all of one blood?" When Joseph reported this conduct of the brothers to his father Jacob, the latter replied, "Reuben did wrong, but he repented. Simeon also did wrong; and Levi was not altogether blameless. . . . But the heart of Judah is princely. Judah hath the soul of a king. His father's children shall bow down before him, and he shall rule over his brethren."

One of Franklin's most interesting experiments with matters of language in a religious work relates to his abridgement of the *Book of Common Prayer*.[19] During the summer of 1773 in England he visited Lord Le Despencer's country residence and there undertook, supposedly with the help of the "noble lord," to improve this well-known liturgy. The preface to this abridgement, written entirely by Franklin, objects to the numerous repetitions and great length of the morning and evening services and especially to the repetitions of the same prayer in the same service, pointing out that Christ had given us "a short prayer as an example" and had "censured the heathen for thinking to be heard because of much speaking." His argument follows practical lines, indicating that it is unhealthy for very old people to remain "for hours in a cold church especially in the winter season" and stating that young people, as well as tradesmen and others, would be more drawn to a shorter service. He omitted the First Lesson entirely, but retained the Second, on grounds that the teaching of the New Testament was "of more immediate importance to Christians." He also shortened the services of Communion, Infant Baptism, Confirmation, Matrimony, and Burial of the Dead. The latter he found "very solemn and moving," but he thought that, "to preserve the health and lives of the living," "this service ought particularly to be shortened." He omitted entirely the Commination: "all cursing mankind, is, we think, best omitted." And he suggested that the Catechism as phrased by eminent divines was "not so well adapted to the capacities of children as might be wished. Only those plain answers, therefore, which express our duty towards God, and our duty towards our neighbor, are retained here." In these and other revisions his tone was modest; he acknowledged the "excellence of our present Liturgy" and added that, "though we have shortened it, we have not presumed to alter a word in the remaining text."

Turning from this practical-minded preface to a simple holiday greeting, we see how heavy-handed Franklin's moralizing could sometimes be. The following example of a Christmas card takes the form of a sermon by Poor Richard in the 1741 almanac: "Let no pleasure tempt thee, no profit allure thee, no ambition corrupt thee, no example sway thee, no persuasion move thee, to do anything which thou knowest to be evil;

so shalt thou always live jollily; for a good conscience is a continual Christmas."

As a writer of religious and philosophical works, Franklin expressed himself in a style which caused one anonymous English critic of the year 1806 to note "the tone of familiarity, of good-will, and homely jocularity; the plain and printed illustrations; the short sentences, made up of short words; and the strong sense, clear information, and obvious conviction of the author himself."[20] A more modern American writer sees Franklin as "a kind of Socrates in small clothes" who preserved ancient irony, the dialogue, and ingenious exposition, but who was incapable of the love of wisdom for its own sake because of his incorrigible flair for the practical.[21]

Several of Franklin's most characteristic utterances on religious topics pop up in his correspondence, and we quote some of his letters here for this reason. In a letter to Priestley (London, September 19, 1772) Franklin mentions "Moral or Prudential Algebra," attempting to make "morality" into an exact science like mathematics. Similarly, in writing (Passy, February 6, 1780) to Dr. Richard Price, a London clergyman, Franklin says: "We make daily improvements in *natural,* there is one I wish to see in *moral* philosophy; the discovery of a plan that would induce and oblige nations to settle their disputes without first cutting one another's throats. When will human reason be sufficiently improved to see the advantage of this? When will men be convinced that even successful wars at length become misfortune to those who unjustly commenced them, and who triumphed blindly in their success, not seeing all its consequences?" In a letter to Sir Joseph Banks in the year 1783 (Passy, July 27), he writes, "In my opinion, *there never was a good war, or a bad peace.* What vast additions to the conveniences and comforts of life might mankind have acquired if the money spent in wars had been employed in works of public utility!"

For further comment about Franklin's ideas of war we should note a letter written (Passy, June 7, 1782) by Franklin to Priestley in which he depicts an angel coming to earth and mistaking it for hell because a war is in progress. The angel's guide, however, tells him that it is really the earth because "Devils never treat one another in this cruel manner; they have more sense, and more of what men vainly call humanity."

There exists an undated letter from Franklin to Tom Paine

(Sparks, *Works*, X, 281-82), warning him against an extremist position in religion. But Paine failed to heed this warning in his fiery and unorthodox Deist production *The Age of Reason*. By this time Franklin had become more orthodox and conservative in his Deism.

Six weeks before he died, Franklin wrote to Ezra Stiles, the president of Yale, a kind of final credo of his religious position: "I believe in one God, Creator of the Universe. That He governs it by his Providence. That He ought to be worshipped. That the most acceptable service we render to Him is doing good to His other children. That the soul of man is immortal and will be treated with justice in another life respecting its conduct in this. These I take to be fundamental principles of all sound religion, and I regard them, as you do, in whatever sect I meet with them."[22] In this same letter Franklin expresses doubt as to the divinity of Christ, as did Paine and other Deists. But Franklin acknowledged that Christ's system of morals was the "best the world ever saw or is likely to see."[23]

The greatness of Franklin as a religious writer is nowhere better expressed than in his attitude of broad tolerance toward sectarianism. "All sects here [Philadelphia], and we have a great variety, have experienced my good will in assisting them with subscriptions for building their new places of worship; and as I have never opposed any of their doctrines, I hope to go out of the world in peace with them all."[24]

Two footnotes on this statement will show that he practiced what he preached. In 1776 Franklin went to Canada with Father John Carroll, his good Catholic friend, who told him of the plight of the Catholic Church in America because of its lack of a bishop. Franklin wrote the Pope and was instrumental in effecting the appointment of Carroll as Superior of the Catholic Clergy in America with many powers of a bishop, in July, 1784. According to one source, Franklin was deeply perturbed over the religious persecutions that existed in some of the American colonies.[25]

On January 29, 1956, there appeared an announcement in the *New York Times* to the effect that Congregation Mikveh Israel had held on this particular day a special service for Benjamin Franklin, who had led a list of subscribers to save its first synagogue from the auction block when it was hard pressed for money immediately following the Revolution.[26]

CHAPTER *9*

Conclusion: A Reassessment of Franklin as a Writer

FRANKLIN'S REPUTATION as a prose stylist is as difficult to assess today as ever. The critics who have treated the subject of his style—and they are legion—show an incorrigible tendency to load his brows with ponderous, and often tritely worded, bouquets.[1] After all, Franklin is a national idol. But honesty in literary criticism demands something more than mere unqualified praise for even the best of writers. It also demands something more than the impassioned defense or ardent rebuttal that usually greets any small adverse comment about Franklin's style, however stupid. Jeffrey's statement in the *Edinburgh Review* for July, 1806, for example, asserts that Franklin could not be expected to write with great polish because of his early education.[2] Such a statement neglects the excellent quality of the *Courant* library and Franklin's early association with those sophisticated satirists. The term "early education" needs defining, of course.

Some qualities of Franklin's style that have been frequently noted by the critics include the following: order, brevity, simplicity, clarity, facility, wit, humor, liveliness, rustic masculinity, grace, urbanity, variety and common sense.[3] Tyler mentions "melody" as a characteristic. While Franklin himself had a musical ear and played the harp, guitar, and violin, his style does not impress us as "melodic,"—a word that conjures up the shades of Milton, Dryden, Coleridge, Poe, and Swinburne.[4] McMaster surprises us by saying that in Franklin's writing "A metaphor, a simile, a figure of speech of any kind, is rarely to be met with."[5] Many of Franklin's satires belie this statement. One could add many more examples of inaccuracies such as these and such as Jackson's mention of Franklin's "short words and sentences."[6] On occasion Franklin could write a sentence like this one taken from *Some Account of the Pennsylvania Hospital*.

About the end of the year 1750 some persons who had frequent opportunities of observing the distress of such distempered poor as from time to time came to Philadelphia for the advice and assistance of the physicians and surgeons of that city; how difficult it was for them to procure suitable lodgings and other conveniences proper for their respective cases and how expensive the providing good and careful nurses and other attendants for want whereof many must suffer greatly, and some probably perish, that might otherwise have been restored to health and comfort and become useful to themselves, their families, and the public for many years after; and considering moreover that even the poor inhabitants of this city though they had homes were therein but badly accommodated in sickness and could not be so well and so easily taken care of in their separate habitations as they might be in one convenient house, under one inspection and in the hands of skillful practitioners; and several of the inhabitants of the province who unhappily became disordered in their senses wandered about to the terror of their neighbors, there being no place (except the house of correction) in which they might be confined and subjected to proper management for their recovery, and that house was by no means fitted for such purposes; did charitably consult together and confer with their friends and acquaintances on the best means of relieving the distressed under those circumstances.

Moreover, in another misleading generalization, Edmund Gosse describes Franklin's style as "notoriously graceful and charming."[7] But the following sentence from *Reflections on Courtship and Marriage* shows that Franklin could write equally well in the rough school of realism fathered by Defoe:

Let us survey the morning dress of some women. Downstairs they come, pulling up their ungartered, dirty stockings; slipshod, with naked heels peeping out; no stays or other decent conveniency, but all flip-flop; a sort of clout thrown about their neck, half on and half off, with the frowsy hair hanging in sweaty ringlets, staring like Medusa with her serpents; shrugging up her petticoats, that are sweeping the ground and scarce tied on; hand[s] unwashed, teeth furred and eyes crusted—but I beg your pardon, I'll go no farther with this sluttish picture, which I am afraid has already turned your stomach.

This is hardly the same style as that of *The Ephemera*, the style praised by Jorgenson for its "curious felicity."[8] It is, rather, "the flexible style of a writer who has learned the craft of expression by studying and imitating the virtues of many writers."[9] To which we must add that the great emotional range one critic has noted in Franklin's writing during the Revolution has parallels in his equally great stylistic differences, the latter being determined by the multifarious occasions, purposes, and periods of his career as a writer.[10] For this reason the generalizations of many critical statements about Franklin's style can usually be easily refuted by reference to a different kind of work or to a work from a different period of his very extensive career.

As a writer Franklin generally concerned himself greatly with the problem of *order*, not only in the main parts of his composition but also in the smaller and finer elements of the sentence itself. The humor (in *Poor Richard's Almanack* and elsewhere), the plain direct diction, the common sense, the rhythmical ease (what he called "smoothness"), the turn and cadence of his finely wrought phrases and sentences, the art that conceals art—these were all constituent parts of the style which in the last analysis was the man, a man of a shrewd, inventive, practical mind who had mastered numerous genres of writing.

Franklin is often enough credited with helping to found a noble political tradition in this country. We forget that he established a tradition of humor and journalistic writing that is peculiarly American. His writing in this tradition was usually distinguished in style, taste, and idiom. In a letter to Hume (September 27, 1760) he wrote: "I hope with you, that we shall always in America make the best English . . . our standard, and I believe it will be so."

Notes and References

If the source is recorded in the bibliography, the footnote is listed only by author and page below. Where more than one work by the author has been used, abbreviated titles have been added for clarity.

Chapter One

1. *Diary of Cotton Mather* (Boston, 1912), II, 639.
2. Worthington C. Ford, p. 346.
3. Labaree and Bell, *The Papers of Benjamin Franklin,* I, 8. Hereafter, *Papers of B.F.* See Ford, p. 349, for other contributors and the number of pieces each contributed, supposedly written by Franklin himself in the margins of the *Courant* (p. 340).
4. Ford, p. 350.
5. Unsigned article, "On the Character of B. Franklin," [Boston] *Monthly Anthology* (Dec. 1806), p. 663.
6. *Ibid.,* p. 664.
7. Davy, p. 6.
8. Ford, p. 341.
9. *Ibid.*
10. Cook, p. 18.
11. *Ibid.,* p. 18.
12. Cook, p. 27.
13. P. 343.
14. *Papers of B.F.,* I, 51-52.
15. Ford, pp. 337n., 350. *Papers of B.F.,* I, 8, for the date of the first issue.
16. Ford, p. 352.
17. Ford, p. 340.
18. *Papers of B.F.,* I, 47-48. The case of James Franklin was considered by the grand jury in May, 1723, but he was not indicted and was soon released.
19. Cook, pp. 13-14.
20. *Ibid.,* p. 12.
21. *Ibid.,* p. 21. See also pp. 20-21 for a more complete list of the books in the *Courant* library.
22. *Ibid.,* p. 23.
23. Sanford, p. 52.
24. Tyler, *Hist. of Am. Lit.,* II, 228.
25. Pp. 227-28.
26. Smyth, *Phila. Magazines,* p. 28.
27. Nye, *Benjamin Franklin's Autobiography and Other Writings,* p. 57. Hereafter, *Autobiog.*

28. *Autobiog.,* pp. 59-60.

29. Nunally Lawton, "Benjamin Franklin, the Newspaperman," *Editor and Publisher,* LVI, No. 33 (Jan. 12, 1924), 3.

30. *Autobiog.,* p. 57.

31. Albert H. Smyth, "Franklin's Place in Literature," *Book News,* XXIV (Jan. 1906), 312.

32. Griswold in Sanford, p. 47.

33. *Ibid.*

34. Crane, *Benjamin Franklin, Englishman and American,* pp. 50-51.

35. *Ibid.,* p. 57.

36. Meyer, *Free Trade in Ideas,* p. 87.

37. *Ibid.*

38. *Ibid.*

39. *Ibid.,* p. 88.

40. *Speech in the Constitutional Convention on the Subject of Salaries 2 June 1787.*

41. P. 60.

42. Farrand, "Self-Portraiture," pp. 407, 414. Hall, p. 78.

43. This quote from a letter to Francis Hopkinson reveals that as late as 1782 Franklin was concerned with the abusive nature of the American press. See Smyth, *The Writings of Benjamin Franklin,* p. 647. Hereafter, *Writings.* See *Papers of B.F.,* I, 370, for a letter in the *Pa. Gaz.,* dated April 11, 1734, commending Franklin for keeping his paper "pretty clear of SCANDAL." See "Apology for Printers" in the June 10, 1731, issue for an even earlier statement against vice, immorality, corrupt taste, and personal defamation in publishing. (*Papers of B.F.,* I, 194.)

44. *Papers of B.F.,* I, 157.

45. Aldridge, "Franklin and Jonathan Edwards," p. 163.

46. *Papers of B.F.,* I, 164, 184-89.

47. *Ibid.,* I, 271.

48. *Ibid.,* I, 271-80.

49. *Ibid.,* I, 219.

50. *Ibid.,* I, 265.

51. *Ibid.,* I, 274.

52. *Ibid.,* I, 219.

53. See *ibid.,* I, 237-48 and Davy, pp. 43-45.

54. Crane, *B. F.'s Letters to the Press,* p. xiv.

55. *Papers of B.F.,* I, 158-59.

56. *Ibid.,* I, 282.

57. Mott, I, 24.

58. *Papers of B.F.,* II, 265.

59. *Ibid.,* II, 305.

60. *The Philadelphia Magazines,* p. 26.

61. *Papers of B.F.*, II, 317-20, 322-27. See also Mott, I, 73-77.

62. Mott, I, 24. See also *Papers of B.F.*, II, 267n.

63. Jorgenson, "Sidelights on Franklin's Principles of Rhetoric," p. 219.

64. *Writings*, II, 242-43, and VIII, 448n.

65. Marie Katherine Jackson, *Outlines of the Literary History of Colonial Pennsylvania* (Lancaster, 1906), p. 64.

66. Cf. Sparks, *The Works of Benjamin Franklin* (Boston, 1840), I, 532, (hereafter *Works*) and E. A. and G. L. Duyckinck, *Cyclopedia of American Literature* (Philadelphia, 1875), I, 120.

67. *Autobiog.*, pp. 10, 12-14, 19, 38-40. Robert or Richard Burton, according to Davy, pp. 146-47, was a penname for Nathaniel Crouch (c. 1632—c. 1725), a popular writer and publisher of historical works. These works were published as late as 1810. See Davy, pp. 163, 163n, for further information on Greenwood's *Grammar*.

68. MacLaurin, pp. 11-12.

69. *Ibid.*, p. 17-18.

70. *Ibid.*, pp. 19, 15.

71. MacLaurin, p. 2.

72. *Ibid.*, p. 20.

73. Newcomb, pp. 162-63.

74. *Autobiog.*, p. 12.

75. *Davy*, pp. 148-49.

76. Lucas, p. 210.

77. Jorgenson, pp. 211-12.

78. Davy, p. 2.

79. Davy, pp. 56-58, 160-62. Cf. *Papers of B.F.*, I, 328.

80. *Ibid.*, p. 153.

81. *Ibid.*

82. MacLaurin, p. 26.

83. Jorgenson, p. 209; Davy, p. 165.

84. *Ibid.*, pp., 168-69. See *Autobiog.*, p. 14, for *The Art of Thinking*.

85. Davy, p. 167.

86. *Ibid.*, pp. 167-68.

87. P. 168.

88. *Papers of B.F.*, II, 194.

89. *Ibid.*, I, 328.

90. *Autobiog.*, p. 13.

91. *Ibid.*

92. Arnold Mulder, "Benjamin Franklin: Teacher of Composition," *Coll. English*, III (Feb. 1942), 482. Pope's "An Essay on Man," IV, 49.

93. *Writings*, I, 37. Quoted by Smyth.

94. *Papers of B.F.*, I, 329-30.

95. *Ibid.*, I, 330.

96. *Ibid.*, I, 256.

97. *Writings*, X, 51.

98. *Papers of B.F.*, I, 99.

99. Davy, p. 151.

100. *Writings*, II, 391.

101. *Papers of B.F.*, I, 329.

102. *Ibid.* All quotations for this paragraph are found in the essay *On Literary Style* (*Papers of B.F.*, I, 329-30.)

103. *Papers of B.F.*, II, 146-49. All quotations for this paragraph are from this essay.

104. *Ibid.*, I, 331.

105. *Ibid.*, Jorgenson, "Sidelights on Franklin's Principles of Rhetoric," p. 217, characterizes Franklin's literary purposes as "basically motivated by a dominant ethicism."

106. *Papers of B.F.*, I, 328.

107. Anonymous, "The Franklin Papers," *Life Magazine*, XLVII (Oct. 5, 1959), 105.

108. Davy, p. 187; Crane, "Three Fables," p. 501; Van Doren, "First American Man of Letters, p. 295.

109. Van Doren in Sanford, p. 96.

110. Van Doren, "First American Man of Letters," p. 284.

111. Farrand, p. 410.

112. See, for example, a manuscript in the library of the Hist. Soc. of Pa. printed in the *Penna. Gaz.* (July 12, 1733) and appearing under the title of "On Ill-Natured Speaking" in *Papers of B.F.*, I, 327n.

113. Donald Grant Mitchell, *American Lands and Letters* (New York, 1887), I, 98.

114. P. 225.

115. Baender, p. 267.

116. *Ibid.*

117. *Ibid.*

118. *Ibid.*

119. *Ibid.*

120. *Ibid.*

121. G. Brown Goode, "The Literary Labors of Benjamin Franklin," *Proc. APS*, XXVIII (April 1890), 4.

Chapter Two

1. Van Doren, "First American Man of Letters," p. 283, and Sanford, p. 98, say so categorically.

2. H. A. Beers, *An Outline Sketch of American Literature* (New York, 1887), p. 48; W. C. Bronson, *A Short History of Amer-*

ican Literature (Boston, 1910), p. 56; Wm. Cabell Bruce, *Benjamin Franklin Self-Revealed* (New York, 1917), p. 499; John B. McMaster, *Benjamin Franklin As a Man of Letters* (Boston, 1887), p. 282; and Max Farrand, "Benjamin Franklin's Memoirs, "*Huntington Lib. Bull.*, X (Oct. 1936), 49.

3. Oral S. Coad, *The Autobiography of Benjamin Franklin* (New York, 1927), p. xx. See also Beers, p. 48; Tyler, *Hist. of Am. Lit.*, II, 252; Rufus B. Griswold, *The Prose Writers of America* (Phila., 1847), p. 58; and Smyth, "Franklin's Place in Literature," p. 314.

4. Farrand, "Self-Portraiture; The Autobiography," p. 411.

5. Goode, p. 6.

6. Anonymous, "On the Literary Character of Benjamin Franklin," *Monthly Anthology* [Boston,] (Dec. 1806), p. 668.

7. *Ibid.*, p. iv.

8. Crane, *Benjamin Franklin, Englishman and American*, p. 48.

9. Farrand, "Self-Portraiture," p. 417. Cf. Edward Engel, *Geschichte der nordamerikanischen Literatur* (Leipzig, 1897), p. 11. Engel regards Franklin as an outstanding representative of American life in the eighteenth century—an apostle of utility, frugality, and shrewdness.

10. Sanford, p. 72.

11. *Ibid.*, p. 71.

12. *Ibid.*, p. 72.

13. *Ibid.*

14. Mark Twain, "The Late Benjamin Franklin," in *Sketches New and Old*, Vol. XIX of *The Writings of Mark Twain*, Hillcrest, ed. (New York, 1899), p. 214.

15. P. 103.

16. *Autobiog.*, p. x.

17. *Ibid.*, p. 100.

18. *Ibid.*, p. 111.

19. P. 70 for both quotations.

20. *Ibid.*

21. *Ibid.*

22. Van Doren, *Autobiographical Writings*, p. 411.

23. *Ibid.*, p. 216.

24. Farrand, "B. F.'s Memoirs," pp. 54, 55.

25. *Autobiog.*, p. xxi; Farrand, "Self-Portraiture," p. 407.

26. *Autobiog.*, p. xxi.

27. Goode, p. 18, explains its goodness in terms of Franklin's "intimate connection with English literary society," whatever this may mean.

28. Farrand, "B. F.'s Memoirs," p. 55.

29. *Ibid.*

30. *Ibid.*, p. 61.

31. *Ibid.*, p. 57.
32. *Ibid.*
33. Farrand, "Self-Portraiture," p. 412.
34. *Ibid.*, for this and the following quote.
35. *Autobiog.*, p. xxi.
36. *Ibid.*
37. *Ibid.*
38. Farrand, "Self-Portraiture," pp. 412-13. "Throughout all the second part one feels a greater emphasis than was noticeable in the first installment that others might well profit by his example." P. 413.
39. *Ibid.*
40. *Ibid.*
41. See Van Doren, *Autobiographical Writings,* pp. 688, 701; Nye, *Autobiog.,* p. xxi; Farrand, "B. F.'s Memoirs," p. 61.
42. Van Doren, *Autobiographical Writings,* pp. 701, 702.
43. *Autobiog.*, p. xxii.
44. Farrand, "B. F.'s Memoirs," *loc. cit.,* p. 61.
45. *Ibid.*
46. *Ibid.*
47. Farrand, "Self-Portraiture," p. 414.
48. Van Doren, *Autobiographical Writings,* pp. v, 777, 779-80.
49. For the history of the MSS of the *Autobiography,* see Van Doren's *Autobiog. Writings,* pp. 777-79; Farrand's "Self-Portraiture," p. 414; and Farrand's "B. F.'s Memoirs," pp. 49-77.
50. Farrand, "Self-Portraiture," p. 49.
51. *Autobiog.*, p. ix.
52. *Ibid.*, Farrand, "Self-Portraiture," pp. 411-12, advances the belief that Franklin was refused social recognition by aristocratic Philadelphia. If this is true, it does not seem to have bothered him much. He was too busy with more important things. Farrand also notes that Franklin's fondness for women and children, a very human and social part of his life, comes out in his personal letters but not in the *Autobiography.*
53. Van Doren, "First American Man of Letters," p. 296.
54. Van Doren, *Autobiographical Writings,* p. v. See also pp. 306-29, 347-99, and 514-83.
55. *Ibid.*, p. v.
56. J. Bennett Nolan, *Benjamin Franklin in Scotland and Ireland* (Philadelphia, 1938), p. 6.
57. Coad, p. vii.
58. *Papers of B. F.,* I, 54.
59. *Ibid.; Autobiography,* pp. 39-40.
60. *Autobiog.*, p. 97.
61. See *Papers of B. F.,* II, 290n, for details.
62. Crane, *Benjamin Franklin, Englishman and American,* p. 139.

63. *Autobiog.* (Nye), p. xi.

64. *Ibid.*, p. vii.

65. *Ibid.*, p. 102. See for further comments on this quality of scientific detachment, among many others, Farrand, "Self-Portraiture," pp. 408, 409, 417, and Robert Chambers, *Handbook of American Literature* (Philadelphia, c.1856), p. 27.

66. P. xii.

67. Coad, p. xviii.

68. Anonymous review of Bigelow's *Life of Benjamin Franklin* (extracted from the *Edinburgh Review*, April, 1880) in Yale Library pamphlet entitled *Benjamin Franklin, 1880*, p. 345.

69. Dixon Wecter, ed., *Benjamin Franklin's Autobiography* (New York, 1948), p. iv. Like Nye (see *supra*) Wecter objects that Franklin's preoccupation with the early part of his life, along with the incompleteness of the book as a whole, has led to an oversimplified image of Franklin in the *Autobiography*.

70. Van Doren, *Meet Dr. Franklin*, p. 5. The journal of an ocean voyage that Franklin kept during his crossing from London to Philadelphia (July 22, 1726-Oct. 11, 1726) is one example of an important part of Franklin's life that is not included in the *Autobiography*. See *Papers of B. F.*, I.

71. Van Doren, "The First American Man of Letters," p. 296.

72. Farrand, "Self-Portraiture," p. 407.

73. *Cyclopedia of American Literature* (New York, 1856), I, 107. All quotations in this paragraph are from this source.

74. James O'Donnell Bennett, in a pamphlet entitled "Best Sellers of the Ages—*The Autobiography of Benjamin Franklin,*" (Chicago: The Franklin Co., n.d.), taken from the Chicago *Tribune* (Sept. 17, 1922), p. 10.

75. Smyth, "Franklin's Place in Literature," p. 314.

76. Van Doren, "First American Man of Letters," p. 296.

77. *Ibid.*

78. *Papers of B. F.*, I, xxxiv.

79. I. Bernard Cohen, *Benjamin Franklin: His Contribution*, p. 68; Henry S. Pancoast, *An Introduction to American Literature* (New York, 1898), p. 90.

80. MacLaurin, p. 34; Francis Underwood, *The Builders of American Literature* (Boston, 1893), p. 46.

81. *Autobiog.*, pp. vii-ix.

82. *Ibid.*, p. viii.

83. MacLaurin, p. 34.

84. Bronson, p. 57.

85. Pancoast, p. 90.

86. "Franklin's Place in Literature," p. 46; Duyckinck, I, 107.

87. P. iii.

88. *Ibid.*, p. vi.

89. Quoted in Howells' review of Bigelow's *Autobiography of B. F.* in *The Atlantic* (July 1868), p. 127.

90. *Ibid.*

91. "Benjamin Franklin's *Memoirs*," p. 74.

92. *Ibid.*

93. *Ibid.*, p. 63.

94. Farrand, "Self-Portraiture," p. 412; Van Doren, "First American Man of Letters," p. 295, says the first part is "richest in anecdotes"; Mitchell, pp. 102-3; *et al.*

95. Van Doren, "The First American Man of Letters," p. 295.

96. Mitchell, pp. 102-3.

97. Van Doren, *B. Franklin*, p. 768.

Chapter Three

1. Ross, p. 794, writes: "The final Richard [the voice of utilitarianism] speaks with the same voice which produced the Autobiography."

2. Pancoast, p. 88. "He [Franklin] tells us that his object is to make people virtuous, but assures us at the same time that the road to virtue lies through the making of money." See p. 89.

3. Van Doren, "First American Man of Letters," p. 283.

4. See Goode, p. 9, for some indication of the numerous foreign editions. In addition, by 1890 there had been at least seventy English editions.

5. Pancoast, p. 87.

6. Van Doren, "First American Man of Letters," p. 288.

7. *Hist. of Am. Lit.*, II, 122. See Newcomb, "Sources," pp. 35-37, for a comparison and discussion of representative writings of those two philomaths. Newcomb disagrees with Tyler.

8. *Papers of B. F.*, I, 280.

9. Newcomb, "Sources," pp. 21-22, is my excellent source for this quotation and for the other material in this paragraph.

10. Ellis Paxson Oberholtzer, *The Literary History of Philadelphia* (Philadelphia, 1906), p. 49.

11. *Papers of B. F.*, I, 281.

12. Newcomb, "Sources," pp. 23-24.

13. *Ibid.*

14. C. William Miller, p. 183.

15. Jackson, p. 66.

16. *Papers of B. F.*, I, 282.

17. Clary, p. 33. "Franklin's two greatest business successes, the *Almanac* and the *Gazette*, were the result not mainly of Franklin's ability as a printer, though this contributed, but of his ability as a writer." P. 34.

18. Van Doren, *Benjamin Franklin*, p. 107. Van Doren also

points out that there was a Philadelphian by the name of Richard Saunders listed in Thomas Denham's account book. Denham was the friend who helped Franklin as a young man to return from London to Philadelphia [see *Papers*, I, 73]. On his return home Franklin worked as a clerk for Denham. Denham died in 1737 and left Franklin a bequest in his will.

19. Newcomb, "Sources," p. 22.
20. *Papers of B. F.*, I, 281.
21. Ross, p. 790.
22. *Ibid.*, p. 793. See also Walter Blair, *Native American Humor* (New York, 1937), pp. 113-15. The change, writes Ross, came after the first six editions of the first six years. P. 791.
23. Newcomb, "Sources," p. 30.
24. *Papers of B. F.*, I, 280.
25. *Ibid.*, I, 312.
26. *Ibid.*, I, 287-310.
27. *Ibid.*, I, 281.
28. Davy, p. 64.
29. Newcomb, "Sources," p. 19.
30. Jorgenson, "The New Science in the Almanacs of Ames and Franklin," *New England Quart.*, VIII (Dec. 1935), 560-61.
31. Goode, p. 8. Cf. Jackson, p. 65; the almanac was "the one form of literature read in every family."
32. Newcomb, "Sources," p. 169, says this definition is from a book entitled *A Collection of Epigrams to which is Prefixed, A Critical Dissertation on this Species of Poetry* (London, 1735).
33. Gallacher, "Franklin's *Way to Wealth*," pp. 238-39.
34. *Autobiog.*, p. 88. See Newcomb, "Sources," Chapter III, for a thorough discussion of definition and history of the proverb.
35. Newcomb, "Sources," p. 93.
36. Gallacher, pp. 238-39.
37. Newcomb, "Sources," appendices I and II.
38. Newcomb discusses all these in the body of his dissertation. Labaree and Bell neglect to list Herbert's *Outlandish Proverbs* in *Papers of B. F.*, I, 281-82, possibly because it was included in *Wit's Recreation*.
39. Newcomb, "Sources," pp. 50, 12.
40. *Ibid.*, p. 51.
41. *Ibid.*
42. *Ibid.*, p. 50.
43. *Ibid.*, pp. 60-61.
44. *Ibid.*, p. 53.
45. *Ibid.*, pp. 109, 112. This source of Fuller, according to Newcomb, contains "only very definite sources of Franklin's sayings" that he cannot "attribute elsewhere." See p. 112.
46. *Ibid.*, p. 101.

47. *Ibid.*, pp. 101-2.
48. *Ibid.*, p. 99.
49. *Ibid.*, p. 84.
50. *Ibid.*, p. 87.
51. Newcomb, "Poor Richard's Debt to Lord Halifax," p. 536. See also pp. 535-39.
52. Newcomb, "Sources," p. 138.
53. *Ibid.*, p. 139.
54. Frank Brady and Martin Price, *English Prose and Poetry 1660-1800* (New York, 1961), p. 41.
55. Newcomb, "Sources," pp. 152-53.
56. *Ibid.*, p. 194.
57. *Ibid.*, p. 203.
58. *Ibid.*, pp. 112-13.
59. *Ibid.*, p. 114. The years of principal borrowing from La Rochefoucauld were 1745 and 1751. See p. 113. The first year mentioned is 1735 (p. 116).
60. *Ibid.*, p. 114.
61. *Ibid.*, p. 112.
62. *Ibid.*, p. 69. Franklin used Charles Cotton's translation. P. 121.
63. *Ibid.*, p. 121.
64. *Ibid.*, p. 71. Jorgenson, "B. Franklin and Rabelais," pp. 538-39, traces the saying, "Lying rides upon debt's back," which previously had been attributed to Herodotus, to Rabelais (Bk. III, Chapter V of *Gargantua*). Franklin's version of this saying was "The second Vice is Lying, the first is running in Debt." Newcomb, "Sources," p. 70, corrects Jorgenson, tracing this version to Fuller rather than to Rabelais.

Jorgenson says that Rabelais gives a version of the sheep that needed carts for their heavy tails, an image which Franklin used in one of his later satires, but adds that Rabelais in turn procured it from Jean Tenaud. See p. 539.

65. Newcomb, "Sources," p. 190.
66. *Ibid.*, p. 98.
67. *Ibid.*, p. 101. Newcomb names the year 1757 as the period of this "substantial" borrowing.
68. *Ibid.*, p. 153.
69. *Ibid.*, pp. 157-58. See also Van Doren, *Autobiographical Writings*, p. 157.
70. Newcomb, "Sources," p. 89.
71. *Ibid.*, pp. 117-18, 204-6, 97, 159. As an instance of Bacon's influence, Labaree and Bell present the following from *Poor Richard* (1738): "Reading maketh a full Man, Meditation a profound Man, discourse a clear Man." *Papers of B. F.*, II, 196.

72. Newcomb, "Sources," p. 90.
73. *Ibid.*, p. 91.
74. *Ibid.*, p. 184. Newcomb agrees with McKillop's identification of the source of Franklin's verses in honor of the deceased Jacob Taylor, an almanac maker. See p. 209n and also McKillop's "Some Newtonian Verses in *Poor Richard*," *New England Quart.*, XXI (1948), 383-85.
75. Newcomb, "Sources," pp. 186, 14. To some of these Franklin added a "distinctively original element by writing four-line morals to them." P. 14.
76. *Ibid.*, pp. 181-82, for a tabulation of forty-one borrowings for the years 1738, 1739, 1741-1756. These epigrams are of the four- to eight-line variety.
77. *Ibid.*, p. 15.
78. *Ibid.*, p. 170, lists thirty-three, eleven couplets, and six miscellaneous poems.
79. *Ibid.*, p. 179n.
80. *Ibid.*, p. 22. The trend of Franklin's borrowing in the first years of *Poor Richard* was towards "an increasing reliance on collections of original aphorisms." Newcomb mentions collections of Savile, Richardson, and Quarles. P. 13.
81. *Ibid.*, p. 31.
82. Newcomb, "Sources," pp. 250-51.
83. *Papers of B. F.*, I, 353.
84. Newcomb, "Sources," p. 246.
85. *Ibid.*, p. 53.
86. Sanford, p. 97.
87. Van Doren, "First American Man of Letters," p. 290.
88. Newcomb, "Sources," p. 245.
89. *Ibid.*, p. 57.
90. *Papers of B. F.*, I, 282.
91. *Ibid.* See pp. 150-51 for revisions of Palmer, and pp. 131-38 for some extensive revisions of Richardson.
92. *Ibid.*, p. 182. Previous to this time in *Poor Richard* he had made "a large number of minor—sometimes major—changes in borrowed verse." P. 14.
93. *Ibid.*, p. 177.
94. *Ibid.*, p. 187.
95. *Ibid.*, p. 211.
96. Gallacher, p. 231.
97. Newcomb, "Sources," p. 106.
98. *Ibid.*, p. 248.
99. *Ibid.*, p. 16.
100. *Ibid.*, p. 239.
101. *Ibid.*, p. 158. The enormous popularity of *The Way to*

Wealth (nearly five hundred editions are known) has been explained by one editor as due "partly to the age-old love for proverbs."

102. Luther S. Livingston, "News for Bibliophiles," *The Nation,* Vol. 96 (May 15, 1913), p. 494.

103. *Ibid.,* p. 495.

104. Newcomb, "Sources," p. 233.

105. Newcomb, "Sources," p. 222.

106. *Ibid.,* p. 220.

107. *Ibid.,* p. 221.

108. *Ibid.*

109. Meister cites both these on p. 161. They are both in *The Way to Wealth.*

110. *Ibid.,* p. 166. Meister mentions two examples in the *Autobiography* where Franklin used a proverb as an excuse for a moral digression or "sermon." He also notes (p. 165) that Franklin quotes more proverbs in the part of the *Autobiography* dealing with his life after 1730 than in that before 1730. He thinks Franklin grew more didactic with age.

111. *Ibid.,* p. 166.

112. *Writings,* III, 318.

113. *Writings,* IV, 243.

114. *Writings,* VIII, 469.

115. *Meister,* p. 162.

116. *Ibid.,* p. 163 for further examples of this method and of the method mentioned in the sentence following.

Chapter Four

1. Crane, *Benjamin Franklin, Englishman and American,* p. 65.

2. *Ibid.*

3. *Ibid.,* p. 72.

4. *Ibid.,* p. 86.

5. See *Papers of B. F.,* I, 161.

6. *Ibid.,* I, 159-61.

7. Crane, *B. F.'s Letters to the Press,* p. xi.

8. Crane, *Benjamin Franklin, Englishman and American,* p. 105.

9. Crane, "Franklin's Political Journalism in England," *Jour. Franklin Inst.,* CCXXXIII (March 1942), 214.

10. V. W. Crane, "Certain Writings of Benjamin Franklin on the British Empire and the American Colonies, *Papers of the Bibliog. Soc.,* XXVII, I (1934), 26. See also, by the same author, "B. Franklin and the Stamp Act," *Pub. Col. Soc. Mass.,* XXXII (Feb. 1934), 62.

11. Crane, "Three Fables by B. Franklin," p. 499. F. B., N. N., Homespun, Pacificus Secundus, Americus, Justice, A Virginian, and

Equity were some of the pennames used by Franklin. See V. W.
Crane, "Franklin's Political Journalism," pp. 213-14, and by the
same author, "B. F. and the Stamp Act," pp. 63-64.

In addition to the forms listed one should add that Franklin also
wrote prefaces for one Dublin and two London editions of John
Dickinson's *Letters of an American Farmer* in the same year as
their American publication in pamphlet form. Tyler, *Lit. Hist. of
the Am. Rev.*, I, 237. According to McMahon, p. 68, these prefaces
amounted to a striking piece of irony, "but one of Franklin's many
devices to get America's viewpoint before the public." Similarly, his
Preface to the Speech of Joseph Galloway attacked the evils of proprietary government. Thus the *Preface* must be numbered among the
literary forms of Franklin's political journalism. Here, too, McMahon
mentions *A Catechism Relating to the English National Debt* as a
rather unusual form. It consisted of nine questions and answers.
See p. 77.

12. Crane, *B. F.'s Letters to the Press*, p. xi.

13. Crane's "F.'s Political Journalism," pp. 210-11, for the background of this entire paragraph.

14. Davy, p. 235.

15. *Ibid.*, p. 113.

16. Crane, "F.'s Political Journalism," p. 214.

17. *Ibid.*, p. 211.

18. *Ibid.*, p. 214.

19. Davy, p. 2.

20. *Ibid.*, p. 174.

21. *Ibid.*, p. 156n, for specific evidence.

22. David Worcester, *The Art of Satire* (Cambridge, Mass.,
1940), p. 8.

23. Davy, p. 1 of abstract and pp. ix-x of preface.

24. *Ibid.*, p. 81.

25. *Ibid.*, p. 234. See also, p. 233.

26. McMahon, p. 85. Two other works less well known as satires
are the *Remarks Concerning the Savages of North America* and the
Captivity of William Henry. Both of these, along with the *Information
for those Who Would Remove to America*, which also contains some
satiric quality, have been discussed elsewhere. See A. O. Aldridge,
"Franklin's Deistical Indians," *Proc. APS*, XCIV, No. 4 (Aug. 1950),
398-410, *Franklin and his French Contemporaries*, pp. 30-38, and
my *Franklin's Wit and Folly*, pp. 75-98.

27. *Ibid.*

28. Crane, *B. F.'s Letters to the Press*, p. xxxvii.

29. *Ibid.*, pp. 262-64, for the complete text.

30. Davy, p. 113n, states that a certain Count Schaumburg
actually served George III in recruiting mercenaries.

31. *Ibid.*, p. 207.

32. *Papers of B. F.*, I, 176.
33. *Writings of B. F.*, IV, 341.
34. I am indebted to Davy for this and the following example. P. 205.
35. Crane, *B. F.'s Letters to the Press*, p. 96. Quoted in Davy, p. 205.
36. Davy, p. 208.
37. *Ibid.*, pp. 1, 221.
38. Crane, "B. F. and the Stamp Act," p. 69.
39. Davy, p. 215.
40. *Ibid.*, pp. 215-16.
41. Crane, *B. F.'s Letters to the Press*, p. 4.
42. Davy, p. 211. See Crane, *B. F.'s Letters to the Press*, p. 4, for another example of the same technique.
43. See Crane, *B. F.'s Letters to the Press*, pp. 14, 19, 108, 110, 120, 138, 141 for examples.
44. Davy, p. 92.
45. Crane, *B. F.'s Letters to the Press*, p. 33.
46. *Ibid.*, p. 34. See note 6 on this same page.
47. Davy, p. 237.
48. P. 240.
49. Davy, p. 270n.
50. Van Doren, *Autobiographical Writings*, p. 296.
51. *Ibid.*, p. 297.
52. George Simson, "Legal Sources for Franklin's 'Edict,'" *American Lit.*, XXXII (May 1960), 153.
53. *Ibid.*
54. *Ibid.*, p. 157. For further historical background of the "Edict," see Merrill Jensen's *American Colonial Documents to 1776*, Vol. IX of *English Historical Documents* (New York, 1955), pp. 414-17, for reference to the Woolen Act, the Hat Act, and the Iron Act.
55. P. 157.
56. Crane, *B. F.'s Letters to the Press*, p. 237.
57. Davy, p. 100.
58. Letter to the Countess Ossory (Oct. 1, 1782) in Mrs. Paget Toynbee's *The Letters of Horace Walpole* (London, 1904), XII, 340-41.
59. Davy, p. 116 and Mott and Jorgenson, p. 541, note 111.
60. *Autobiog.*, p. 143.
61. *Ibid.*, p. 272.
62. Crane, *B. F.'s Letters to the Press*, p. 235.
63. Davy, p. 248.
64. Crane, *B. F.'s Letters to the Press*, p. 14.
65. *Ibid.*, pp. 158-59.
66. Davy, p. 267.

67. Smyth, *Writings*, X, 88.
68. Smyth, *Writings*, VI, 408, 218.
69. Davy, p. 245.
70. Van Doren, *Autobiographical Writings*, p. 173.
71. See Mott and Jorgenson, pp. 168-69.
72. Reproduced in Crane, *B. F.'s Letters to the Press.*
73. V. W. Crane, "Three Fables by B. F.," p. 501. See also *Papers of Bibliog. Soc. of America*, XXVIII, Part 1 (1934), pp. 1-27.
74. P. 56.
75. Smyth, "Franklin's Place in Literature," p. 314.
76. See *Papers of B. F.*, I, 139-41 for the historical background of *A Modest Enquiry.*
77. P. 57.
78. V. W. Crane, "F.'s Political Journalism," p. 213.
79. Quoted in Goode, p. 15.
80. *Proc. APS*, LXIII (April 24, 1924), 9.
81. "Sidelights on B. F.'s Principles of Rhetoric," p. 220.
82. Allan Nevins, *The American States During and After the Revolution, 1775-1789* (New York, 1924), p. 12.
83. P. 65.
84. Tyler, *Lit. Hist. of the Am. Rev.*, II, 373.
85. Crane, "B. F. and the Stamp Act," p. 65. See also, by the same author, *B. F.'s Letters to the Press*, pp. 63-73, for the outline of another pamphlet Franklin had apparently projected, the completion of which was interrupted by the repeal of the Stamp Act.
86. *B. F.'s Letters to the Press*, pp. xxiv, 35.
87. I. Bernard Cohen *in* Sanford, p. 85.
88. *Autobiography*, p. 113.
89. *Ibid.*
90. *Ibid.*, pp. 113-14.
91. *Ibid.*, p. 103.
92. *Ibid.*, p. 109.
93. *Papers of B. F.*, I, xxxi. The quote comes from Stuart P. Sherman, "Franklin," *Camb. Hist. Am. Lit.* (New York, 1917), I, 109.
94. *Autobiography*, p. 120.
95. I. B. Cohen *in* Sanford, p. 89.
96. *Ibid.*, p. 90.
97. I. B. Cohen, *Benjamin Franklin: His Contribution*, p. 46.
98. Maurice J. Quinlan, "Dr. Franklin Meets Dr. Johnson," in F. W. Hilles' *New Light on Dr. Johnson* (New Haven, 1959), p. 111.
99. *Ibid.*, p. 114, from the account of the minutes of February 2, 1764, of *Dr. Bray's Associates*, at which meeting Franklin's letter of this date was read.
100. P. 143.
101. P. 269.

102. Baender, p. 279.
103. *Ibid.*
104. McMahon, p. 86.

Chapter Five

1. See Thrall, Hibbard, and Holman, *A Handbook to Literature* (New York, 1960), pp. 183-89, for a fuller history of this genre. For an even more complete history of the essay, see R. S. Crane and W. F. Bryan's *The English Familiar Essay* (Boston, 1916), pp. xi-lx.
2. Horner, pp. 501-2.
3. *Ibid.*, p. 522.
4. *Ibid.*, p. 502.
5. *Ibid.*, p. 521.
6. *Papers of B. F.*, I, 9.
7. Horner, p. 521.
8. *Ibid.*, p. 511.
9. *Papers of B. F.*, I, 12-13.
10. *Ibid.*, I, 30, 32, 37, 39.
11. *Papers of B. F.*, I, 24n.
12. *Ibid.*, I, 27.
13. Davy, p. 29.
14. In *Papers of B. F.*, I, 32n, Labaree and Bell see Defoe's *An Essay Upon Projects* (1697), pp. 132-41, as the source.
15. *Ibid.*, I, 45n.
16. Horner, p. 501.
17. Davy, p. 31; *Autobiog.*, p. 17.
18. Davy, p. 32.
19. Wright, p. 215.
20. *Papers of B. F.*, I, 114.
21. See *ibid.*, I, 114n, for further information on Breintnall.
22. *Ibid.*, I, 111-12.
23. *Ibid.*, I, 112.
24. *Ibid.*
25. *Ibid.*
26. *Ibid.*, I, 113.
27. *Ibid.*, I, 121.
28. Davy, p. 36.
29. *Papers of B. F.*, pp. 177-81.
30. *Franklin and His French Contemporaries*, p. 251, note 38.
31. *Ibid.*, pp. 159-60; Davy, p. 119n.
32. Van Doren, *B. F.*, p. 147.
33. In Sanford, p. 94. See also Van Doren, "First American Man of Letters," p. 284, for further comment on Franklin's drinking songs.

34. Joseph Priestley, *Observations on the Increase of Infidelity* (London, 1796), note to pp. 29-30.
35. Mott and Jorgenson, p. 540.
36. "Franklin in Literature," p. 102. See also Van Doren, *B. F.*, p. 663, and Smyth, *Writings*, VII, 427-33, for text of *The Lord's Prayer* and the *Proposed New Version of the Bible*.
37. Amacher, pp. 67-69.
38. Granger, "We Shall Eat Apples of Paradise," p. 41.
39. *Ibid.*, p. 38.
40. *Ibid.*
41. Chinard, p. 739.
42. *Ibid.*
43. Amacher, p. 48.
44. Blair, Hornberger, and Stewart, *The Literature of the United States*, I, (New York, 1953), 224.
45. P. 755.
46. *Ibid.*, pp. 741-44 and 759.
47. Cairns, p. 55.

Chapter Six

1. Van Doren, "First American Man of Letters," p. 291.
2. *Ibid.*, p. 292, for the entire paragraph.
3. *Ibid.*, p. 294.
4. Coad, p. xvi.
5. Wecter, p. xi.
6. *Papers of B. F.*, I, xxxi.
7. Labaree and Bell, *Mr. Franklin*, p. xv.
8. Duyckinck, I, 109. See Smyth, *Writings*, X, 511-35, for a list of Franklin's correspondents.
9. Labaree and Bell, *Mr. Franklin*, p. xv.
10. Goode, p. 11.
11. Sanford, p. 96.
12. Respectively Coad, p. xvii; Van Doren, "The First American Man of Letters," p. 283; and Tyler, *Lit. Hist. of the Am. Rev.*, I, 13.
13. See, among others, anonymous, "On the Literary Character of Dr. Franklin," [Boston] *Monthly Anthology* (December, 1806), p. 668; McMaster, p. 280; Bronson, p. 56; Sanford, p. 95; Van Doren, "First American Man of Letters," p. 292.
14. Van Doren, *Letters and Papers of B. F. and Richard Jackson*, p. 2.
15. *Ibid.*, pp. 5-6.
16. *Ibid.*, p. 17.
17. *Ibid.*, p. 19.
18. *Ibid.*, pp. 19, 27.

19. *Ibid.,* pp. 9-16.
20. *Ibid.,* p. 7.
21. Van Doren, *Autobiographical Writings,* p. 139.
22. Labaree and Bell, *Mr. Franklin,* p. 21.
23. Bridenbaugh, pp. 153, 135.
24. Van Doren, *Autobiographical Writings,* p. 139.
25. Letter dated Philadelphia, November 20, 1786, reproduced in MS form in Brander Mathews' *An Introduction to the Study of American Lit.* (New York, 1896), pp. 34-35.
26. Robert L. Kahn, "Three Franklin-Raspe Letters," in W. E. Lingelbach's "Studies on B. Franklin," *Proc. APS,* XCIX, No. 6 (Dec. 15, 1955), pp. 397-400.
27. Clary, p. 10.
28. *Ibid.,* pp. 43, 45.
29. *Ibid.,* p. 46.
30. *Ibid.,* pp. 46-47.
31. "F.'s Political Journalism in England," p. 210.
32. *Ibid.*
33. *Ibid.*
34. *B. Franklin,* pp. 539-40.
35. *Ibid.,* p. 540.
36. *Clary,* p. 82.
37. Sanford, p. 49.
38. McMahon, pp. 68-69.
39. *Ibid.,* p. 70.
40. Sanford, p. 31.
41. *Papers of B. F.,* I, xxxiii.
42. See Labaree and Bell, *Mr. Franklin,* pp. 52-53.
43. Quoted in *ibid.,* p. 48.
44. *Ibid.*
45. *Ibid.,* p. 49.

Chapter Seven

1. P. 153.
2. Diller, p. 16.
3. S. P. Sherman in Sanford, pp. 76-77.
4. Cohen, *Franklin and Newton,* pp. 79-80.
5. Smyth, *Writings,* III, 99-100.
6. Quoted by Cohen, *F. and Newton,* p. 79.
7. Quoted in *ibid.,* p. 79.
8. Diller, pp. 20, 28.
9. Cohen, *F. and Newton,* p. 80.
10. P. 18.
11. *Autobiography,* p. 108.
12. *Ibid.*

13. All these are listed in the APS *Classified Index to Publications* as published at one time or another either in the *Transactions* or *Proceedings* of the APS.

14. Jackson, p. 69.

15. Cairns, p. 54.

16. Smyth, "Franklin's Place in Literature," p. 313, and Rufus W. Griswold, *The Prose Writers of America* (Philadelphia, 1847), p. 62, respectively. See also Griswold, p. 59.

17. Quoted, *Works*, I, 457-58, and in Duyckinck, I, 109.

18. *Franklin and Newton*, p. 78.

19. Quoted in Smyth, "Franklin's Place in Literature," p. 314.

20. "Sidelights on B. F.'s Principles of Rhetoric," p. 213.

21. MacLaurin, p. 21.

22. Quoted in Nye, *Autobiography*, p. viii.

23. P. 19.

24. Farrand, "Self-Portraiture," pp. 410-11, for both quotations.

25. Tyler, *Hist. of Am. Lit.*, II, 317.

26. Letter dated Philadelphia, April 23, 1752, quoted in anonymous article, "America's Pioneer Man of Science," *Life Magazine*, XLVIII (February 29, 1960), 56.

Chapter Eight

1. Crane, *B. F. and a Rising People*, p. 205.

2. J. M. Stiffer, *The Religion of B. F.* (New York, 1925), p. 47.

3. Cohen, *B. F.: His Contribution*, p. 112.

4. Crane, *Benjamin Franklin, Englishman and American*, pp. 39-40.

5. *Ibid.*

6. *Papers of B. F.*, I, 58.

7. See Mott and Jorgenson, *B. F.*, pp. cxvii-cxxviii for a more detailed background of Franklin's readings that turned him towards Deism.

8. *Papers of B. F.*, I, 58n.

9. *Ibid.*, I, 57.

10. *Autobiography*, pp. 38-39. See also *Papers of B. F.*, I, 58-59n.

11. "B. F. and Philosophical Necessity," pp. 308-9. XII, No. 3 (September 1951), pp. 308-9.

12. *Papers of B. F.*, I, 264.

13. *Ibid.*, I, 101, n7.

14. *Papers of B. F.*, I, 101n.

15. *Autobiography*, p. 75.

16. *Ibid.*

17. Amacher, p. 153.

18. *Ibid.*, pp. 152-55, and Aldridge, *F. and His French Contemporaries*, pp. 174-75.

19. See Smyth, *Writings*, VI, 165ff., for Franklin's preface to this work. Also, *Works*, X, 207-12.

20. "On the Literary Character of Dr. F.," [Boston] *Monthly Anthology*, p. 668.

21. Vincent Buranelli, "Colonial Philosophy," *William and Mary Quarterly*, 3rd series, XVI (July 1959), 351.

22. Letter dated March 9, 1790.

23. *Ibid.*

24. *Ibid.*

25. Harry Cohen, *The Religion of B. F.* (New York, 1957), pp. 11-12.

26. *Ibid.*, p. 37.

Chapter Nine

1. See, for examples, "On the Literary Character of Dr. F.," p. 667; Tyler, *Lit. Hist. of the Am. Rev.*, II, 365, 381.

2. Jeffrey commends, however, the general style of Franklin's letters. See XIII, 327.

3. Tyler, *Lit. Hist. of the Am. Rev.*, II, 375; Sherman, p. 109; Lingelbach, "F.'s *American Instructor*," p. 373; Smyth, "F.'s Place in Literature," p. 313; Fisher, pp. 27-28; Farrand, "Self-Portraiture," p. 410; *et al.*

4. Tyler, *Lit. Hist. of the Am. Rev.*, II, 365. See also Smyth, *Writings*, I, 210.

5. P. 276.

6. P. 77.

7. *A History of Eighteenth Century Literature* (London, 1888), p. 398.

8. Jorgenson, "Sidelights on B. F.'s Principles of Rhetoric," p. 222.

9. Sherman, pp. 108-9.

10. Tyler, *Lit. Hist. of the Am. Rev.*, II, 381.

Selected Bibliography

This bibliography, both in its primary and secondary sources, can obviously be only highly selective. Students interested in a more complete listing are referred to the statement on manuscripts and collections and also to that on collected and uncollected works in Van Doren, *B. Franklin*, pp. 785-86. For bibliographies of some of the principal collections mentioned by Van Doren, see Richard Amacher, *Franklin's Wit and Folly: the Bagatelles*, pp. 177-78.

I *Primary Sources*
(Arranged in order of importance.)

LABAREE, LEONARD W. and WHITFIELD J. BELL, JR., eds. *The Papers of Benjamin Franklin*. Vols. I, II. New Haven: Yale University Press, 1959–to present.

SMYTH, ALBERT HENRY. *The Writings of Benjamin Franklin*. 10 vols. New York: Macmillan, 1907.

SPARKS, JARED. *The Works of Benjamin Franklin*. 10 vols. Boston: Hilliard Gray, 1840.

MOTT, FRANK L. and CHESTER E. JORGENSON. *Benjamin Franklin: Representative Selections*. New York: American Book Co., 1936.

NYE, RUSSEL B., ed. *Benjamin Franklin. Autobiography and Other Writings*. Boston: Houghton Mifflin, 1958.

VAN DOREN, CARL. *Benjamin Franklin's Autobiographical Writings*. New York: Viking, 1945.

CRANE, VERNER W., ed. *Benjamin Franklin's Letters to the Press, 1758-1775*. Chapel Hill: University of North Carolina, 1950.

COHEN, I. BERNARD, ed. *Benjamin Franklin: His Contribution to the American Tradition*. New York: Bobbs-Merrill Co., 1953. An anthology of selections compiled by a skillful editor who has carefully and successfully arranged the readings to show Franklin's great contributions to the American tradition.

STIFLER, JAMES M., ed. "My Dear Girl": the Correspondence of Benjamin Franklin, Polly Stevenson, Georgiana and Catherine Shipley. New York: George H. Doran Co., 1927.

ROELKER, WILLIAM GREENE. *Benjamin Franklin and Catharine Ray Greene*. Philadelphia: American Philosophical Society, 1949.

LABAREE, LEONARD W. and WHITFIELD J. BELL, JR., eds. *Mr. Franklin, A Selection from His Personal Letters*. New Haven: Yale University Press, 1956.

AMACHER, RICHARD E., ed. *Franklin's Wit and Folly: the Bagatelles*. New Brunswick: Rutgers University Press, 1953.

II *Secondary Sources*
(Arranged alphabetically within categories of interest.)

1. *General*

BRIDENBAUGH, CARL and JESSICA. *Rebels and Gentlemen: Philadelphia in the Age of Franklin*. New York: Reynal & Hitchcock, 1942. Excellent general description of culture and literary conditions in Franklin's Philadelphia.

FAY, BERNARD. *Franklin, The Apostle of Modern Times*. Boston: Little, Brown, and Co., 1929. Despite its rather romantic style and some inaccuracies, this book remains a standard reference. The section on the bagatelles (pp. 453-500) is exceptionally good; pp. 517-33, a useful bibliography.

LINGELBACH, WILLIAM E., *et al.* "Studies on Benjamin Franklin. The Two Hundred and Fiftieth Anniversary of His Birth, Jan. 17, 1956," *Proceedings of the American Philosophical Society*, XCIX, No. 6 (December 15, 1955). Pp. 359-473. A commemorative issue of excellent scholarly quality.

LUCAS, F. L. *The Art of Living: Four Eighteenth-Century Minds*. London: Cassell & Co., 1959. Pp. 203-61. Little new, but a fairly good, short summary of Franklin's entire career from the standpoint of an English don.

MOTT, FRANK L. and CHESTER E. JORGENSON, eds. *Benjamin Franklin: Representative Selections*. New York: American Book Co., 1936. The excellent introduction and bibliography (pp. xiii-clxxxviii) of these editors deal with such matters as the historical background of the enlightenment, Franklin's theories on education, literary practice, economy, politics, science, and religion as well as his role as printer and journalist.

SANFORD, CHARLES P., ed. *Benjamin Franklin and the American Character*. Boston: D. C. Heath, 1955. An American Studies source book presenting thirteen different points of view of such writers as I. Bernard Cohen, Carl Van Doren, Whitney Griswold, *et al.*

TYLER, MOSES C. *A History of American Literature During the Colonial Time*. 2 vols. New York: G. P. Putnam's Sons, 1890. Revised edition. Standard and authoritative reference work. Gives attention to Franklin's reputation as a writer during the period ending in 1765. Tyler apparently intended a study of Franklin as a writer, but never undertook it. See II, 253.

————. *The Literary History of the American Revolution, 1763-1783*. 2 vols. New York: Barnes and Noble, 1941. Monumental source book on writers of this period. Useful but not very critical.

WRIGHT, THOMAS GODDARD. *Literary Culture in Early New England*,

1620-1730. New Haven: Yale University Press, 1920. Primarily historical rather than literary, but nonetheless interesting and useful as a reference book.

VAN DOREN, CARL. *Benjamin Franklin*. New York: Viking, 1938. The best biography to date.

————. *Meet Dr. Franklin*. Philadelphia: The Franklin Institute, 1943. Introductions by various specialists.

2. *Autobiography*

FARRAND, MAX. "Benjamin Franklin's Memoirs," *Huntington Library Bulletin*, X (October, 1936). Pp. 49-78. Presents the very complicated history of the composition, copying, translation, and publication of the *Autobiography*. One of the most valuable pieces of research work on Franklin during our time.

————. "Self-Portraiture: The Autobiography," *General Magazine & Historical Chronicle*, XLII, No. 4 (July, 1940). Pp. 403-17. Explains Franklin's motives in writing the *Memoirs* and why the autobiography is so remarkably human. Gives history of the MS. A perceptive analysis.

3. *Poor Richard and The Way to Wealth*

GALLACHER, STUART A., "Franklin's *Way to Wealth*: A Florilegium of Proverbs and Wise Sayings," *Journal of English and Germanic Philology*, XLVIII (1949), 229-51. Good introduction to subject of Franklin's borrowing and reworking of the *Poor Richard's* sayings. Lists various sources for *The Way to Wealth*, 242-51.

L[IVINGSTON], L[UTHER] S., "News for Bibliophiles," *The Nation*, XCVI (May 15, 1913), 494-96. A study of the editions and scholarly problems connected with various editions of *The Way to Wealth*.

McKILLOP, ALAN D. "Some Newtonian Verses in Poor Richard," *New England Quarterly*, XXI (September, 1948), 383-85. A note on Franklin's borrowing for the preface of *Poor Richard Improved* (1748) and for *Poor Richard* (1756).

MEISTER, CHARLES W. "Franklin as a Proverb Stylist," *American Literature*, XXIV (May, 1952), 157-66. Deals with problems of how Franklin tended to express proverbs in certain forms and of how he "incorporated proverbial material into his persuasive rhetoric." Newcomb finds Meister "frequently deficient in attributing exact sources." (*Sources of B. F.*, p. 4.)

NEWCOMB, ROBERT. "Benjamin Franklin and Montaigne," *Modern Language Notes*, 489-91. Instances of Franklin's borrowing from Montaigne's essays in *Poor Richard* and in a letter to Priestley (June 7, 1782).

————. "Poor Richard's Debt to Lord Halifax," *Publications of the Modern Language Association,* LXX (June, 1955), 535-39. Finds the source for thirty-two sayings in Halifax's *Character of King Charles the Second.*

————. "The Sources of Benjamin Franklin's Sayings of Poor Richard," unpublished dissertation, University of Maryland, 1957. In this excellent dissertation, which deserves publication, Newcomb makes an original contribution to our knowledge of Franklin's borrowings. The only extensive study of its kind, it covers the poetry as well as the sayings of *Poor Richard.*

Ross, John F. "The Character of Poor Richard: Its Source and Alteration," *Publications of the Modern Language Association,* LV (September, 1940), 785-94. Shows that Franklin depended more on the Partridges than on Isaac Bickerstaff for his portrait of Richard and Brigit Saunders. Points out that the character of Poor Richard changed with age, became less entertaining and more didactic.

4. Political Career and Writings

Baender, Paul. "The Basis of Franklin's Duplicative Satires," *American Literature,* XXXII (November, 1960), 267-79. Suggests that Franklin's use of resemblances in three political satires is his general method as a writer—a plausible hypothesis that needs further testing. The "basis" referred to is Franklin's assumption of the distinction between virtuous and selfish men, on which his entire rhetorical system seemed to depend.

Butler, Ruth L. *Doctor Franklin, Postmaster General.* New York: Garden City, 1928. Useful and reliable reference work.

Crane, Verner W. *Benjamin Franklin and a Rising People.* Boston: Little, Brown and Co., 1954. Compact historical approach to the biography of Franklin. Fascinating reading.

————. "Benjamin Franklin and the Stamp Act," *Publications of the Colonial Society of Massachusetts,* XXXII (February, 1934), 56-77. Franklin's "imperialistic views concerning the British empire underwent a radical change during the period of the Stamp Act controversy and after its repeal." Also useful for understanding Franklin's anonymous propaganda.

————. *Benjamin Franklin, Englishman and American,* the Colver Lectures at Brown University for 1935. Baltimore: Williams and Wilkins Co., 1936. A lucid, readable little book by an outstanding scholar. Presents historical and other issues clearly and effectively.

————. "Three Fables by Benjamin Franklin," *New England Quarterly,* IX (September, 1936), 499-504. Points out that Franklin's habits of slow, careful composition were not really violated by John Adams' story of the improvisation of the fable about the cat and the eagle.

DAVY, FRANCIS X., "Benjamin Franklin, Satirist: the Satire of Franklin and Its Rhetoric," unpublished dissertation, Columbia University, 1958. The most penetrating and complete work yet accomplished on Franklin's satire. An excellent piece of work with a fine bibliography; deserves publication.

GRANGER, BRUCE INGHAM. *Political Satire in the American Revolution 1763-1783.* Ithaca: Cornell University Press, 1960. A well-written, highly readable study of 530 American satires in their historical context.

MCMAHON, WINIFRED T. "Forms Used in Franklin's Political Writings," *Franklin Lectures,* Harvard University, I, No. 1 (June, 1935), 44-100. This published M.A. thesis contains brief, well-written summaries of many of Franklin's most famous political writings, effectively presented in terms of backgrounds and arguments.

MEAD, EDWIN. *Washington, Jefferson and Franklin on War.* Boston: World Peace Foundation, 1913. See Vol. III, No. 5, pp. 7-10, of this pamphlet for Franklin's increasing pacifism from 1780 to 1788.

MEYER, GLADYS. *Free Trade in Ideas: Aspects of American Liberalism Illustrated in Franklin's Philadelphia Career.* New York: Kings Crown Press, 1941. Conceives of Franklin as an eighteenth-century liberal. Treats the influence of social and economic life of Boston as well as Philadelphia on both the early and late phases of his career. An excellent scholarly work, showing insight into the particular nature of Franklin's true greatness.

PITT, STUART A. "Franklin and William Penn's *No Cross, No Crown,*" *Modern Language Notes,* LIV (June, 1939), 466-67. Useful note, showing how Franklin elaborated, in the 81st number of the *Courant,* on Penn's attack on titles in the 9th chapter of the latter's *No Cross, No Crown* (1669).

QUINLAN, MAURICE J. "Dr. Franklin Meets Dr. Johnson," in *New Light on Dr. Johnson,* ed. by F. W. Hilles. New Haven: Yale University Press, 1959. Pp. 107-20. Franklin met Johnson on May 1, 1760, at a club called Dr. Bray's Associates for Founding Clerical Libraries and Supporting Negro Schools.

ROSENGARTEN, J. G. *American History from German Archives with Reference to German Soldiers in the Revolution and Franklin's Visit to Germany.* Lancaster, Pa.: Pennsylvania German Society, 1904. Pp. 50-61 describe Franklin's visit to Germany during the summer of 1766.

SIMSON, GEORGE. "Legal Sources for Franklin's 'Edict,'" *American Literature,* XXXII (May, 1960), 152-57. Calls attention to the acts of parliament used by Franklin in writing this satire.

5. *History of Journalism*

BRIGHAM, CLARENCE S., "Bibliography of American Newspapers," *Proceedings of the American Antiquarian Society,* Worcester, Mass., n.s. XXXII (1923), 136, 157-68, 198, 213-14. Pages 157-68 contain history, contents, and present location of surviving numbers of the *Pa. Gaz.*

CLARY, WILLIAM W. *Benjamin Franklin, Printer and Publisher.* Los Angeles: Los Angeles Club of Printing House Craftsmen, 1935. Contains valuable letters from Franklin to Strahan and part of one from Strahan to Franklin.

COOK, ELIZABETH C. *Literary Influences in Colonial Newspapers, 1704-1705.* New York: Columbia University Press, 1912. Pp. 8-28, 93-100. This monograph presents good background material on the *N. E. Courant* and colonial libraries. Lists some of most important literary works in library of the *Courant* and describes some numbers of the *Pa. Gaz.*

FORD, PAUL L. "History of a Newspaper, the Pennsylvania Gazette," *Magazine of American History,* XV (New York, 1886), 452-56. Useful reference work on *Pa. Gaz.*

FORD, WORTHINGTON C. "Franklin's *New England Courant,*" *Massachusetts Historical Society Proceedings,* LVII (February-April, 1924), 336-53. Valuable presentation of Franklin's personally annotated file of *N. E. Courant.* Good for background of Franklin's literary career and state of literature in Boston. Discusses work of other *Courant* writers—Checkley, Dr. Douglass, Gardner, Capt. Taylor, etc.

HUDSON, FREDERIC. *Journalism in the United States from 1690 to 1872.* New York: Harper & Bros., 1873. Provides history of Franklin's press.

MILLER, C. WILLIAM. "Benjamin Franklin's Philadelphia Type." Papers, Biblio. Soc., University of Virginia, in *Studies in Biblio.,* XI (1958), 179-206. Excellent study of Franklin's three kinds of type: Philadelphia, 1728-1766; Non-Philadelphia, used to stock houses of his partners; Passy (1776-1785), sold to Francis Childs, a New York printer.

MILLER, DANIEL. *Early German American Newspapers.* Lancaster, Pa.: Pennsylvania German Society, 1911. A pamphlet reprinted from *Proceedings and Addresses, Pennsylvania German Society,* XIX (1908), 9, 10, 14-26. Reproduces copies of the *Philadelphische Zeitung* for May 6, 1732, and June 24, 1732. Briefly discusses Franklin's connections with other German-English publications.

MOTT, FRANK L. *A History of American Magazines (1741-1850).* New York: D. Appleton, 1930. Best work of its kind; it is authoritative, but contains little information on Franklin as a writer.

SMYTH, ALBERT H. *The Philadelphia Magazines and their Contributors, 1741-1850.* Philadelphia: R. M. Lindsay, 1892. Superseded by later work, but contains some good background material on eighteenth-century journalism.

6. *Essays, Bagatelles, and Letters*

ALDRIDGE, A. OWEN. *Franklin and His French Contemporaries.* New York: New York University Press, 1957. Excellent scholarly treatment of Franklin's reputation, writings, and friends in France. Distinguishes between Franklin's "legendary and his actual character."

————. "The Sources of Franklin's 'The Ephemera,'" *New England Quarterly,* XXVII (September, 1954), 388-91. Traces this famous *bagatelle* to two British periodicals, *The Free Thinker* and *The Universal Instructor.*

AMACHER, RICHARD E., ed. *Franklin's Wit and Folly: the Bagatelles.* New Brunswick, N. J.: Rutgers University Press, 1953. Introduction, bibliography, and notes contain historical and textual material.

CHINARD, GILBERT. "Random Notes on Two 'Bagatelles,'" *The American Philosophical Society Library Bulletin,* CIII, No. 6 (December, 1959), 727-60. Collates the recently discovered Cornell University MS of *The Ephemera* in English with the APS MS in French and with the two Passy imprints (Yale University); gives a brief history of texts and editions. Corrects Livingston's dating of MSS of *The Elysian Fields,* Franklin's letter to Mme. Helvétius.

GRANGER, BRUCE INGHAM. "We Shall Eat Apples of Paradise," *American Heritage,* X (June, 1959), 38-41, 103-4. Well-written introduction to the *bagatelles.*

HALL, MAX. *Benjamin Franklin and Polly Baker: The History of a Literary Deception.* Chapel Hill: University of North Carolina Press, 1960. Readable account of this famous hoax, showing how the French writers Raynal, Diderot, and Brissot made Polly Baker into "an important symbol of the revolutionary spirit."

HORNER, GEORGE F. "Franklin's Dogood Papers Re-examined," *Stud. in Phil.,* XXXVII (1940). Pp. 501-23. Stresses the original elements; gives religious, social, political, and commercial background necessary to understand them.

MASON, WILLIAM S. *Franklin and Galloway, Some Unpublished Letters.* Pamphlet reprinted from *Proceedings of the American Antiquarian Society* (October, 1924). Worcester, Mass: American

Antiquarian Society, 1925. This pamphlet contains some of the
Franklin-Galloway correspondence (1757-1760), a period during
which they combined resistance to the proprietaries.

PHILBRICK, FRANCIS S. "Notes on Early Editions and Editors of Franklin," *Proceedings of the American Philosophical Society*, XCVII
(October, 1953), 525-64. Deals with "twenty collections of letters to and from Franklin, and other writings by him and others,
which were published down to 1834." Useful to researchers of
early Franklin editions. Covers period 1751-1834.

VAN DOREN, CARL. *Jane Mecom*. New York: Viking Press, 1950.
Much interesting primary source material worked into an entertaining narrative for the general reader interested in Franklin's
correspondence with his favorite sister.

————. *The Letters and Papers of Benjamin Franklin and Richard
Jackson, 1753-1785*. Philadelphia: American Philosophical Society, 1947. Fertile source book for historical and political information since Jackson was an American sympathizer. Throws considerable light on contents and methods of Franklin's letter-
writing.

7. *Scientific Writings*

ALDRIDGE, A. OWEN. "Benjamin Franklin and Jonathan Edwards on
Lightning and Earthquakes." *Isis*, XLI (July, 1950), 162-64.
Indicates a probable common source for both Edwards and
Franklin in their theories on these subjects (Chambers' *Cyclo-
pedia*, London, 1728). Points out Franklin's heavy reliance on
Chambers.

COHEN, I. BERNARD. *Benjamin Franklin's Experiments: A New Edition of Franklin's "Experiments and Observations on Electricity."*
Cambridge, Mass.: Harvard University Press, 1941. A bibliography of early editions of Franklin's book on electricity (English,
French, Italian, German). Presents the 5th English edition,
which he says was personally supervised by Franklin. Useful
to students of Franklin's scientific style.

————. *Franklin and Newton: An Inquiry into Speculative Newtonian Experimental Science and Franklin's Work in Electricity
as an Example Thereof*. Philadelphia: American Philosophical
Society, 1956. A monumental study by a leading expert on the
history of science, replete with an excellent bibliography. Not
for the beginner, although clearly written and well organized.

DILLER, THEODORE. *Franklin's Contribution to Medicine*. Brooklyn:
Albert T. Huntington, 1912. Makes clear Franklin's importance
to the medical profession in early America, not only as a writer
on scientific subjects but also as a publisher of medical books.

8. *Religious and Philosophical Works*

ALDRIDGE, A. OWEN. "Benjamin Franklin and Philosophical Necessity," *Modern Language Quarterly*, XII (September, 1951), 292-309. Philosophical background of Wollaston and others to which Franklin's dissertation was a retort from the Deists. Useful, although approach is philosophical rather than literary.

9. *Reputation as a Writer*

CAIRNS, WILLIAM B. *British Criticisms of American Writings, 1783-1815, A Contribution to the Study of Anglo-American Literary Relationships.* Pamphlet reprinted from *University of Wisconsin Studies in Language and Literature*, No. 1. Madison: University of Wisconsin Press, 1918. Pp. 8, 16-18, 47, 53-56, 61. Traces Franklin's reputation as a writer for period 1783-1815.

EDDY, GEORGE SIMPSON. *Dr. Benjamin Franklin's Library.* Reprint from *Proceedings of the American Antiquarian Society* (October, 1924). Worcester, Mass.: American Antiquarian Society, 1925. Has ascertained titles of 1,350 of the 4,276 volumes in Franklin's library, but does not give list. Of interest to Franklin specialists.

JACKSON, MARIE K. *Outline of the Literary History of Colonial Pennsylvania.* Lancaster, Pa.: New Era Printing Co., 1906. A published Columbia University dissertation, containing useful information on Franklin's reputation as a writer.

JORGENSON, CHESTER. "Benjamin Franklin and Rabelais," *Classical Journal*, XXIX (April, 1934), 538-40. Follows Parton in thinking the synonyms for "intoxicated" in *Dogood* 12 may have been suggested by word catalogues in *Gargantua*. Demonstrates Franklin's knowledge of Rabelais.

————. "Sidelights on Benjamin Franklin's Principles of Rhetoric," *Revue Anglo-Américaine*, XI (February, 1934), 208-22. Devoted mainly to influences of Franklin's style and his ideals of good writing rather than to techniques of persuasion.

LINGELBACH, WILLIAM E. "Franklin's *American Instructor*, Early Americanism in the Art of Writing," *American Philosophical Society Library Bulletin* (1952). Pp. 367-88. Useful, but deals mainly with Franklin's handwriting.

MACLAURIN, LOIS M. *Franklin's Vocabulary.* New York: Doubleday, Doran, 1928. A careful and useful study.

VAN DOREN, CARL. "The First American Man of Letters," *Quarterly Review of the Michigan Alumni*, XLV (July 22, 1939). A defense of Franklin as a man of letters.

Index

(This index is limited to a listing of important persons and writings of Franklin. It does not include items in the Chronology on pp. 11-13.)

Sowter, John, 64
Spectator, The, 17, 28, 29, 32, 33, 104, 105, 106
Steele, Richard, 17, 28, 34, 64, 104, 106
Stevenson, Polly, 120, 133, 134, 135
Stiles, Ezra, 155
Strahan, William, 136-37
Swift, Jonathan, 19, 20, 28, 29, 30, 53, 60, 61, 71, 72, 73-77
Swinburne, Algernon, 156

Tatler, The, 104
Taylor, Jacob, 169
Tenaud, Jean, 168
Tennent, Gilbert, 27
Thomas, Gov. (Pa.), 143
Thompson, Charles, 138
Thompson, James, 27, 28
Tillotson, John, 19, 28, 109
Twain, Mark, 39, 40

Vaughan, Benjamin, 33, 42, 43, 73, 143
Vergenne, Charles Gravier, Comte de, 138
Vicq-d'Azyr, Felix, 142

Walpole, Horace, 89
Waterhouse, Benjamin, 142
Watson, Sir William, 142
Watts, Isaac, 27, 28
Washington, George, 67, 130
Webb, George, 114
Webb, John, 15
Webbe, John, 26, 27
Whitfield, George, 27, 45
Whitefoorde, Caleb, 136
Woodfall, Henry S., 88
Wollaston, William, 27, 147, 148

Xenophon, 27, 30

Young, Edward, 28, 59, 61